The Life of JOHN TAYLOR

THIRD PRESIDENT OF THE CHURCH

By

B.H. ROBERTS

This book manuscript is considered public domain, and to the best of our knowledge, is complete and accurate in its entirety. The book content reflects the thoughts and opinions of the author, and not necessarily that of the publisher. Minor edits have been added for ease-of-reading and to meet electronic and publication formatting requirements. Latter-day Strengths Publishing makes frequent quality checks of each of our books to ensure that it is formatted properly.

COVER DESIGN: Bryan A. Hunt
IN-HOUSE EDITOR: A. J. Alexander

Latter-day Strengths is an independent publisher of books, eBooks, audiobooks and photography for Latter-day Saints, and is not owned or operated by the Church of Jesus Christ of Latter-day Saints.

Latter-day Strengths Publishing
San Tan Valley, AZ 85143
LatterDayStrengths@gmail.com
Latterdaystrengths.com
Etsy.com/shop/LatterDayStrengths
Amazon.com/latter-daystrengths

Originally published in 1892 at Salt Lake City, Utah.
Original title: THE LIFE OF JOHN TAYLOR: THIRD PRESIDENT OF THE CHURCH OF JESUS CHRIST OF LATTER-DAY SAINTS

Printed in the U.S.A.

A special thanks to The Mormon Texts Project (www.mormontextsproject.org) for assisting in the initial preparation of this manuscript.

We donate a portion of every sale to support full-time missionaries of the Church of Jesus Christ of Latter-day Saints.

The Gospel: An Exposition of its First Principles

The Life of John Taylor

Succession in the presidency of the church

A New Witness for God, Vol 1

A New Witness for God, Vol 2

A New Witness for God, Vol 3

The Missouri Persecutions

The Rise and Fall of Nauvoo

Corianton a Nephite Story

Outlines of Ecclesiastical History

Mormon Doctrine of Deity

Defense of the Faith and the Saints, Vol 1

Defense of the Faith and the Saints, Vol 2

Joseph Smith the Prophet-Teacher

The Mormon Battalion

"The great man is he who chooses the right with invincible resolution"

John Taylor

To the family of the late President John Taylor this work is respectfully dedicated, with the hope that it will inspire in the minds of his numerous and ever-increasing posterity an emulation of his virtues.

TABLE OF CONTENTS

B.H. ROBERTS

Biographical Sketch

(1857 – 1933)

Brigham Henry Roberts was born in 1857 in Wolverhampton, England, of itinerant and soon separated parents. His convert mother immigrated to Zion when he was five years old, leaving him in the care of foster parents. When he was ten he too reached Utah, having walked nearly all the way across the plains. Once in Utah he moved from one mining camp to another, remaining illiterate until his mid-teens. His only formal schooling was one year at the University of Deseret, but added considerable self-education and became one of the most articulate and eloquent orators and writers in the Church's history.

Roberts edited and published the seven-volume 4,500 page "documentary" ***History of the Church*** *also known as* ***History of Joseph Smith.*** Later Roberts authored and published the 3,400-page six-volume history of the first century of the Church, known as ***A Comprehensive History of the Church***. In addition he authored the three-volume ***New Witnesses for God***, which he regarded as "the fullest treatise on the Book of Mormon yet published." This, he said in retrospect, was his "finest work." He authored, in addition, more than fifty tracts, articles, and pamphlets revolving around the Book of Mormon, its origins, its content, its meaning, its purposes, and its power as a sacred document.

Robert's multi-volume work made B. H. Roberts the foremost Latter-day Saint historian of the first century of the Church's existence.

Roberts became a member of the First Quorum of the Seventy in 1888 at the age of 31. He was elected to the United States House of Representatives in 1898 but was not allowed to take his seat because of the controversy over his involvement in polygamy.

Beyond the age of 60 he was a chaplain in America and France for Utah Soldiers serving in World War I during 1917-1918.

PREFACE

If the preface to a book be looked upon as the author's excuse for writing it, then this book should have no preface, for the author has no excuse to make. Justice to the character and labors of John Taylor demanded that his life be written. The annals of the Church could not be recorded without devoting large space to the part he took in her affairs; but no notice of his life and labors, however extended in a general history, could do justice to his great career: for of course there is much in that career peculiar to himself, and of a character, too, to make it worthy of a separate volume.

The author is of the opinion that John Taylor would have had a remarkable history even if Mormonism had not found him; for he possessed those qualities of mind which would have made him a leader and a reformer among men. It is quite probable, too, that in the event of Mormonism not finding him, he would have won more of the honors and applause of men; for while his connection with the Church of Jesus Christ of Latter-day Saints threw him into prominence, the disrepute in which that Church is held brought reproach and odium upon him from the world. Had the courage and unselfish devotion which he brought to the support of Mormonism been given to some reform movement less odious in the estimation of mankind, his conduct would have called forth the highest encomiums from all men; but as those virtues were displayed for the interest and advancement of Mormonism, the world either refused to recognize them at all, or accounted them fanaticism merely, for which no praise was due.

The praise of the world, however, is a small matter. It often praises those least worthy; it neglects or abuses those who are its chief benefactors. Our generation like many that have preceded it, garnishes the sepulchers of the ancient prophets, saying, "Had we lived in their day, we would not have persecuted and killed them." And yet with strange inconsistency they hunt to the death the living prophets whose memory future generations will honor. But the praise or censure of the world had little influence over the mind of John Taylor where truth was concerned. The more men despised it the more intense seemed his devotion.

In that most beautiful of all his poems entitled "An Irishman's Address to his Mistress"—the poem is an allegory, the mistress is the Irish Catholic Church—Thomas Moore represents the Irishman as saying that through grief and through danger the smile of his mistress had cheered his way, till hope seemed to spring from thorns that round him lay; the darker their fortunes, the brighter their pure love burned, until shame into glory and fear into zeal was turned. The mistress had a rival. That rival was honored, while the mistress was wronged and scorned; her crown was of briars, while gold the rival's brows adorned. The rival wooed him to temples, while the mistress lay hid in caves; the former's friends were all masters, while the latter's, alas! were all slaves. "Yet," said the faithful devotee, "cold in the earth at thy feet I would rather be, than wed what I love not, or turn one thought from thee!" Such was the love of John Taylor for the Church of Christ to which he devoted his life.

The author has but one reason to give for undertaking the pleasing task of writing this book—he loved the subject. To him John Taylor was the embodiment of those qualities of mind and heart which most become a man. He therefore applied to the family of the late President John Taylor—they being the parties most interested in such an undertaking—for the privilege of writing his history. They gave a ready assent, and the work was begun. Of the difficulties attending the production of this history I need not speak. They are such as attend all similar undertakings. The journals of President Taylor were very incomplete, covering only fragments of his life at best; but the chief events of his life were so closely interwoven with the history of the Church that his movements and labors could be followed in the Church publications; so that I feel reasonably certain that no important fact is omitted.

To George J. Taylor—the eldest son of President Taylor—I am indebted for many valuable items of information; and he has taken an abiding interest in the work from its commencement.

At my request the first Presidency of the Church appointed a committee to read the manuscript and pass upon it critically in respect to its doctrinal and historical correctness. That committee was Elders John Jaques and L. John Nuttall, the former assistant Church historian, the latter for a number of years secretary to President Taylor. The position these brethren occupied made them intimately acquainted with the subject, and they were enabled to render me valuable assistance in my work, for which I am deeply grateful to them.

The work is now presented to the public in the hope that it will meet with approval, and preserve to the present and future generations a true history of John Taylor, the third President of the Church of Jesus Christ of Latter-day Saints.

-THE AUTHOR

CHAPTER 1 - BIRTH AND ANCESTRY

The leading spirits whom the Prophet Joseph Smith gathered about him in his brief but glorious career, were remarkable men. Not remarkable for illustrious birth, for they were of humble origin; not for scholarly attainments, for such were the conditions of their early life that scholastic education of a very high order was out of the question: but they were remarkable for character—that mysterious something which exists independent of birth, education or fortune.

It has become proverbial that all great movements, all reformations, all revolutions must produce their own leaders; and this is as true of the great work of the last days, the establishment of the Church of Christ on the earth, as it is of any other great movement. Leaders in established usages and institutions, political, social or religious, are very seldom converted to innovations. They usually consider it to their interest to oppose changes, especially those changes which from their very nature cast any shadow of doubt upon the correctness of existing customs or institutions with which they are connected. Hence it happened that the Jewish rabbis, the priests, the scribes, the members of the great Sanhedrin—leaders in their nation—did not accept the doctrines of Messiah and become the chief apostles, seventies and elders of the new church. On the contrary, this class was the stubbornness opponents to the doctrines taught by the Son of God, and His most implacable enemies. It was the common people who heard Him gladly: and from their number He chose the apostles, who, through the God-given powers of the priesthood conferred upon them, shook the old systems of morals and religion from their foundations.

Nor can it be doubted that the hand of the Lord is in this matter of choosing men to be His messengers, His prophets and His rulers. Many of them are chosen before they are born in the flesh. The messenger that was to prepare the way for the coming of the Son of God, John the Baptist, was so chosen. Jeremiah was ordained a prophet to the nations before he was born. Cyrus the Great, the war prince of Persia, was selected to be the deliverer of Israel from Babylonian bondage more than a century before his birth. Indeed, we are given to understand from the revelations of God, that from among the nobler class of spirits that dwell in His presence, the Father hath chosen those who are to be His rulers.

From the very nature of things it must be necessary that men whose minds are unwarped by prevailing customs and traditions, should be selected to establish a new order of religion, of government or of society. How could the Jewish priests and rabbis, bound by long custom to a slavish adherence to the outward forms and ceremonies of the Mosaic ritual, the spirit and purpose of which had long been made of no effect by the rubbish of false traditions, open their minds to receive the larger and nobler doctrines of the gospel of Christ, unmixed with the pomp and circumstance which they of that age and nation considered essential to religion?

Can men educated to an attachment for despotic government, and whose interests are bound up with its maintenance, be expected to look with favor on democratic principles, or become the champions of a republic?

Finally, to wander no further from the subject in hand, were the religious leaders of the early part of the nineteenth century, educated to the idea that revelation had ceased; that the voice of prophecy was forever silenced; that the ministration of angels was ended; that the miraculous powers of the Holy Ghost were done away; that the ancient organization of the church was no longer needed; and further, believing that God was a substance merely, without form, without a body, or parts, or passions—were such men, filled with pride which the learning of this world too often infuses into the hearts of those who possess it—were such men qualified to stand at the head of, and become the leading actors in, the Dispensation of the Fullness of Times? A dispensation which was to be opened by the personal visitation of the Father and the Son, followed by numerous visitations of angels, the re-establishment of the church of Christ, with all its doctrines, ordinances, priesthoods, powers, promises and blessings; and ending, eventually, with the full restoration of the house of Israel and the complete redemption of the earth and all its righteous inhabitants?

Such a work was too large, too high and too deep for minds filled with false, sectarian ideas. Hence God chose His servants in these last days from men whose minds were unwarped by false education, but men of large capacity; possessing breadth and freedom of thought, of sanguine, fearless temperament: children of nature were they, with consciences unseared by worldly guile, and strangers to motives other than those dictated by an honest purpose; and, withal, full of implicit confidence in God—a confidence born of a living faith in the fact of Deity's existence, and a consciousness of the rectitude of their own intentions and lives.

It was these qualities which made the men whom the Prophet Joseph Smith gathered about him, and who were his trusted counselors, remarkable; and of that coterie of men there was not one who more completely united in his own character all those qualities which made the group remarkable than John Taylor. Nor was there one more devoted in his friendship for the prophet, or more zealous in his efforts to spread abroad the glad tidings that the gospel of the Son of God in its fullness was restored to the earth to bless mankind. Neither was there one whose experience was more varied, or whose life was more crowded with thrilling events, or whose position in the Church was more exalted than his. He proclaimed the gospel in many lands; and as the champion of truth, stood ready to meet all who assailed it; and whether he met his opponents in the forum, before a multitude steeped full of prejudice against him, or in the columns of the public press, he was equally successful in vanquishing them by his powerful statement of the truth, backed by a peculiar ability to expose the weakness of his opponent's position.

So prominent was the career of John Taylor in the Church, as a trusted friend of the Prophet Joseph Smith, with whom he may be said to have shared martyrdom; as a founder and editor of Church periodicals; as a preacher of the gospel; as an apostle; as a pioneer of Utah; as a legislator; and, finally, as President of the Church during one of the most trying periods through which she has passed in her eventful career, that the literature of the Church would be incomplete without his history. And if the lives of her leading men be the history of the Church, as some aver, then that history would be extremely imperfect if the life of her third President in this dispensation were not written.

JOHN TAYLOR was born November 1st, 1808, in Milnthorpe, a small town near the head of Morecombe Bay, and not far from Windemere, the "Queen of English Lakes," in the county of Westmoreland, England. His father's name was James Taylor, whose forefathers for many generations had lived on an estate known as Craig Gate, in Ackenthwaite. James Taylor's mother was the second wife of his father, Edward Taylor. By his first wife Edward Taylor had two sons and three daughters; by his second wife, whose name was Elizabeth, he had one son, James, and three daughters, named Mary, Jane and Agnes. Edward Taylor, the grandfather of the subject of this writing, died before his son James was born; and owing to the English law of primogeniture, the eldest son took the estate and left the younger branches of the family to provide for themselves as best they could.

Though James Taylor was deprived of any share of his father's estate, he acquired a good English education, some proficiency in the Latin and Greek languages, and the higher branches of mathematics. What he had lost by an unjust law, in the sudden demise of his father, was made up to him by the munificence of an uncle (on his mother's side), William T. Moon, who bequeathed to him a small estate in Hale, Westmoreland.

John Taylor's mother's name was Agnes; her maiden name was also Taylor. Her grandfather, Christopher Taylor, lived to be ninety-seven years of age. His son John, father of Agnes, held an office in the excise under government, from his first setting out in life to the age of about sixty. He was between seventy and eighty when he died. The maiden name of Agnes Taylor's mother was Whittington, a descendant of the family made famous by Richard Whittington, the younger son of Sir William Whittington. (Sir William died intestate shortly after his son Richard was born; and this circumstance, under the English law of primogeniture, left him without a fortune. Nothing discouraged by this event, Richard went to London to engage in trade. He apprenticed himself to a mercer and appears to have risen rapidly in the world. He was made an alderman in the city of London, then high sheriff; thrice was he chosen lord mayor of London, and afterwards was elected member of parliament for the city. He stood in high favor with the king, who conferred on him the honor of knighthood. He was diligent and exceedingly prosperous in business, upright and liberal in character, "a virtuous and godly man, full of good works, and those famous," says an old chronicler. In many respects he was considerably in advance of his times and conferred a lustre on his family's name which will live forever in English story. This illustrious man was born, as nearly as may be ascertained, about 1360.)

To James and Agnes Taylor were born ten children—eight sons and two daughters. Three of the sons died while young. John Taylor was the second son, but as his eldest brother, Edward, died at the age of twenty-two, John stood next to his father, the head of the family.

John Taylor's father had received an appointment under government in the excise, and the nature of his office was such that he had to move from place to place. In 1819, however, he left government employ and removed from Liverpool, where he had lived five years, and settled on his estate in Hale.

CHAPTER 2 - SPIRITUAL MANIFESTATIONS

John Taylor was eleven years old when his father settled on his estate in Hale. He attended school at Beetham, about a mile from Hale, and only a few miles south of his birth place. It was in these boyhood days at home that he got "mixed up," as he puts it, "with ploughing, sowing, reaping, hay-making and other farm work; and I have indelibly impressed on my mind," he continues, "some of my first mishaps in horsemanship in the way of sundry curious evolutions between the horses' backs and *terra firma*."

At the age of fourteen he was bound an apprentice to a cooper, in Liverpool. In about twelve months his employer failed and young Taylor returned home. He afterwards went to learn the business of turner in Penrith, Cumberland. Penrith is situated near the middle of a beautiful, fertile valley sloping northwesterly to the Solway firth, and drained by the Eden river; the valley because of its rare scenery, is called the Vale of Eden. It is one of the most romantic districts in all England. On the east is the Pennine range of mountains, which in this locality attain their greatest altitude. On the west is the Cumbrian group, where the highest summits in England are found. The highest mountain is Scawfell, the loftiest of whose four peaks is 3,229 feet above the sea. A little to the east of this, and hence nearer Penrith, is Mount Helvellyn 3,118 feet; and to the north Skiddaw 3,058 feet.

Nestling at the feet, or in basins between these mountain peaks, are the most famous lakes in England, fifteen in number, varying in size from one mile to ten in length, and from one-third to one mile in width. Ulleswater is the lake nearest to Penrith, and while it has little of the soft beauty that has made Lake Windemere famous, its rugged surroundings and especially Mount Helvellyn at its south west extremity, give to it a grandeur that verges on sublimity.

The climate of this lake region is very damp, and on the higher mountain peaks snow lies for six and in some seasons even eight months in the year. The excessive rain-fall, however, gives great freshness and luxuriance to vegetation.

Besides the beauty and grandeur of the surrounding country, Penrith and vicinity are rich in historical associations and monuments of a past civilization. Lying near the Scotch border it was frequently invaded by that hardy race during their unhappy conflicts with England; the town was well-nigh destroyed by them in the time of Edward III.; and was again sacked in the time of Richard III.

In the immediate vicinity are a number of Druidical remains, among which is the great Druidic monument Long Meg, a monolith eighteen feet high and fifteen feet in circumference; while about her, in a circle one hundred and fifty yards in diameter, are sixty-six other monuments, inferior to her in size, called her daughters. Nearby is Lowther Castle with its beautiful park; Eden Hall, the seat of the ancient family of Musgrave; Arthur's Round Table, and Shap Abbey, are also within a radius of five or six miles.

It was in the midst of this splendid scenery, made doubly enchanting by historic associations and the monuments of those weird people, the Druids, that John Taylor spent the days of his youth, from his fifteenth to his twentieth year; and no doubt these surroundings had a powerful effect on his then forming character, and did much to develop the poetical impulses of his mind, for the power of poetry was not among the least of his natural gifts. Thence, too, comes the splendid imagery so frequently dashed into his sermons and writings. It was there he saw the "water nymphs playing with the clouds on mountain tops, frolicking with the snow and rain in rugged gorges, coquetting with the sun and dancing to the sheen of the moon;" there, too, he saw the drifting clouds wrapping mountain peaks in solemn gloom, while the flower-flecked vale below was flooded with warm sunlight. These scenes and the impressions they formed he treasured up, and afterwards made them clothe in splendid drapery an eloquence which held thousands enchanted by the magic of its spell.

The religious nature of John Taylor began early to develop. His parents were members, nominally, of the Church of England, and he was told that that Church was the true one, and that the "Roman Catholics were a dreadful set of fellows." Indeed, it may be said that part of the Church of England's creed in those days, though unwritten, was "down with the Pope." He learned the catechism and the prayers of the church. In a fine vein of satire he says: "I repeated week after week—'We have erred and strayed from Thy ways like lost sheep. We have left undone those things which we ought to have done; and we have done those things which we ought not to have done, and there is no health in us; have mercy upon us, miserable sinners.'"

He was baptized into the church when an infant; a god-father and god-mother promised and vowed for him that he would renounce the devil and all his works—the pomp and vanity of this wicked world, and all the deceitful lusts of the flesh; that he should believe all the articles of the Christian faith, and keep God's holy laws and commandments, and walk in the same all the days of his life. "How far I have filled their pledges," he says, "I must leave others to judge."

In childhood and youth he was naturally vivacious, and seems to have had but little regard for the stiff formula of church creed, and was without any definite idea of correct religious views; still he had a deep reverence for God; with him it was an intuition, and he dreaded nothing so much as offending Him.

When about sixteen he heard the Methodist doctrines taught, and as he perceived more spiritual light and force in their teachings than in the cold, set services of the Church of England, he became a Methodist. He was strictly sincere in his religious faith, and very zealous to learn what he then considered to be the truth. Believing that "every good and perfect gift proceedeth from the Lord," he prayed frequently in private. Most of his leisure hours were spent in reading the Bible, works on theology and in prayer. For the latter purpose he usually resorted to secluded places in the woods and fields. The missionary spirit about this time began to develop in him. He induced a number of boys about his own age to join with him in secret prayer, but they generally soon forsook him. He relates a circumstance that must have occurred about this time, which still further gives evidence of the missionary spirit working within him. Living in the same neighborhood was an old gentleman whom he greatly respected; he was a good man, a praying man, but he had a wife who did not want to pray, and also interfered with his devotions. She was restless and turbulent, a kind of thorn in his flesh. Under these circumstances he did not get along very well, but it used to drive him to the Lord. After a while she died, and he married again; this time to a very amiable lady. His wife was so pleasant and agreeable, that the change in his circumstances was very great. Being thus comfortably situated he became remiss in his religious duties; and among other things gave way to the temptations of liquor. Observing the course he was taking, young Taylor took up a labor with him. He felt a little abashed on account of his youth, but because of long friendship, and out of respect for the old gentleman's many good qualities, he felt it his duty to call his attention to his neglect of Christian precepts. He told him how he had seen him drunk a few days previously, and how it had hurt his feelings, as his course hitherto had been exemplary. The old gentleman appreciated the good feelings, the respect and courage of his young friend, deplored his weakness and promised amendment.

Young Taylor possessed a portion of the spirit of God and was very happy. Manifestations of its presence were frequent, not only in the expansion of his mind to understand doctrines and principles, but also in dreams and visions. "Often when alone," he writes, "and sometimes in company, I heard sweet, soft, melodious music, as if performed by angelic or supernatural beings." When but a small boy he saw, in vision, an angel in the heavens, holding a trumpet to his mouth, sounding a message to the nations. The import of this vision he did not understand until later in life.

At the age of seventeen he was made a Methodist exhorter, or local preacher. His first appointment was at a small country town some seven miles from Penrith. A brother in the same church accompanied him; and when the two had walked about a mile from Penrith, young Taylor suddenly stopped, overpowered by a peculiar influence, and as he stood there in the road, he remarked to his companion, "I have a strong impression on my mind, that I have to go to America to preach the gospel!" At the time he knew nothing of America but what he had learned in his geography at school; and emigration to that country had not been thought of then by his family. So strong was the voice of the spirit to him on that occasion that it continued to impress him as long as he remained in that land; and even after he arrived in Canada, a presentiment that he could not shake off, clung to him that he had some work to do which he did not then understand.

At the age of twenty, having mastered the business of turner, young Taylor left Penrith, and in the town of Hale started business for himself, under the auspices of his father. Shortly after this, in 1830, his father and family emigrated to Upper Canada, leaving him to dispose of some unsold property and settle the affairs of the estate.

In about two years he completed the business entrusted to him and followed them. While crossing the British channel the ship he sailed in encountered severe storms, which lasted a number of days. He saw several ships wrecked in that storm, and the captain and officers of his own ship expected hourly that she would go down. But not so with our young emigrant. The voice of the Spirit was still saying within him, "You must yet go to America and preach the gospel." "So confident was I of my destiny," he remarks, "that I went on deck at midnight, and amidst the raging elements felt as calm as though I was sitting in a parlor at home. I believed I should reach America and perform my work."

CHAPTER 3 - EMBRACE THE GOSPEL

Landing in New York, he remained there and in Brooklyn and Albany a few months before going on to Toronto, Upper Canada, where he was to rejoin his parents.

After his arrival in Toronto he connected himself with the Methodists in that city, and began preaching under the auspices of their church organization. It was while he was engaged in this work that he met Leonora Cannon, to whom he was married on the 28th of January, 1833.

Leonora Cannon was a daughter of Captain George Cannon (grandfather of President George Q. Cannon) of Peel, Isle of Man. Captain Cannon died while Leonora was yet in her girlhood; the old homestead in Peel was rented to strangers, and she went to reside in England with a lady named Vail. Later she became an inmate of Governor Smelt's family, residing in Castle Rushen, Castletown, Isle of Man. Here she frequently met with many distinguished people from England. Finally in the capacity of companion to the wife of Mr. Mason, the private secretary of Lord Aylmer, Governor General of Canada, she went to Toronto, and being a devout Methodist, associated with that church and there met Mr. Taylor, who became her class leader.

His first proposal of marriage was rejected; but afterwards, through a dream in which she saw herself associated with him, she was convinced that he would be her husband. Therefore, when he renewed his proposal, he was accepted.

Refined both by nature and education, gentle and lady-like in manner, witty, intelligent, gifted with rare conversational powers, possessed of a deep religious sentiment, and, withal, remarkable for the beauty of her person, she was a fitting companion to John Taylor.

Mrs. Taylor frequently accompanied her husband in filling his appointments to preach on the Sabbath, and he often alluded to the singular revelation he had received in his youth, about his having to preach the gospel in America.

"Are you not now preaching the gospel in America?" Leonora would ask.

"This is not the work; it is something of more importance," he would answer.

As a preacher in the Methodist church, both in England and Canada, he was very successful, and made many converts. "My object," he remarks, "was to teach them what I then considered the leading doctrines of the Christian religion, rather than the peculiar dogmas of Methodism." His theological investigations had made him very much dissatisfied with existing creeds and churches, because of the wide difference between modern and primitive Christianity, in doctrine, in ordinances, in organization and above all, in spirit and power.

He was not the only one on whom the Spirit was operating in this manner. There were several others, chiefly men belonging to the same Church, in or near Toronto, and engaged in the same calling. They were gentlemen of refinement and education, and generally talented.

It was their custom to meet several times a week to search the scriptures, and investigate the doctrines of the Christian religion as contained in the Bible. They were all familiar with the various systems of theology as accepted by the Christian sects of the day, and as they had more or less distrust regarding each of them they agreed, in their investigation, to reject every man's opinion and work, and to search the scriptures alone, praying for the guidance of the Holy Spirit.

On these lines they investigated the claims of each sect of religion, as to its being the Church of Christ. The result of that investigation was that they were driven irresistibly to the conclusion that all sects were in error, and without authority to preach the gospel or administer its ordinances. "If modern Christianity is true," said they, "then the Bible is false," and *vice versa*. Fortunately they clung to a firm belief in the Bible; and further believed in a restoration of pure principles and a true church. They believed that men should be called of God as in former days, and ordained by proper authority; and that in the Church there should be apostles and prophets, evangelists and pastors, teachers and deacons; in short, that the primitive organization of the Church of Christ should be perpetuated.

They believed that men who accepted the gospel should have bestowed upon them the Holy Ghost; that it should lead them into all truth, and show them things to come. They believed also in the gift of tongues, the gift of healing, miracles, prophecy, faith, discerning of spirits and all the powers, graces and blessings as experienced in the Christian Church of former days. They believed that Israel would be gathered, the ten tribes restored; that judgments would overtake the wicked, and Christ return to the earth and reign with the righteous; they believed in the first and second resurrection, and in the final glory and triumph of the righteous. But while they believed all these things, they recognized the fact that they had no authority to act in the premises and organize a church, incorporating these views in its doctrines and organization. True, they might organize a church with apostles and prophets, and all other officers, and teach the letter of their principles; but whence should they look for the Spirit to give it life, and make their dream of a restored, perfect Christian church a reality? It was evident to them they could not perform this work unless called of God to do it, and they were painfully conscious of the fact that not one among them was so called. They could only wait, and pray that God would send to them a messenger if He had a Church on the earth.

So wide and thorough an investigation of religion, by such a body of men, could not fail to attract some attention, especially from the church with which the most of them were nominally connected. The leading men in the Methodist church called a special conference to consider the principles of these heterodox brethren. The meeting was called and presided over by some of the most prominent leaders in the Methodist persuasion in Canada, among whom were the Rev. Mr. Ryarson and Rev. Mr. Lord, of the British conference. The hearing was not a trial *pro forma*, but rather a friendly discussion of those principles held by the brethren in question.

The hearing continued through several days; and in the debates the "heterodox" held their own against the learning and talent of the church leaders; and at the conclusion of the investigation expressed themselves as being more fully confirmed in their doctrines since their learned opponents had been unable to refute them by the word of God. The conclusion reached by the conference was thus stated by the president:

"Brethren, we esteem you as brethren and gentlemen; we believe you are sincere, but cannot fellowship your doctrine. Wishing, however, to concede all we can, we would say: You may believe your doctrines if you will not teach them; and we will still retain you in fellowship as members, leaders and preachers."

These conditions the "heterodox" could not conscientiously comply with, so they were deprived of their offices but retained as members. Since they considered the Methodist Church without authority, taking from them their offices was not regarded by them as a hardship.

Meantime, their fastings and prayers, their longing for the Kingdom of God, came up in remembrance before the Lord, and He sent a messenger to them. Parley P. Pratt, an Apostle of the Church of Jesus Christ, called upon Mr. Taylor, with a letter of introduction from a merchant acquaintance of his, Mr. Moses Nickerson. As soon as he learned that Mr. Pratt was a "Mormon," he thought his acquaintance had imposed upon him a little by sending him such a character; for then, as now, and as in the days of the ancient apostles, the Saints were everywhere spoken against, and Mr. Taylor had heard the evil rumors circulated about them; and because of these rumors, he had been led to regard "Mormonism" as anything but a *religious* system. He treated Apostle Pratt courteously, as he considered himself bound to do, because of his letter of introduction; but the reception he gave him could not be called cordial.

It was a strange message the Apostle had to deliver—this story of the revelation of the gospel: how God had passed by the great, and learned, and eloquent theologians of the day, and had revealed Himself to an unlearned youth, reared in the backwoods of New York; how, subsequently, He sent to him an angel, who made known to him the existence of the hidden record of the ancient inhabitants of America—the Book of Mormon; how that angel met him annually in the month of September for four successive years, and taught him the gospel and many things concerning the work of the Lord in these last days; and then delivered into his keeping those records, which he translated into the English language by the gift and power of God; how this same young man, during the progress of the work of translation, was visited by John the Baptist, who conferred upon him and Oliver Cowdery the Aaronic Priesthood, which gave them the authority to preach repentance and baptize for remission of sins; how, subsequently, the ancient apostles, Peter, James and John came and conferred upon the young Prophet the apostleship, which gave him the right and power to ordain other men to be Apostles, Seventies, High Priests and Elders; to lay on hands for the gift of the Holy Ghost—in short, which gave him the right to preach the gospel in all the world, and establish the Church of Christ on the earth.

But if this story was strange, the circumstance which led to the Apostle coming among them, though of less importance than the main message he had to deliver, was stranger still. He told them how Heber C. Kimball, and others, came to his house one night, in Kirtland, after he and Mrs. Pratt had retired. Heber C. Kimball requested him to get up as he had a prophecy to deliver concerning him. Apostle Pratt arose and his visitor thus addressed him:

"Brother Parley, thy wife shall be healed from this hour, and shall bear a son, and his name shall be Parley; and he shall be a chosen instrument in the hands of the Lord to inherit the priesthood, and to walk in the footsteps of his father. He shall do a great work on the earth in ministering the word and teaching the children of men. Arise, therefore, and go forth in the ministry, nothing doubting. Take no thought for your debts, nor the necessaries of life, for the Lord will supply you with abundant means for all things. Thou shalt go to Upper Canada, even to the city of Toronto, the capital, and there thou shalt find a people prepared for the gospel, and they shall receive thee, and thou shalt organize the Church among them, and it shall spread thence into the regions round about, and many shall be brought to a knowledge of the truth, and shall be filled with joy; and from the things growing out of this mission, shall the fullness of the gospel spread into England, and cause a great work to be done in that land."

To understand the boldness of this prediction the reader ought to be informed that Apostle Pratt had been married to his wife ten years, but they had never been blessed with offspring; and for six years his wife had been considered an incurable consumptive.

As before stated Mr Taylor did not receive Apostle Pratt very cordially. While seeking for the truth he did not propose being led away by every wind of doctrine, nor by the cunning craftiness of men who lie in wait to deceive. He was very cautious, remembering that an ancient apostle had said:

"If there come any unto you, and bring not this doctrine, [the gospel] receive him not into your house, neither bid him God speed; for he that biddeth him God speed is partaker of his evil deeds."

He therefore rendered Elder Pratt no assistance, until he began to discover that there were good grounds for believing he was a messenger sent of God.

Elder Pratt applied to all the ministers of Toronto, and the city officials having charge of public buildings, for a place in which to deliver his message, without avail. Disheartened at his unpropitious reception, he was about to leave a city where he could see no prospect of making an opening. In this spirit he called on Mr. Taylor to say farewell.

Mr Taylor's turning shop adjoined his house, and it was here that Elder Pratt found him. While talking to him, valise in hand ready to depart, a Mrs. Walton called on Mrs. Taylor in the adjoining room. The latter told Mrs. Walton about Elder Pratt and his strange mission, and how, failing to get an opportunity to preach, he was on the eve of departing. "He may be a man of God," said Leonora, "I am sorry to have him depart."

At this Mrs. Walton expressed her willingness to open her house for Elder Pratt to preach in, and proposed to lodge and feed him. Here at last was an opening. He began holding meetings at Mrs. Walton's, and was soon afterwards introduced to the investigation meetings held by Mr. Taylor and his religious friends.

They were delighted with his preaching. He taught them faith in God, and in Jesus Christ; called upon them to repent of their sins, and to be baptized in the likeness of Christ's burial, for the remission of them, and promised them the Holy Ghost through the laying on of hands, together with a full enjoyment of all its gifts and blessings. All this, and much more that he taught, was in strict harmony with what they themselves believed; but what he had to say about Joseph Smith and the Book of Mormon perplexed a great many, and some of their members even refused to investigate the Book of Mormon, or examine the claims of Apostle Pratt to having divine authority to preach the gospel and administer in the ordinances thereof.

It was at this juncture that the noble independence and boldness of spirit, so conspicuous in John Taylor throughout his life, asserted itself. He addressed the assembly to the following effect:

"We are here, ostensibly in search of truth. Hitherto we have fully investigated other creeds and doctrines and proven them false. Why should we fear to investigate Mormonism? This gentleman, Mr. Pratt, has brought to us many doctrines that correspond with our own views. We have endured a great deal and made many sacrifices for our religious convictions. We have prayed to God to send us a messenger, if He has a true Church on earth. Mr. Pratt has come to us under circumstances that are peculiar; and there is one thing that commends him to our consideration; he has come amongst us without purse or scrip, as the ancient apostles traveled; and none of us are able to refute his doctrine by scripture or logic. I desire to investigate his doctrines and claims to authority, and shall be very glad if some of my friends will unite with me in this investigation. But if no one will unite with me, be assured I shall make the investigation alone. If I find his religion true, I shall accept it, no matter what the consequences may be; and if false, then I shall expose it."

After this, John Taylor began the investigation of Mormonism in earnest. He wrote down eight sermons which Apostle Pratt preached, and compared them with the scripture. He also investigated the evidences of the divine authenticity of the Book of Mormon and the Doctrine and Covenants. "I made a regular business of it for three weeks," he says, "and followed Brother Parley from place to place." The result of his thorough investigation was conviction; and on the 9th of May, 1836, himself and wife were baptized. "I have never doubted any principle of Mormonism since," was the comment he made in relating, when well advanced in life, how he came to accept the gospel.

CHAPTER 4 - THE IMPOSTER

Shortly after his baptism, John Taylor was ordained an Elder in the Church, and began his labors in the ministry. He was now preaching the gospel in America in fulfillment of the revelation he received in his youth.

So rapidly did the work spread in Canada, that Apostles Orson Hyde and Orson Pratt were sent to assist Parley. The country was excited on the subject of "Mormonism," and the ministers alarmed. Public discussions were frequent and the truth everywhere triumphed. All through the summer of 1836, Elder Taylor was actively engaged in the ministry; and when in the autumn the apostles departed for Kirtland, he was appointed to preside over the churches they had founded.

In March of the following year, Elder Taylor visited Kirtland, and there met the Prophet Joseph Smith, who entertained him at his house and gave him many items of information pertaining to the work of the Lord in this dispensation. At that time there was a bitter spirit of apostasy rife in Kirtland. A number in the quorum of the Twelve were disaffected towards the Prophet, and the Church seemed on the point of disintegration. Among others, Parley P. Pratt was floundering in darkness, and coming to Elder Taylor told him of some things wherein he considered the Prophet Joseph in error. To his remarks Elder Taylor replied:

"I am surprised to hear you speak so, Brother Parley. Before you left Canada you bore a strong testimony to Joseph Smith being a Prophet of God, and to the truth of the work he has inaugurated;

and you said you knew these things by revelation, and the gift of the Holy Ghost. You gave to me a strict charge to the effect that though you or an angel from heaven was to declare anything else I was not to believe it. Now Brother Parley, it is not man that I am following, but the Lord. The principles you taught me led me to Him, and I now have the same testimony that you then rejoiced in. If the work was true six months ago, it is true today; if Joseph Smith was then a prophet, he is now a prophet."

To the honor of Parley, be it said, he sought no further to lead Elder Taylor astray; nor did he use much argument in the first place. "He with many others," says Elder Taylor, "were passing under a dark cloud; he soon made all right with the Prophet Joseph, and was restored to full fellowship."

It was about this time that Elder Taylor first came prominently before the Church. The apostates met frequently in the temple, and on one of these occasions, on a Sunday—the Prophet Joseph was absent—Warren Parrish made a violent attack upon the character of the Prophet, which was warmly sustained by many of those present. Towards the close of the meeting, Elder Taylor asked the privilege of speaking. It was granted him. He referred, in opening his remarks, to the ancient Israelites, and to their murmurings against God and Moses, and then asked:

"From whence do we get our intelligence, and knowledge of the laws, ordinances and doctrines of the kingdom of God? Who understood even the first principles of the doctrines of Christ? Who in the Christian world taught them? If we, with our learning and intelligence, could not find out the first principles, which was the case with myself and millions of others, how can we find out the mysteries of the kingdom? It was Joseph Smith, under the Almighty, who developed the first principles, and to him we must look for further instructions. If the spirit which he manifests does not bring blessings, I am very much afraid that the one manifested by those who have spoken, will not be very likely to secure them. The children of Israel, formerly, after seeing the power of God manifested in their midst, fell into rebellion and idolatry, and there is certainly very great danger of us doing the same thing."

While the apostates were neither convinced nor silenced by the remarks of Elder Taylor, the faithful Saints were strengthened, and saw in that fearless defender of the prophet, a champion of innocence and truth. While on his part, in commenting on this circumstance, Elder Taylor remarks: "I was pained on the one hand to witness the hard feelings and severe expressions of apostates; while on the other, I rejoiced to see the firmness, faith, integrity and joy of the faithful."

Elder Taylor returned to Canada in company with Isaac Russell and others. Being detained in Queenstown on Sunday, the brethren determined to hold meeting. Before seeking for a place to preach in, at the suggestion of Elder Taylor, the party repaired to a secluded spot under a high cliff, just below Niagara Falls. While engaged in prayer, there, within hearing of the mighty cataract, Elder Taylor spoke in tongues for the first time. Comforted by this manifestation of the power of God which was with them, the party, full of joy, re-entered Queenstown, secured a place to meet in, and Elder Taylor preached. Next day they continued their journey and arrived at Toronto.

Not long after Elder Taylor's return to Canada, Doctor Sampson Avard, a high priest, presented himself in Toronto, and by virtue of an appointment signed by his quorum, claimed the right to preside over the churches in that district. Elder Taylor was absent from Toronto when Avard arrived, but that officious person at once assumed the responsibility of presiding; and boasted of his great power, and what marvelous things he intended to accomplish. Elder Taylor had been cautioned by the apostles, before their departure, not to allow any person to take his place, unless he came commissioned by proper authority. But when on his return Avard showed his authority from the high priest's quorum, Elder Taylor thought that sufficient, gave up his presidency and went into Whitby County to preach.

It was in August of that year, 1837, that the Prophet Joseph, accompanied by Sidney Rigdon and Thomas B. Marsh, then President of the Twelve Apostles, visited Canada. The course of the Prophet was in marked contrast with that of the self-sufficient high priest,

Sampson Avard. The latter at once assumed the presidency of the churches, and commenced regulating affairs without consulting or even seeing Elder Taylor; the former, though acknowledged and sustained as the President of the Church in all the world, and Prophet, Seer and Revelator thereto, called for him, and would not move in any business concerning the churches in Canada until he had seen him. Although Elder Taylor was some distance from Toronto, the Prophet sent for him, and patiently awaited his coming. On his arrival, to the great surprise of Elder Taylor, the Prophet began to counsel with him as to the best mode of procedure in relation to holding some conferences during their visit. Elder Taylor told the prophet that Elder Avard was presiding. It was Joseph's turn to be surprised now. Avard had never been sent to preside in Canada by his consent. Elder Taylor told him of the credentials that Avard had presented from the high priests' quorum. Joseph insisted that there must be some mistake; an imposition had been practiced, at which he was much annoyed.

Obtaining a carriage, Elder Taylor accompanied the Prophet and his associates in visiting the churches. "This was as great a treat to me as I ever enjoyed," he remarks. "I had daily opportunity of conversing with them, of listening to their instructions, and in participating in the rich stores of intelligence that flowed continually from the Prophet Joseph."

A conference was held in the County of Whitby, in a large barn owned by Edward Lawrence, which was numerously attended. The spirit of God was present, the hearts of the Saints were made to rejoice, and many who were out of the Church believed.

Another conference was held in Scarboro with similar results. At the latter conference Doctor Avard was present, and the Prophet reproved him severely for coming to that place with fictitious papers. He also censured Elder Taylor for yielding up his office on so flimsy a pretext; but palliated it on account of his youth and inexperience. He gave him a strict charge never again, on any account, to give up any office or calling unless he received orders from a legitimate source that could be relied upon; otherwise he would be held responsible for any evil that might accrue from it. The apostate party at Kirtland had appointed Doctor Avard to supercede Elder Taylor. They remembered the fearless speech the latter had made in Kirtland, in the early spring, and doubtless thought it to their interest to have a man presiding in Canada who was less staunch in his friendship for the Prophet than he.

Before the Prophet and his companions left Canada, they ordained Elder Taylor a High Priest, on the 21st of August, 1837, and reappointed him to preside over the Churches.

The work spread rapidly on every hand in Canada. The Lord labored with His servants, confirming their words by signs following the believers. The sick were healed; and many possessed the spirit of prophecy. Among the latter was a boy living in Toronto, who, shortly after his baptism, prophesied that the people of Canada would soon have war, and that armed men would arrive in the city of Toronto on a steamer, and stack their arms on the wharf.

As at that time their was no prospect whatever of war, many of the enemies of the Church laughed at what they called the impertinence of the young prophet. The prophecy however was fulfilled.

At that time Canada was divided into two Provinces, Upper and Lower Canada. A governor was appointed by the English crown, for each province, and to assist him in his duties there was also appointed an executive council. In addition to these executive officers there was a legislative council, appointed by the crown, and an assembly, the members of which were elected by the people. This latter body formed the lower branch of the provincial legislature, and the former the higher.

For years the people had petitioned the British government for the abolishment of the executive council, and demanded that the legislative council be made elective. The British Parliament refused these alterations in the Canadian constitution, whereupon one Mackenzie, the leader of a party that had urged complete separation from the British government, considered the times ripe for a revolution, and suddenly assembled five hundred men at Montgomery's tavern, four miles from Toronto, with a view of attacking that town. The loyalists as suddenly assembled to defend the town, and a few days later defeated the rebels in an open engagement. Mackenzie escaped to Buffalo, in the United States, and there succeeded in kindling a great enthusiasm for the cause of his party; and in a short time returned to Canada and mustered into service over a thousand men.

He took up a position on Navy Island, situated in the Niagara Channel. Fortifications were commenced which were defended by thirteen cannon, and for a time the insurgents baffled all attempts of the government to dislodge them. The uprising, however, was finally suppressed.

It was during this rebellion that all the terms of the young prophet's predictions were fulfilled. War broke out as he had said it would; and during the time it existed, troops entered Toronto harbor, were disembarked and stacked their arms on the wharf. Elder Taylor and his wife witnessed the arrival of the ships, the landing of the troops, and saw them stack their arms on the wharf.

Speaking of prophecy, it may be well to state here that the remarkable prophecy of Heber C. Kimball on the head of Parley P. Pratt was literally fulfilled. He found a people in Canada prepared to receive the gospel; they assisted him to sufficient means to relieve him from his temporal embarrassments: his wife, contrary to all natural prospects, bore him a son, though she died at his birth; and from Canada the work of the Lord spread into England in the following manner:

At the request of Elder Joseph Fielding, Elder Taylor wrote a letter to his brother, a minister in the town of Preston, England, giving an account of the restoration of the gospel through the ministration of angels to the Prophet Joseph Smith. This was doubtless the first announcement of these things in England, by an authorized servant of God.

Subsequently, in this same year, 1837, Elder Fielding accompanied Apostles Kimball and Hyde to England; and it was in his brother's chapel, in Preston, that Apostle Heber C. Kimball preached the first public discourse, in this dispensation, on the gospel in that land.

CHAPTER 5 - THE CALL

The spirit of apostasy so prevalent in Kirtland, in 1837 and 1838, resulted in many prominent leaders being excommunicated from the Church. Among those who fell in those dark days were a number of the Twelve Apostles.

About the same time several business enterprises which the Saints inaugurated at Kirtland, including a banking establishment, went down before the wave of financial disaster which swept over the country; and as the Presidency of the Church were heavily involved in consequence of these failures, Elder Taylor was appointed to collect funds in the district over which he presided, to relieve them from their embarrassment. He accomplished this labor to the entire satisfaction of the Presidency.

In the fall of 1837, Elder Taylor received word from the Prophet Joseph that he would be chosen to fill one of the vacancies in the quorum of Apostles.

This call to the Apostleship, found Elder Taylor busily engaged in the ministry. He had previously received a manifestation that he would be called to that high office in the Church, but fearing that it might be from the devil he wisely kept it hidden in his own breast. Now, however, he had been chosen to that place by the voice of God through His Prophet; but while his heart rejoiced at the thought that he was known of the Lord, and considered worthy by Him to stand in this exalted station in the Church of Christ, he bore his new honors with becoming modesty. Commenting upon the appointment, and the prospect which now opened before him, he remarks:

"The work seemed great, the duties arduous and responsible. I felt my own weakness and littleness; but I felt determined, the Lord being my helper, to endeavor to magnify it. When I first entered upon Mormonism, I did it with my eyes open. I counted the cost. I looked upon it as a life-long labor, and I considered that I was not only enlisted for time, but for eternity also, and did not wish to shrink now, although I felt my incompetency."

Having received notice of his appointment, and instructions from the Prophet to make his way to Far West as soon as possible, he appointed a time to leave, and in the interim made a farewell visit to the branches of the Church he had presided over, for the purpose of setting them in order.

Some time previous to being called to the Apostleship, in connection with a brother by the name of Henry Humphrey, Elder Taylor had purchased a house and barn and five acres of land within a quarter of a mile of the Kirtland Temple, where they had anticipated going into business together as soon as he should be released from presiding in Canada. This, with his expenses during nearly two years that he had been preaching in Canada without remuneration, left him with very little means. "But," he writes, "I put my trust in the Lord."

He told his wife to make preparations for leaving at a certain time.

"But how are you going to perform a journey of thirteen or fourteen hundred miles by land, and to a wilderness country without means?"

"I don't know; but the Lord will open out the way."

Everywhere he went, he told the Saints about the time he expected to leave for Far West, but still no visible prospect of getting there was yet in sight. Three or four days before the time appointed for his departure, he called upon a Brother John Mills, who had previously talked of going with him to Kirtland when the time came that he could leave Canada. Elder Taylor now told him that he would have to give up going to Kirtland as he had received word from the Prophet to go to Far West.

"Well, I'll go to Far West too," said Brother Mills, "won't you go with me, Brother Taylor, I have plenty of teams?"

Elder Taylor.—"Brother Mills, I have nothing to pay you with for taking me."

Brother Mills.—"That makes no difference."

Elder Taylor.—"But I have no money to pay my expenses."

Brother Mills.—"I have plenty, and it is at your service."

Elder Taylor.—"That is very kind of you, but I object to getting into debt without the prospect of being able to pay."

Brother Mills.—"But you need not pay."

Elder Taylor.—"Well, if you'll clear me of all responsibility in the matter, and take the Lord for your paymaster, I'll go with you."

Brother Mills.—"Oh, I am quite willing to agree to that."

And so it was arranged right then that they would travel together to Far West. Before the day of their departure had come, the Saints sent to Elder Taylor plenty of supplies, flour, cakes and hams; and as it was the winter season, and such things would keep, they furnished him enough roasted geese, ducks, and other cooked provisions to last himself and several other families hundreds of miles on the journey. Others sent him money and clothing, so that he had an abundance of everything; and as Brother Mills had supplied the necessary conveyance for the journey, it would appear that he had not trusted in the Lord in vain.

They fitted up a covered sleigh for their families to ride in, while their goods were conveyed in wagons. In this way they traveled to Kirtland.

CHAPTER 6 - DEFIANCE TO THE MOB

On arriving in Kirtland Elder Taylor found that the Presidency of the Church and many of the Saints had removed to Far West, Missouri. This alone was calculated to make a great alteration in the place, and surround it with a spirit of loneliness. But other causes had also been operating to bring about marked changes since his former visits to this shrine.

Only a year or two before, everything in and about Kirtland had been prosperous. The Saints abounded in everything their hearts could desire. The men wore expensive raiment, ornamented with velvets and silks of the richest and rarest quality. It may be taken for granted that the sisters were not a whit behind them. They were arrayed in their silks, satins, lace, veils and jewelry; and amid all their piety, manifested a full share of vanity and pride.

Speculation was rife all over the United States at that time, and the Saints did not escape the contagion. They started a banking institution, engaged in mercantile pursuits and land speculation. For a time they were prosperous and wealth rapidly accumulated among them. Sidney Rigdon declared, in a burst of enthusiasm, that the glory of the latter-days was now being ushered in, and that Zion would soon become the glory of the whole earth; when the Lord for silver would bring gold; for iron, brass; and for stones, iron. But a wave of financial disaster swept over the entire country. Banking institutions went down before it; thousands of merchants were hopelessly ruined; and in the general disaster Kirtland did not escape. Like the inhabitants of other towns her people were overwhelmed with financial embarrassment. "Distress, ruin and poverty," says Elder Taylor, "seemed to prevail. Apostates and corrupt men were prowling about as so many wolves seeking whom they might devour. They were oppressive, cruel, heartless; devising every pretext that the most satanic malignity could invent to harass the Saints. Fraud, false accusation and false swearing, vexatious law suits, personal violence, and bare-faced robbery abounded. They were truly afflicted, persecuted and tormented."

As snow failed them at Kirtland Elder Taylor and company had to abandon their sleigh and take to their wagons. The roads were so very bad, however, that they had only gone some twenty or thirty miles when they concluded it would be wise to stop until they should become dryer. In the village where they stopped Elder Taylor took a job of varnishing some furniture for a cabinet maker. While here he formed the acquaintance of a number of infidels with whom he frequently conversed, and they desired to hear him preach. He consented. They could not obtain the use of the Methodist Church, though they had assisted to build it; but nothing daunted, they cleared out and seated a cabinet maker's shop, and here the Elder held forth.

He proved the Bible true, and then taught them its principles. He proved the Book of Mormon true, and then preached from that. They were highly delighted with his lectures; and when the time came that he had to leave them, they deeply regretted his departure. One of the number took him by the hand and said: "Mr. Taylor, God bless you wherever you go."

Among them was a gentleman to whom the Prophet Joseph had gone to school. He spoke very highly of him as an exemplary, moral young man. He had never investigated the evidences concerning the Book of Mormon; but he knew the Prophet's character was misrepresented by pious frauds, jealous of his influence and the spread of Mormonism.

Near Columbus, the capital of Ohio, they stayed at a town where a number of brethren resided, and all were anxious to hear Elder Taylor preach. As they had no hall, it was arranged that he should speak in the open air.

A little before meeting time a number of the brethren came running to the house where he was stopping with the information that the whole town was gathering and that a number of men had proposed tar and feathers, and boasted they would dress him with them if he undertook to preach. The brethren advised him not to attempt it as they were not strong enough to protect him. After a moment's reflection, however, he decided to go and preach. The brethren remonstrated; they knew the tar and feathers were prepared and that he could not escape. He replied that he had made up his mind to go; they could go with him if they chose, if not, he would go alone.

A very large concourse of people had assembled to listen to him. He began his remarks by informing them that he had lately come from Canada—a land under monarchical rule; that standing as he then did on free soil, among free men, he experienced peculiar sensations.

"Gentlemen, I now stand among men whose fathers fought for and obtained one of the greatest blessings ever conferred upon the human family—the right to think, to speak, to write; the right to say who shall govern them, and the right to worship God according to the dictates of their own consciences—all of them sacred, human rights, and now guaranteed by the American Constitution. I see around me the sons of those noble sires, who, rather than bow to the behests of a tyrant, pledged their lives, fortunes and sacred honors to burst those fetters, enjoy freedom themselves, bequeath it to their posterity, or die in the attempt.

"They nobly fought and nobly conquered; and now the cap of liberty is elevated on the tops of your liberty poles throughout the land, and the flag of freedom waves from Wisconsin to Louisiana—from Maine to Missouri. Not only so, but your vessels—foremost in the world—sail over oceans, seas and bays; visiting every nation, and wherever those vessels go your flag flutters in the breeze, a hope is inspired among the down-trodden millions, that they, perchance, if they cannot find liberty in their own land, may find it with you. Gentlemen, with you liberty is more than a name; it is incorporated in your system; it is proclaimed by your senators; thundered by your cannon; lisped by your infants; taught to your school-boys; it echoes from mountain to mountain; reverberates through your valleys, and is whispered by every breeze. Is it any wonder, gentlemen, under these circumstances—having lately emerged from a monarchical government, that I should experience peculiar sensations in rising to address you?

"But, by the by, I have been informed that you purpose to tar and feather me, for my religious opinions Is this the boon you have inherited from your fathers? Is this the blessing they purchased with their dearest hearts' blood—this your liberty? If so, you now have a victim, and we will have an offering to the goddess of liberty." Here he tore open his vest and said: "Gentlemen come on with your tar and feathers, your victim is ready; and ye shades of the venerable patriots, gaze upon the deeds of your degenerate sons! Come on, gentlemen! Come on, I say, I am ready!"

No one moved, no one spoke. He stood there drawn to his full height, calm but defiant—the master of the situation.

After a pause of some moments he continued his remarks and preached with great boldness and power for some three hours.

At the conclusion of his discourse, he was waited upon by some of the leading citizens of the place who expressed their pleasure at what they had heard, and disclaimed, in behalf of the people, any intention of tarring and feathering him; but the brethren still insisted that such was the intention of the crowd, and that the tar and feathers had been provided; but they had been awed into silence by the boldness of Elder Taylor.

Near Indianapolis, Indiana, Brother Mills and the other brethren who had joined their company, obtained employment, and Elder Taylor and his family stayed at the house of a Brother Miller. While there his second son, Joseph James, was born.

During the two months that he remained in that place, he worked at his craft and also made a carriage for himself. He preached the gospel in Indianapolis and raised up a small branch of the Church. His wife having recovered from child bed, he continued his journey to the west, parting company with Brother Mills who was not ready to go.

Approaching De Witt, Caroll County, Missouri, about fifty miles from Far West, as he was holding back his horse, while descending a hill, his foot slipped and he fell from his carriage. The wheels passed over his arm, inflicting a serious injury, and he was again detained.

In DeWitt there was a number of Saints who had purchased land and settled there, and Elder Taylor stayed at the house of a Brother Humphreys. It was while at DeWitt that he had his first experience with mobs. It was late in the summer of 1938 when he arrived there, and the persecutions which were to terminate in the expulsion of the Saints from Missouri were just beginning.

The mob that first came upon the Saints at DeWitt, was led by two alleged ministers of the gospel, Sashiel Woods and Abbot Hancock. "This was the first mob I had ever seen," remarks Elder Taylor, "and the whole affair was new to me, especially when I considered the kind of officers they had. I had heretofore looked upon gospel ministers as messengers of peace; here they came not only in a war-like capacity, but as the leaders of an armed mob—a gang of marauders and free-booters, with the avowed object of driving peaceful citizens—men, women and children—from their homes."

It would appear that while Elder Taylor did not believe in fighting for slight infringements of his rights, he did believe to the fullest extent in self-defense; and the ease with which he adapted himself to the new circumstances in which he was placed, exhibited the character of the man. "I had no arms," he continues in his account of this affair at DeWitt, "and heretofore considered that I needed none in a Christian civilized land; but I found I had been laboring under a mistake. The civilization here was of a very low order, and the Christianity of a very questionable character. I therefore threw off the sling and bandages from my lame arm, suppressed my repugnance to fighting, borrowed a gun, bought a brace of pistols, and prepared myself at least for defensive measures."

There were twenty four of the brethren, and about one hundred and fifty of the mob. The little band, nothing daunted at the superior forces of the enemy, organized under a captain and prepared for the onset. "These *reverend* gentlemen," says Elder Taylor's narrative, "concluded that it was best to have a parley, and by a little strategy throw us off our guard. Having captured a stray Saint, they sent by him a message informing us that they would like three or four of our leaders to come and treat with them. To this we returned answer that they had come in the capacity of banditti, to interfere with our rights when in the peaceful prosecution of our daily avocations; that we could have no confidence in men occupying so questionable a position; that their *ruse* to divide us would not work; and though inferior to them in numbers, if they attempted to molest us, we should protect ourselves as best we could."

After some further parleying, the mob gave the Saints ten days in which to leave, threatening that if they were not gone in that time, they would return with increased forces, kill every man, woman and child, and throw their goods into the Missouri.

This affair having ended for the time being, Elder Taylor continued his journey, and finally reached Far West, where he met the Prophet Joseph, several of the Twelve and other leading brethren. The mob did not return in ten days upon the people of De Witt, but they did return early in October and the Saints at last had to abandon their homes there, although they had purchased their lands from the general government.

The history of the prominent men in the Church is so closely interwoven with that of the Church, that it is difficult to write the one without also writing the other; and in order to understand the scenes which the subject of this writing was now in the midst of, it will be necessary to relate as briefly as may be, the events which befell the Saints in the state of Missouri up to the time that Elder Taylor joined them, in the autumn of 1838.

From the Book of Mormon, the Saints learned that upon the continent of America the people of God, in the last days, are to build a holy city, the "New Jerusalem," or "Zion." In July, 1831, the Lord revealed the place where the city should be located and a temple built. That place was Independence, near the western boundary of Missouri; and there the Saints were commanded to gather, purchase the land and dedicate it unto the Lord. This commandment they began to fulfill, whereupon the jealous rage of the old settlers was aroused against them. It was the meeting of two elements that had little or no affinity with each other.

The old settlers were from the slaves states of the south, the Saints were from the free states of the north, and many of them from New England. The former were idle, indifferent to their surroundings, and the development of their lands; the latter were industrious, frugal, eager to make good homes, develop, build up and beautify the country—in short, make it the Zion of God in very deed. The Missourians were habitual Sabbath breakers; horse racing, cock-fighting and gambling being the "pleasures" they indulged in on that day, attended with the drunkenness and blasphemy which usually go hand in hand with such sports. Of course the Saints could not engage with them in this kind of life, their early training, no less than their religion, forebade it. The result was a coolness between the Saints and the old settlers, followed by suspicion on the part of the latter that they would be supplanted by the new comers. From that conviction to a resolution to prevent it was a short step, and they made haste to take it.

Although some of the Saints were, doubtless, unwise in much of their talk, they were guilty of no overt act against the peace and good order of the community in which they settled; nor did they in any way interfere with the old settlers, further, perhaps, than to remonstrate with them on their manner of life, and surely that was no act that called for violence.

But if there was no real cause for violence, it was easy to create an imaginary one, and this was done. All manner of false accusations were brought against the Saints. They were accused of tampering with the negro slaves, with a view to creating a servile insurrection; and of having a design to possess themselves of the land by force.

But it was their religion that was made the chief rock of offense. It was denounced as blasphemy—"derogatory of God and religion, and subversive of human reason;" and this because the Saints claimed and enjoyed, to some extent at least, the power and blessings which attended the gospel of Christ in ancient days. For these reasons(?) the old settlers determined to rid themselves of the Saints, "peaceably if they could, forcibly if they must;" and to the performance of this unlawful action, they pledged their "bodily power, their lives, fortunes and sacred honors." They organized mobs; and, finally, with acts of cruelty and violence that would bring the blush of shame to the cheek of a savage, they drove the Saints from Jackson County; stole or destroyed their goods, burned their houses and appropriated to their own use the lands the Saints had purchased. There were some twelve hundred Saints, men, women and children thus expelled by violence from Jackson County.

This first driving took place in December, 1833.

The exiles found a temporary resting place in Clay County, and while there petitioned the governor of the state to reinstate them in their lands, and give them protection when so reinstated. The governor replied that he could call out the militia and escort them back to their homes; but he considered that he had no authority to detail any force for their protection after he had thus reinstated them. As to go back under those circumstances would be exposing themselves to more violence from their enemies, they could not avail themselves of the governor's proffered assistance to return.

The Saints remained scattered through Clay and the surrounding counties until 1836, when, at the request of the citizens of Clay County, who had kindly received them in their affliction, they moved northward and petitioned for the forming of a new county. The new county was called Caldwell, and the county seat, Far West.

The rapidity with which the new county increased in population and prosperity, aroused the jealousy of the people in surrounding counties; and as the inhabitants of Jackson had despoiled the Saints with impunity, it encouraged others that were like-minded to attempt the same thing. Especially was this the case when they saw those who had taken a prominent part in expelling the Saints from Jackson County, holding high positions in the state.

The fact that the religion of the Saints was different from that professed by their neighbors was of itself sufficient to arouse the hatred and jealousy of the sectarian ministers, who throughout all the Missouri troubles took not only an active but a leading part. A leading part in what? In murdering, plundering, driving, imprisoning, whipping and turning out of their homes their fellow men! A fine occupation for ministers of the gospel truly! And for what? Because the Saints bore witness that God had restored to the earth the gospel of Jesus Christ in its fullness; that the Priesthood to administer in its ordinances was again conferred on men; and they announced it as their intention to beautify the earth and prepare a portion of it for the coming of the Son of God. For this they were hated by the Missourians, and considered the legitimate prey of the despoiler.

Another circumstance that increased the hatred and jealousy of the Missourians against the Saints was the growing political power of the latter; and it was at a political election in Gallatin, Daviess County—a county joining Caldwell on the north—that the troubles in the autumn of 1838 began.

A number of the Saints had settled in Daviess County, and being citizens of the United States, and of the state and county where they lived, and possessing all the qualifications of voters, they essayed to cast their ballots at the aforesaid election, but some of the old settlers sought forcibly to prevent them; a thing which the brethren would not quietly submit to, and a disturbance was the result. Upon that difficulty the mob founded their pretext for the commencement of open hostilities. The clouds which had been gathering hatred and jealousy for so long, burst almost without warning upon the unprotected heads of the Saints.

Scenes of mob violence were of almost daily occurrence; property was destroyed, men were tied up and beaten until blood streamed down their backs; the chastity of women was forcibly outraged; cattle and hogs were wantonly shot down; houses were ruthlessly burned in the presence of their owners; fields of grain destroyed—but this was not the worst—helpless women and children were brutally murdered together with defenseless old men, some of whom had fought in the continental army during the American Revolution. Elder Taylor, in relating these scenes some thirty years after they had occurred, refers to one who had been of the class last named:

"My mind wanders back upwardly of thirty years ago," he says, "when in the state of Missouri, Mr. McBride, a gray-haired, venerable veteran of the Revolution, with feeble frame and tottering steps, cried to a Missouri patriot: 'Spare my life, I am a revolutionary soldier, I fought for liberty, would you murder me? What is my offense, I believe in God and revelation?' This frenzied disciple of a misplaced faith said, 'Take that you God d—d Mormon,' and with the butt of his gun he dashed his brains out, and he lay quivering there, his white locks clotted with his own brains and gore, on the soil that he had heretofore shed his blood to redeem—a sacrifice at the shrine of liberty!"

Taking advantage of the disturbance at the election in Gallatin, some of the old settlers at Millport, in the same county, set fire to their log huts and then fled southward, spreading the report that the Mormons had burned their houses and driven them from their lands. At this rumor, false though it was, a wave of popular indignation passed through the state, which Governor Boggs took advantage of to issue an exterminating order, and called out the militia of the state to execute it.

Governor Boggs was the more ready to issue this infamous order, because he himself had imbibed a hatred of the Saints, and had been an active participant against them in the Jackson County troubles.

By this edict the Governor virtually converted the mobs that had been plundering the Saints into the state militia, and gave them full license to continue the war on the Saints, which they did in the most brutal manner.

The result of these outrages was that some four hundred of the Saints were either murdered outright or died from exposure and hardship inflicted upon them in this unhallowed persecution; from twelve to fifteen thousand citizens of the United States were expelled from the state of Missouri—from the lands they had purchased of the general government; while their homes were destroyed, and their stock and much other property were confiscated. Many of the leaders in the Church, among them the Prophet Joseph and his brother Hyrum, were cast into prison.

Elder Taylor was a witness of these high-handed and unlawful proceedings, and a sufferer in some of them. One circumstance he relates which I do not remember to have seen elsewhere, and hence give it here:

"On one occasion, when some thirty-five hundred of the mob forces were approaching Far West, our officer, Colonel Hinkle, sought to betray us, and as a preliminary step, ordered us to retreat. 'Retreat!' exclaimed Joseph Smith. 'Why, where in the name of God shall we go?' Then turning to our men he said: 'Boys, follow me.' About two hundred men went out on the open prairie to meet the thirty-five hundred. While these forces faced each other, a flag of truce came in from the mob bearing the message that it was their intention to destroy Far West; but there was a man and his family—of the name of Lightner—not Mormons, who had friends among the attacking party, and they desired this family to leave the city before it was destroyed. This message was sent to the family. They replied that they had always been treated with consideration by the Mormons, and they would stay with them. This reply the Prophet Joseph took in person to the flag of truce man; and just then a troop of cavalry, two hundred strong, was seen approaching, and Joseph added this to the answer sent by the non-Mormon family: 'Go tell your general for me that if he does not immediately withdraw his men, I will send them to hell!'"

Notwithstanding their superiority in numbers the mob beat a hasty and inglorious retreat.

Such were the scenes enacted in Missouri during the stay of Elder Taylor in that state; and it was in the midst of such scenes as these, on the 19th of December, 1838, that he was ordained an Apostle of the Lord Jesus Christ, by Brigham Young and Heber C. Kimball.

CHAPTER 7 - PROPHESY FULFILLED

The Saints, after their expulsion from the State of Missouri, found a temporary resting place in Quincy, Illinois, and to that city, after visiting the Prophet Joseph Smith in Liberty prison, the place of his incarceration, Elder Taylor made his way.

Several of the Apostles who met there held a consultation in respect to the revelation which had been given the July previous, commanding their quorum to take leave of the Saints in the city of Far West, on the 26th day of April, 1839, at the building spot of the Lord's house, previous to crossing the Atlantic on a mission to foreign lands. It had been the constant boast of the mob from the time the revelation was made known, that this was one of "Joe Smith's" revelations that should fail of fulfillment if no other did. But the several Apostles who took part in the above mentioned consultation, among whom was Elder Taylor, were determined that the revelation should not fail, and agreed to return to Far West by different routes, and meet at the temple site on the day appointed.

Their undertaking was successful. Five of the Apostles were at the temple site before daylight of the day appointed, together with a number of high priests, elders and priests. At this meeting they excommunicated a number of persons from the Church, ordained Wilford Woodruff and George A. Smith apostles, and others were ordained to the office of seventy. Prayer was offered up by the apostles in the order of their standing in their quorum. It was a brilliant, moonlight night, according to Elder Taylor, and out on the still air, strong and clear rose that glorious song of Zion—

ADAM ONDI-AHMAN

This earth was once a garden place,
With all her glories common;
And men did live a holy race,
And worship Jesus face to face—
    In Adam-ondi-Ahman.
We read that Enoch walked with God,
Above the power of mammon;
While Zion spread herself abroad,
And saints and angels sang aloud—
    In Adam-ondi-Ahman.
Her land was good and greatly blest,
Beyond old Israel's Canaan;
Her fame was known from east to west,
Her peace was great, and pure the rest
    Of Adam-ondi-Ahman.
Hosanna to such days to come—
The Savior's second coming,
When all the earth in glorious bloom
Affords the saints a holy home,
    Like Adam-ondi-Ahman.

At the conclusion of the hymn, Elder Alpheus Cutler, the master workman of the Lord's House, laid the south-east corner stone in its position, and stated that in consequence of the peculiar situation of the Saints it was deemed prudent to discontinue further labor on the house until the Lord should open the way for its completion. The Apostles then took leave of some seventeen Saints who were present, and started on their way to fill their missions beyond the Atlantic.

On their way they stopped at Quincy, where they met the Prophet Joseph, who had lately escaped from the hands of his enemies in Missouri. The Prophet heartily approved the labors of the Twelve, and their course received also the commendation of the Church in a general conference assembled at Quincy.

The Saints that same spring began settling at Commerce, afterwards Nauvoo, on the east bank of the Mississippi, in Hancock County, Illinois. By this time the reaction from the excitement in which they had lived for more than a year, set in, and almost the entire people sank down from exhaustion, and became an easy prey to the malaria prevalent in the district at that time.

In the midst of this sickness, poverty and general wretchedness, Elder Taylor made his preparations to continue his journey to England. He had secured quarters for his family, in connection with others, in miserable, old log barracks in Montrose, a small settlement opposite Nauvoo, in what was then the Territory of Iowa.

It was the 8th of August that he left Montrose to fill his mission. He dedicated his wife and family to the care of the Lord, and blessed them in His name: "The thought of the hardships they had just endured," he remarks, "the uncertainty of their continuing in the house they then occupied—and that only a solitary room—the prevalence of disease, the poverty of the brethren, their insecurity from mobs, together with the uncertainty of what might take place during my absence, produced feelings of no ordinary character. These solicitations, paternal and conjugal, were enhanced also by the time and distance that was to separate us. But the thought of going forth at the command of the God of Israel to revisit my native land, to unfold the principles of eternal truth and make known the things that God had revealed for the salvation of the world, overcame every other feeling."

In Nauvoo Elder Taylor joined Wilford Woodruff, who was scarcely able to drag himself along, and who remarked that he felt and looked more like a subject for the dissecting room than a missionary. After taking leave of the Prophet and his counselors, Sidney Rigdon and Hyrum Smith, Elder Taylor and his sick companion left Nauvoo.

On the outskirts of the settlement they passed Parley P. Pratt and Heber C. Kimball, who were building a log house. Parley, who, it will be remembered, had carried the gospel to Elder Taylor, was stripped—bare headed and bare footed. He hailed the brethren as they were passing and gave them a purse, it was all he had. Elder Heber C. Kimball, who was but a short distance away, stripped as Elder Pratt was, came up and said, "As Brother Parley has given you a purse, I have a dollar I will give you to put in it." Then mutually blessing each other, they said farewell. Elders Taylor and Woodruff were the first of their quorum to start on their mission.

At Macomb they found Brother Zebedee Coltrin, who proposed taking them as far as Cleveland, Ohio, in his wagon, a proposition they gladly accepted. At this place a Brother Miller, whom Elder Taylor baptized while there, gave them a horse, and another a saddle and bridle. At Springfield a broker sold his horse for him, and with the proceeds he published a pamphlet on the persecutions of the Saints in Missouri. The edition was 2,000. A portion of these pamphlets were left in the hands of Elder Coltrin to dispose of, the proceeds to be given to Sisters Taylor and Woodruff.

Elder Taylor's strong constitution and iron will had carried him through the Missouri troubles and the trying scenes of poverty and sickness which prevailed that summer about Nauvoo; but as he traveled eastward his health began failing him. Approaching Indianapolis he was taken with violent vomiting and afterwards fainted by the wagon in the road. It was with some difficulty that his companions resuscitated him and conveyed him to the house of Brother Horace S. Eldredge, where he received the kindest treatment. Notwithstanding there were rest and attention for him at the home of Brother Eldredge until he should be restored, weak as he was, he continued his journey next morning. He would travel all day and frequently preach at night, though scarcely able to stand upon his feet.

At Germantown, in Indiana, his strength again failed him; and seeing no prospect of immediate recovery, he advised Brothers Woodruff and Coltrin to proceed on their journey without him. This they reluctantly did.

The name of the proprietor of the hotel in Germantown where he stopped was Jacob Waltz; both from himself and his wife Elder Taylor received the kindest attention.

After a severe illness of two weeks, during which time he was reduced to a mere skeleton, he began to recover; and with returning health came the old burning desire to preach the gospel; and before he was fairly able to stand he obtained the court house adjacent to his hotel and began holding meetings, though he had to sit part of the time while delivering his discourses.

One thing that much surprised those who listened to him was that, although he was a long distance from his home and friends, and had been prostrate with sickness among strangers, and on expenses, he never alluded to these things or begged for assistance. What a contrast between this servant of God and the sectarian priests of the day! Had one of their number been similarly situated, what a tale of woe would have been told of his heroic suffering for the gospel's sake, and what pathetic appeals would have been made to the generous who, loved the Lord, for assistance! But this Apostle of Jesus Christ bore all patiently, more anxious to deliver the message he bore than secure his own comfort. At last a gentleman waited upon him, and asking to be excused for the liberty he was about to take, referred to the above matters in the following manner:

"Mr. Taylor, you do not act as most preachers do; you have said nothing about your circumstances or money, yet you have been here some time sick; your doctor's, hotel and other bills must be heavy. Some friends and myself have talked these matters over and would like to assist you, though we do not wish to give any offense."

In replying to this Elder Taylor thanked the gentleman, and said:

"I preach without purse or scrip, leaving the Lord to manage those matters you speak of in His own way; and as you have been prompted by the Lord and your own generous impulses, I shall thankfully receive whatever assistance you are disposed to render me."

The gentleman then presented him a small sum of money, which, with what he had, was sufficient to settle all his bills and enable him to pursue his journey.

Commenting upon the above incident, Elder Taylor says: "I would rather put my trust in the Lord than in any of the kings of the earth."

Bidding farewell to his kind host and other friends in Germantown, he started for Dayton, Ohio. The first day out he reached the town of Richmond, at 5 o'clock, and two hours later he was lecturing to a large audience on the "Mormon Difficulties in Missouri," and the next day was on his way to Dayton.

Here he remained a few days preaching the gospel, and then had a serious relapse which confined him to the house of a friend, a Brother Brown, for two weeks. As he was recovering from his illness and preparing to leave Dayton, he was agreeably surprised to learn of the arrival of his fellow Apostle, George A. Smith, and others. Elder Smith was on his way to England also, and as there was room in his wagon, he invited Elder Taylor to ride with him—a proposition that was gladly accepted.

Together they traveled to Kirtland where they met Elders Brigham Young and Heber C. Kimball. Here Elder Taylor was again stricken down by sickness; but through the blessings of God he recovered sufficiently to accompany his brethren on their way to New York. They arrived in that city in due time, and were cordially welcomed to the house of Parley P. Pratt, whom Elder Taylor had left in Nauvoo a few months before, putting up a log house; but who was now presiding over a large branch of the Church in the metropolis of the United States.

I have been particular to relate the details of this trying journey from Nauvoo to New York, that the readers of this work may have a knowledge of the difficulties encountered by Elder Taylor, in his efforts to comply with the requirement of God to preach the gospel in his native land. Truly he went forth weeping, but bearing precious seed; and we shall see, anon, how he returned rejoicing, bringing his sheaves with him.

CHAPTER 8 - PLENTY OF MONEY

When Elder Taylor arrived in New York, Elder Woodruff had been there some time, and was all impatience to embark for England, but as yet the former had no means with which to pay for his ocean passage. Although supplied with all the means necessary on his journey thus far, after paying his cab-fare to the house of Brother Pratt he had but one cent left. Still he was the last man on earth to plead poverty, and in answer to inquiries of some of the brethren as to his financial circumstances, he replied that he had plenty of money.

This was reported to Brother Pratt, who the next day approached Elder Taylor on the subject:

Elder Pratt: "Brother Taylor, I hear you have plenty of money?"

Elder Taylor: "Yes, Brother Pratt, that's true."

Elder Pratt: "Well, I am about to publish my 'Voice of Warning' and 'Millennial Poems,' I am very much in need of money, and if you could furnish me two or three hundred dollars I should be very much obliged."

Elder Taylor: "Well, Brother Parley, you are welcome to anything I have, if it will be of service to you."

Elder Pratt: "I never saw the time when means would be more acceptable."

Elder Taylor: "Then you are welcome to all I have."

And putting his hand into his pocket Elder Taylor gave him his copper cent. A laugh followed.

"But I thought you gave it out that you had plenty of money," said Parley.

"Yes, and so I have," replied Elder Taylor. "I am well clothed, you furnish me plenty to eat and drink and good lodging; with all these things and a penny over, as I owe nothing, is not that plenty?"

That evening at a council meeting Elder Pratt proposed that the brethren assist Elder Taylor with means to pay his passage to England as Brother Woodruff was prepared and desired to go. To this Elder Taylor objected and told the brethren if they had anything to give to let Parley have it, as he had a family to support and needed means for publishing. At the close of the meeting Elder Woodruff expressed his regret at the course taken by Elder Taylor, as he had been waiting for him, and at last had engaged his passage.

Elder Taylor: "Well, Brother Woodruff, if you think it best for me to go, I will accompany you."

Elder Woodruff: "But where will you get the money?"

Elder Taylor: "Oh, there will be no difficulty about that. Go and take a passage for me on your vessel, and I will furnish you the means."

A Brother Theodore Turley, hearing the above conversation, and thinking that Elder Taylor had resources unknown to himself or Brother Woodruff, said: "I wish I could go with you, I would do your cooking and wait on you."

The passage to be secured was in the steerage—these missionaries were not going on flowery beds of ease—hence the necessity of such service as Brother Turley proposed rendering. In answer to this appeal, Elder Taylor told Brother Woodruff to take a passage for Brother Turley also.

At the time of making these arrangements Elder Taylor had no money, but the Spirit had whispered him that means would be forthcoming, and when had that still, small voice failed him! In that he trusted, and he did not trust in vain. Although he did not ask for a penny of anyone, from various persons in voluntary donations he received money enough to meet his engagements for the passage of himself and Brother Turley, but no more.

Elder Taylor and his two companions embarked on the 10th of December, 1839, and after a very prosperous voyage arrived in Liverpool, January 11th, 1840. Two days later they went to Preston, Lancashire.

In 1837, Apostles Heber C. Kimball and Orson Hyde and several other Elders had opened the door of the gospel in England, and raised up several branches of the Church, the principal one being in Preston. Elder Willard Richards had been left in charge of the mission in England, after the return of Elder Kimball in the spring of 1838; and Elder Joseph Fielding, an old Canadian friend of Elder Taylor's,—at whose instance he had written an account of the restoration of the gospel to England some years before—presided over the branch at Preston.

A council of the priesthood within reach was held at Preston, at which it was decided that Elder Taylor should labor in Liverpool, with Elder Fielding to assist him. After receiving this assignment the brethren at once repaired to Liverpool and began their labors.

A few words here relative to the opening of this English mission. In England, as in Canada, the servants of God found a people looking for and prepared to receive the gospel. They believed the major part of those things which the Elders of Israel had come into their midst to proclaim, as the company of gentlemen did with whom Elder Taylor was associated in Toronto. The people were in that peculiar frame of mind that made them realize that great changes in systems were about to take place. The Spirit of God was moving upon the righteous, and when they heard the gospel they were ready to receive it.

Among those so situated was a Mr. Matthews, a brother-in-law to Elder Joseph Fielding, and formerly a Church of England minister; but he had resigned his position because he saw how far that church had departed from the gospel of the New Testament; and how destitute it was of the gifts and powers of the Holy Ghost; and because it was not making any preparations for the coming and reign of Christ on earth. He had heard the gospel preached by Elders

Richards and Goodson, in Bedfordshire; he testified of its truth to his congregation; and went so far as to appoint a time when he would be baptized with a number of his followers. For some cause he failed to put in an appearance at the appointed time, his mind became darkened and he opposed the Elders, but adopted their principles and began preaching them on his own account. In this way he raised up a number of congregations, one of which was located in Liverpool.

Elder Taylor and his companion diligently searched these people out and presented the gospel message to them. Some gladly received the word, and others rejected it with great bitterness. Against some of this latter class the brethren washed their feet as a witness against them. The manner in which they complied with this ordinance appointed unto them is described by Elder Taylor as follows:

"We washed our feet and then knelt before the Lord and bore testimony of it, saying: 'O Lord, our Heavenly Father, we Thy servants have borne testimony to the truth of those things which Thou hast revealed to Mr. S—, and he has rejected our testimony. O, Father, Thou knowest we have no hard feelings toward the man; if Thou canst forgive him and lead him to the truth, do so, we pray Thee. O, Father, we do this that we may fulfill Thy word, and bear testimony before Thee according to Thy commandment; and now, O, Lord, we leave him in Thy hands, praying Thee to guide us into all truth, in the name of Jesus. Amen.'"

When the Sabbath came they attended services at a chapel in Hope Street, where Mr. Matthews usually held forth. He was absent on this occasion, but a young man, whom Elder Taylor describes as very devout, preached. He lamented the state of the church, its pride, its vanity, its lack of spiritual power; prayed for the blessings of the Holy Ghost to be again made manifest, and for the coming of Christ's kingdom.

Such an opening as this was not neglected by Elder Taylor. At the close of the meeting he arose and requested the privilege of speaking. He was told, however, that he had better repair to the vestry and there a hearing would be accorded him. He accepted the proposition. Some sixteen or twenty class-leaders and elders were present who seemed anxious to learn what sect the brethren were of. Setting aside that matter, Elder Taylor thus addressed them:

"Gentlemen, friends and brethren; I have listened with deep interest to the things that I have heard this morning. I have observed with peculiar emotions the deep anxiety, the fervent prayer and the strong solicitude manifested by you in relation to obtaining the Holy Ghost. I have been pleased with the correct views you entertain in regard to the situation of the world. We believe in those things as you do. We hear that you believe in baptism and the laying on of hands, so also do we. Brethren and friends, we are the humble followers of Jesus Christ and are from America. I lately arrived in this place, and have come five thousand miles without purse or scrip, and I testify to you, my brethren, that the Lord has revealed Himself from heaven and put us in possession of these things you are so anxiously looking for and praying that you may receive." ("Glory be to God," was shouted by many present, and great emotion manifested.)

"That thing has taken place which is spoken of by John in the Revelations, where he says: 'I saw another angel fly in the midst of heaven, having the everlasting gospel to preach unto them that dwell upon the earth, and to every nation and kindred and tongue and people, saying with a loud voice, Fear God and give glory to him, for the hour of his judgment is come.' Brethren, we the servants of God are come to this place to warn the inhabitants of their approaching danger, and to call upon them to repent and be baptized in the name of Jesus Christ, and they shall receive the gift of the Holy Ghost.

"I feel an anxious desire to deliver this testimony. I feel the word of the Lord like fire in my bones and am desirous to have an opportunity of proclaiming to you those blessings that you are looking for, that you may rejoice with us in those glorious things which God has revealed for the salvation of the world in the last days."

This speech filled many with exceeding great rejoicing, some even wept for joy, while others were equally filled with zealous rage. The class so affected demanded to know if they were not Mormons.

"No," replied Elder Taylor, "we belong to the Church of Jesus Christ of Latter-day Saints, called by our enemies the 'Mormon Church.'"

When this was known some said they had heard an unfavorable opinion of that people. Others said that their pastor, Mr. Matthews, had declared the thing was from hell, etc.; and in answer to the application for the chapel to preach in, an unfavorable reply was made.

In the afternoon Elder Taylor and companion attended a meeting of the non-communion Baptists. The brethren made themselves known to the leader of the meeting and asked for the use of the house, telling him he might make collections and keep the money for his society if he would grant them the privilege of speaking. He excused himself on the grounds that the Baptist society was so rigid that they would refuse to hear; but he treated them very kindly.

In the evening they again attended service at Mr. Matthews' chapel. "There are many who will become Saints among them," predicted Elder Taylor, "but they, like others, are sadly under the influence of priests." That night after meeting one of the preachers of the society, of the name of William Mitchell, came to Elder Taylor and invited him to his home, and during the next week opened his house for him to hold meetings in. And notwithstanding all the efforts on the part of Mr. Matthews' preachers and class-leaders to prevent their members from going, the house was filled. At the first meeting Mr. Mitchell and his wife expressed their determination to receive the message, and others soon followed. A hall in Preston Street was taken, capable of seating about three hundred, and the first night it was well filled.

Elder Taylor's text was from Jude:

"It was needful for me to exhort you, that ye should earnestly contend for the faith which was delivered to the Saints."

He referred to the laudable efforts of such reformers as Luther, Melancthon, Calvin, Wesley, Whitfield and others who had tried to bring about the ancient order of things, but by reference to the gospel as contained in the New Testament, showed that they had failed to accomplish it. This was followed up by an account of how the gospel had been restored to the earth in the present age by the ministration of angels and the revelations of God to the Prophet Joseph Smith. He showed them how what they had been praying for was now accomplished, and exhorted them to receive it.

The effect of his discourse was overwhelming. Exclamations of praise and thanksgiving were heard in various parts of the house, while the weeping of others testified to the emotion they could not otherwise express. Ten offered themselves for baptism at the close of the meeting, and many others expressed a friendly disposition.

Meantime the news had reached Mr. Matthews that his sheepfold had been invaded by the "Mormons," and he wrote back a letter warning his flock against "Mormonism," but to no purpose. The ten were baptized, among them Mr. Mitchell, and a great many who attended to witness the ceremony of baptism expressed a desire to obey the message the next time a day was appointed for baptisms. Thus the work was begun in Liverpool.

CHAPTER 9 - FIRST BAPTISM

Elder Taylor continued calling upon ministers and other gentlemen in Liverpool, bearing testimony to them of the restoration of the gospel. For this purpose he called upon an aged Methodist minister who accompanied Doctor Coke in some of his missionary tours, and who was with him when he died.

The conversation with him was very pleasant, but he did not receive the message of the gospel. He inquired if his visitor intended calling upon all the ministers in the city, to which the Elder replied that it was his determination to deliver the message he had been commissioned with; he had called upon some ministers and intended to see others; and if there was liberality enough among the Methodists or other denominations to open their chapels, he would preach. To this the minister replied that he thought the doctrines Elder Taylor had to advocate would not agree with theirs, and that he would have to do as the venerable founder of Methodism had done—go into the highways and the fields.

"But when Paul, the despised Christian, went into the synagogues of the Jews, bigoted and fallen as they were," replied the Elder, "they said to him and his companions, 'Brethren, if ye have any word of exhortation for the people, say on."

"That is what I say," answered the Methodist, "say on."

"Yes," replied Elder Taylor, "but this is not in your synagogue, sir."

To this gentle hint he could only say that he thought the trustees would not consent to it. In parting, he shook the Elder by the hand and wished him God-speed.

Elder Taylor also called upon Mr. Radcliff, agent for the Bible Society and superintendent of the School of Arts. In a conversation lasting over of three hours, that gentleman made many admissions relative to the condition of the religious world, which, when his visitor began to make use of them to show the necessity of a re-opening of the heavens and a restoration of the ancient gospel, he stopped alarmed, and observed that "Mormonism led to tremendous conclusions!"

"I am aware that it does," quietly replied his visitor, "but the words I have used are not mine, but the words of God."

There was present at this interview a Miss Brannan, from the Isle of Man, who expressed a fear of Elder Taylor's religion; and who, as the conversation drew to a close, ventured to censure him because he condemned others.

"No, he does not," said Mr. Radcliff, "he only says they have been wrong ignorantly, and that they have doubtless lived up to the best light they had."

Miss Brannan did not relish this remark, and relapsed into silence.

Before leaving them, Elder Taylor remarked to her that he was thinking of going to the Isle of Man, and he would be pleased to call upon her. She would be glad to see him, but not as a religious teacher. Or if he was like other preachers, she would be pleased to receive him. To this the Elder replied that he should visit the Isle of Man whether she desired him to or not; that there were others there who would receive the gospel if she rejected it, and as to the matter of being like other ministers, it reminded him of the story of the Prophet Micah, who was told to speak as the other prophets of king Ahab had spoken, and it would be well with him; but Micah replied: "As the Lord liveth, even what my God saith, that will I speak." So, likewise, he could only declare that which God had revealed; if that came in conflict with the doctrines and practices of men, so much the worse for their doctrines and practices.

In this manner Elder Taylor continued to labor day after day, neither avoiding the poor and lowly nor shunning the high and the learned. Conscious that he possessed the truth, he fearlessly came in contact with all sorts and conditions of men; and so gentlemanly and pleasing was his bearing that it compelled men to listen to the message he delivered with respectful attention.

On the 6th of April, 1840, Apostles Brigham Young, Heber C. Kimball, Parley P. Pratt, Orson Pratt, George A. Smith and Elder Reuben Hedlock arrived in Liverpool, from America. The next day they found Elder Taylor, who was overjoyed to see them. In a few days they repaired to Preston and held a council—seven of the quorum of Apostles being present.

The first business of the council was to ordain Willard Richards an Apostle, and receive him into the quorum. This addition made eight Apostles in the council. Brigham Young presided; Elder Taylor was made clerk. The former was also sustained as the President of the Twelve Apostles, he being next in seniority of ordination to Thomas B. Marsh, the former President, who apostatized in Missouri.

It was resolved that a periodical should be published and called the *Latter-day Saints' Millennial Star*, of which Parley P. Pratt was appointed editor. A hymn book was also to be published, John Taylor being one of a committee of three to select the hymns. It was also decided to print an edition of the Book of Mormon.

In appointing the several Apostles to fields of labor, it was decided that Elder Taylor continue to preach in Liverpool and vicinity.

On his return to that city, the work spread more rapidly than before the council at Preston. Opportunities for preaching were plentiful, and baptisms frequent. In May he called those who had been baptized together, and ordained a number of the brethren Priests and Elders, which gave them the right to preach the gospel and to administer the ordinances thereof. These brethren, filled with zeal, went out into the public parks, to the commons, the fields and even the streets, proclaiming everywhere the gospel and bearing testimony of its truth.

When the opposition of the priests increased in bitterness, and they sought by every conceivable device to hinder the work and disturb the meetings, Elder Taylor instructed several of the most zealous of the brethren to hold auxiliary meetings simultaneously on the public thoroughfares—just prior to the time appointed for the main central meeting—and announce to their hearers that a discourse would be delivered in the public hall, engaged for that purpose. In this way an interest was awakened in the work, and the meetings crowded with people, notwithstanding all the efforts of the hostile ministers to prevent it.

These labors, and assisting in selecting the hymns suitable for the worship of the Saints, together with reading the proofs and superintending the printing of the Book of Mormon, occupied the early summer of 1840.

In July, however, Elder Taylor took the Music Hall in Bold Street, a large hall, capable of seating some fifteen hundred people, in which he proposed delivering a course of lectures.

Pending the opening of this hall for the lectures, he went to Ireland to proclaim the restoration of the gospel in that land. Among many others he baptized in Liverpool was a Mr. McGuffie, who had some acquaintances in Newry, County Down, Ireland. This man and a Brother William Black he took with him as his companions.

A large company of Saints went with them to the dock to see them off. It was but natural that Elder Taylor should contrast his situation, now that he was departing for Ireland, with what it was when he landed in England a few months before. Then he was friendless, unknown and among strangers; now he was surrounded by a multitude of friends, anxious to administer to his necessities and willing to assist him in his mission, while few men in Liverpool were more sought for, or filled a larger space in public attention.

The company remained on the pier-head waving their adieux until they could no longer be seen.

The day after sailing, Elder Taylor and companions arrived in Newry, a beautiful Irish village nestled among rolling hills, characteristic of that part of Ireland. Brother McGuffie obtained the Court House to hold a meeting in, and sent around the bell-man to give notice of it. A congregation of six or seven hundred gathered in at seven o'clock in the evening, and Elder Taylor preached to them. This was the introduction of the gospel into Ireland.

An appointment was given out for the next evening, but only a few attended, and Elder Taylor turned the meeting into a sort of conversational, promising to explain anything those present wished to know respecting the message he had delivered to them the night before. Thus the evening was passed.

It was determined that night—as his stay in Ireland could only be brief, in consequence of his appointments in Liverpool—that the next day they would proceed to the other points they had proposed to visit.

In the night Elder Taylor in a vision saw a gentleman approach him and ask him to stay, saying he would be pleased to hear him. The next morning, as himself, Brothers McGuffie and Black and a gentleman of the name of Thomas Tate were leaving the village in a jaunting car, the same man whom Elder Taylor had seen in the vision stopped them and requested him to remain; but as Brother McGuffie expected to return to Newry and remain there some time, Elder Taylor concluded to go on his way.

After a ride of seven miles through a beautiful, fertile, undulating country, cut up into small farms by green hedges closely trimmed, and plentifully dotted with neatly white-washed cottages, they arrived at the four towns of Bellimacrat, where, in the evening, Elder Taylor preached in a barn owned by a Mr. Willie. The following morning they started on foot for the town of Lisburn, Mr. Tate going with them to assist in carrying their valises. This Mr. Tate Elder Taylor had met in Liverpool, and prophesied that he would be the first person to be baptized in Ireland. As he and Elder Taylor walked on, side by side, that beautiful, fresh morning they left Bellimacrat, the latter opened the scriptures to his understanding and taught him the gospel in its simplicity. The listener was carried away with admiration for the plan of redemption which God had established for the salvation of His children, and as conviction of its truth had taken hold of his mind, he was ready to receive it; and on reaching the summit of a hill, which suddenly brought them in full view of the beautiful Lock Brickland, he cried out in ecstacy:

"There is water, what doth hinder me being baptized?"

At this the party stopped, and Elder Taylor, going down into the water, baptized him. He was the first to receive the gospel in Ireland in this dispensation.

In the town of Lisburn Elder Taylor preached four times in the market place to large and attentive crowds.

The preaching in Market Square created considerable interest in that place, but no one applied for baptism. The whole of County Down had been considerably excited by the meetings held, and before leaving Lisburn Elder Taylor learned that Brother McGuffie on his return to Newry had begun to baptize.

Having thus opened the door of salvation to the Irish nation by the proclamation of the gospel, Elder Taylor, on the 6th of August, took passage on a steamer at Belfast for the city of Glasgow. On board he formed the acquaintance of a gentleman who had met with Elder Orson Pratt in Edinburgh, where that Apostle was laboring; and also with an Irish gentleman from Belfast. The latter was a friend of a Mr. Mulholland, of Illinois, who had written him an account of the persecutions of the Saints in Missouri. He had the letter published in one of the Belfast papers.

On arriving in Glasgow, Elder Taylor met with Elders Hedlock, Clark and Mulliner, and the following Sunday preached to the Saints there, and ordained two brethren Elders. He also visited a small branch of the Church in Paisley, Renfrewshire. Here that love which the gospel inspires in the hearts of those who receive it was abundantly manifested. Though Elder Taylor was a stranger to the Saints there, they gathered about him, pleaded with him to remain in their midst and teach them something further concerning the Kingdom of God. Failing to persuade him to remain longer, as the time for him to be in Liverpool drew near, they flocked about him for his blessing, and it was not until the night was gone and day was approaching that he could get a chance to retire to rest.

CHAPTER 10 – REFLECTIONS

Returning to Liverpool Elder Taylor delivered his course of lectures in the Music Hall, Bold Street. The course covered the principal events connected with the work of the Lord in these last days. The transgression of the laws of the gospel; the changing of its ordinances; the breaking of the covenant thereof after its introduction by the personal ministration of the Son of God; the restoration of the gospel through the ministration of angels; the restoration, and the powers and authority of the Holy Priesthood; the coming forth, character and value of the Book of Mormon; the gathering of Israel and final redemption of the earth, etc., etc. The lectures were numerously attended and created considerable interest in religious circles.

During his absence in Ireland and Scotland the local Elders in Liverpool had been very active, and a number had been added to the Church. He also found that Elders Curtis and Winchester had arrived from New York. Both these Elders were able ministers of the word. The latter had distinguished himself by his labors in Philadelphia, the former in New York, near which city was his home. Elder Curtis was sent to Ireland to continue the work commenced there.

Considerable opposition ran side by side with the labors of Elder Taylor in Liverpool. The ministers belonging to the churches founded by Mr. Matthews and his chief supporter, Mr. Aitkins, were the principals in this opposition. They had been very near the truth at one time—not far removed from the Kingdom of God; but having made up their minds to reject it, the light they once possessed departed from them. They were filled with bitterness, jealousy and hatred, and in their madness descended to methods of opposition unworthy of those who profess to be gentlemen, to say nothing of men who professed to be followers and ministers of the Son of God. They raised commotions in some of the meetings where Elder Taylor held forth that would have disgraced the meetings in the very heart of a political campaign. They denounced him whose doctrines they could not refute by the word of God or by reason, as a liar, a wolf in sheep's clothing, a hypocrite, a false prophet, and every other vile epithet that the malice of men or the ingenuity of Satan could invent. Truly having rejected the truth, they were given up to a hard heart and a reprobate mind.

Seeing that everything was moving along satisfactorily in Liverpool, Elder Taylor determined to make his long contemplated visit to the Isle of Man. He started on the 16th of September, 1840, having for companions Elder Hiram Clark and Brother William Mitchel, one of the first to receive his testimony in Liverpool. The party arrived in Douglas the next day.

It was but natural that his arrival in this island should awaken his remembrance of "Nora," as he affectionately called his wife, Leonora. Here she had spent her youthful days in the home of her father. Here, amid the green hills and flower-flecked vales, which everywhere abound in this delightful island, she had wandered in girlhood, buoyant with hope and joy; or with a pleasing fear had seen the storm-clouds gather about her island home, and saw old ocean's mighty waves lashed into fury, break into harmless spray on Mona's rugged shores. These thoughts suggested others. He dwelt in fond remembrance on the occasion of her becoming his wife, and called to mind her trust and love, and all the happy scenes and hours they had shared together.

Recollection once at work, stopped not at their joys, but brought up to his vision their sorrows, their afflictions and the persecutions they had passed through for the sake of the truth—for the cause of God; and in conclusion he exclaimed:

"Thou hast passed through trials, Nora, but thou shalt rejoice! Thou hast been driven from thy home for the truth's sake, but thou and thy children shall have a home in the Kingdom of God! Thou hast suffered the bereavement of thy husband—the tender association has been severed—that others may be made partakers of endless life; but thou and thy husband shall yet reign together in the celestial kingdom of God. A few more struggles and the battle will be fought, the victory will be ours, and with the redeemed out of every nation we will sing, 'Glory, and honor, and power, and might, and majesty, and dominion be ascribed to Him that sitteth upon the throne, and to the Lamb, forever and forever?'"

A day or two after their arrival it was decided that Elders Clark and Brother Mitchel should go to Ramsey and Elder Taylor remain to labor in Douglas. He accompanied the two brethren a short distance on their journey, and before separating they repaired to a lovely spot in a field, some distance from the road, and there engaged in prayer. The burden of that prayer was that an effectual door might be opened to them in that island for the proclamation of the gospel; that gainsayers might be put to shame, and that the word might be confirmed by signs following the believers. After prayer they each sought a stone and placed it at the foot of a tree, on which Elder Taylor carved their names and the date of their being there. He also ordained Brother Mitchel a Deacon; and at the request of Elder Clark he also laid hands upon his head that he might have the gift of tongues and the interpretation thereof; and afterwards Elder Clark blessed Elder Taylor. For some time they spoke in tongues, sang, prophesied, and finally separated to their respective fields of labor, each to thrust in his sickle and reap.

Elder Taylor, on returning to Douglas, called on Mr. Cain, a book-binder and seller, and a Primitive Methodist preacher. Although he was a minister, he was sensible that his church fell far short of having a fullness of truth, and hence was ready to listen to one who claimed to have the fullness of the gospel.

He also called upon a number of his wife's girlhood friends, some of whom were pleased to see him. In this way he made a large circle of acquaintances, and taught them the gospel. Finally he engaged the Wellington Rooms, the largest hall in Douglas, capable of seating one thousand persons.

In this hall he delivered several lectures amid considerable opposition from sectarian priests. One of their number, Rev. Thomas Hamilton, was particularly offensive and made some disturbance, but the Elder found many who befriended him, and indeed, the people generally seemed indignant at the course pursued by his opponents. At length Mr. Hamilton sent a challenge to meet him in public discussion, the body of which was as follows:

"SIR:—Conceiving that the principles advocated by you in the lectures which you delivered in the Wellington Rooms have no support from the word of God, but are diametrically opposed to it, and as you *misquoted that word, mutilated it, took from* and *added* to it; I hereby invite you to a public discussion of the truth of what I conceive to be mere assertions, and design to prove you guilty of blasphemy against God and of decoying souls to perdition."

To this Elder Taylor made the following reply:

"I am not aware of having mutilated, misquoted, taken from or added to the word of God, or of speaking or teaching blasphemy, or trying to lead men to perdition, as I am charged with in your note; but have been conscientiously discharging a duty devolving upon me in unfolding the principles of eternal truth. But as I never shrink from the task of supporting those principles, in the strength of the Lord, I comply with your request on the following terms:

"First. That each of us choose a chairman for the preserving of order in the meeting.

"Second. That the lectures I have delivered in the Wellington Rooms be the subject of debate, and that you engage to prove that in those lectures I have advanced doctrines that are unscriptural.

"Third. That the word of God be the test.

"Fourth. That you have an hour to repudiate those supposed errors, and that I have the same time to reply; that you then have half an hour to speak and that I have half an hour to reply, and that the meeting then close for the evening.

"As you have not said anything in your note about the room being taken by you, I propose that we take it between us, and make a collection to pay the charge for its use.

"If these propositions, sir, should meet with your approbation, you may expect me there at the appointed time.

"As I am a stranger in the town I have not as yet made choice of a chairman, but as Mr. Cain, in the midst of the confusion the other evening, spoke a few words in my favor, perhaps I may choose him, if he will accept it."

The discussion came off in accordance with this arrangement, and Mr. Hamilton was vanquished. "No great honor, however," says Elder Taylor, in his account of this affair, "as he was a very ignorant man."

Another minister delivered a course of lectures against him, to which he replied in his own hall—the Wellington Rooms. Another—a Mr. J. Curran—published a series of newspaper articles against Mormonism, to which he replied. At the same time the Rev. Robert Heys, a Wesleyan Methodist, published three pamphlets in opposition to his doctrines, to each of which he published a reply. Unfortunately, only one of these pamphlets—the second—has been preserved; but from it we may learn something of Elder Taylor's power as a debater, the power by which he earned his title of "Champion of Truth." It is not my purpose to follow the discussion in all its details, or even give an outline of it, but simply introduce a single paragraph that is a specimen of Elder Taylor's cogent reasoning.

His reverend opponent stoutly objected to Mormonism because it was based on a new revelation, and in his view the day of revelation had passed—the volume thereof was complete; and he maintained that the Bible itself forbids any more revelation being added to it, and as Mormonism claimed to have come into existence through revelation, it violated the prohibitions of the Bible, and therefore Mormonism was an imposture.

In support of this argument, he quoted three passages of scripture: First from Deuteronomy, "Ye shall not *add* unto the word which I command you, neither shall ye diminish aught from it, that ye may keep the commandments of the Lord your God which I command you;" second from Proverbs, "Every word of the Lord is pure, *Add* thou not unto his words, lest he reprove thee, and thou be found a liar;" lastly, from Revelation, "I testify unto every man that heareth the words of the prophecy of this book, if any man shall *add* unto these things, God shall add unto him the plagues that are written in this book."

To this argument Elder Taylor replied:

"With astonishing confidence in the infallibility of his skill in biblical lore, Mr. Heys rapidly carries his readers along with him through the Old and New Testaments, and then, after showing them why they were written, he reveals the perfection of his knowledge by giving publicity to the following, which, for aught I know, he may consider a new discovery: 'Now of this complete and infallible rule (meaning the HOLY BIBLE) God has decreed and declared that *nothing shall be either added to it or taken from it!*' This certainly must be a *new revelation*, for such a *decree* or *declaration* is not to be found in the whole of the sacred writings! It is true, he quotes three passages—one from Deuteronomy, one from Proverbs, and another from Revelation; but not one of them contains the decree! That in Deuteronomy refers exclusively to the Book of the Law. If they declared the revelation of God to be *complete*, the other scriptures could never have been written. That in Proverbs refers to the portion of the sacred writings then in existence. If it is declared the Holy Scriptures were *complete*, there would not have been afterwards a continued written revelation. That in the Revelation refers to the Apocalypse alone, it being, when written, a separate book, unconnected with the other books of the New Testament which were not then collected; it could not, therefore, have reference to any other book or books of the Holy Scriptures. According to his own interpretation of the above scriptures, in quoting from Proverbs, he would reject the New Testament and all the prophets that prophesied after Solomon's day; and in his quotation from Deuteronomy, he would reject all the Bible but the five books of Moses. But let Mr. Hays take care that he himself is not incurring the curse by altering the meaning of the words of the very books to which the prohibition positively and particularly refers!"

Thus he followed his opponent in all his wanderings, as he promises to do in the beginning of the reply from which the above is taken—"lest he should 'pervert the truth' and 'darken counsel by words without knowledge.'" "And while pursuing him," he continues, "it will afford me no small degree of satisfaction and delight to observe the mists of error which he has spread around him, dissipated by the clear light of the gospel, and to behold the fair flowers of Paradise rising again unhurt in all their native beauty, from beneath the ruthless tread of his unhallowed feet."

Despite all the opposition that raged against him, Elder Taylor found a goodly number who were seeking for the truth, and sufficiently susceptible to the influence of God's Holy Spirit to receive his testimony and be baptized. These he organized into a branch of the Church, and, having placed the work in this island on a substantial footing, he returned to Liverpool.

CHAPTER 11 - THE POWER OF GOD

The remainder of Elder Taylor's time while on his first mission to England was employed mostly in preaching in Liverpool and in assisting the Saints who were beginning to emigrate to Nauvoo.

There was something singular in this movement among the British Saints. When the Apostles started on their missions, the Prophet Joseph had instructed them to say nothing, for the present, in relation to the gathering of the people. It was doubtless the unsettled state of the Church at that time which led him to give such counsel. The instructions were, of course, followed by the Apostles; but no sooner were the people baptized than they were seized with a desire to gather with the main body of the Church. "I find it is difficult to keep anything from the Saints," writes Elder Taylor, "for the Spirit of God reveals it to them. Some time ago Sister Mitchel dreamed that she, her husband and a number of others were on board a vessel, and that there were other vessels, loaded with Saints, going somewhere. She felt very happy and was rejoicing in the Lord." Another sister had a similar dream, and was informed that all the Saints were going. Neither of these sisters, nor any of the Saints at that time, knew anything about the principle of gathering, yet all were anxious to leave their homes, their kindred and the associations of a lifetime, to join the main body of the Church in a distant land, the members of which were total strangers to them.

Not only had this desire to gather with the Church taken hold of them, but those who had means were moved upon to assist those who were poor. Altogether more than eight hundred Saints left

England before the Apostles turned their faces homeward, and Elder Taylor was of material service to them in Liverpool, as he secured for them the best possible terms for their passage; organized them into companies, appointing the most experienced and wisest among them to take charge, that the inexperienced might not be a prey for sharpers and rogues to feast upon.

In addition to these labors, Elder Taylor visited Manchester, Birmingham, Sheffield and many other cities, everywhere preaching the gospel with great success, everywhere preaching the gospel with great success, converting the unbelieving and strengthening and encouraging the Saints. Thus the autumn and winter of 1840—41 passed away.

The object for which the Apostles had visited Great Britain was accomplished. They had established the Church there on a sound basis. The Book of Mormon and the Hymn Book had been published; a periodical to advocate and defend the faith delivered to the Saints established; a permanent shipping agency founded to aid the Saints in gathering to Zion; branches had been organized in nearly all the principal towns of the kingdom, and some eight thousand souls had been baptized. In all this labor Elder Taylor had taken an active, prominent part; and now, in company with his fellow Apostles, Brigham Young, Heber C. Kimball, Orson Pratt, Wilford Woodruff, George A. Smith and Willard Richards, he sailed on the ship *Rochester* for America.

Elder Taylor arrived in Nauvoo on the 1st of July, 1841. Here a great sorrow was awaiting him—his faithful, patient Leonora was sick nigh unto death. The hardships in Missouri, the separation from her husband,—on whose strong arm and steadfast courage she was wont to lean,—and the consequent increase of care in watching over her family, had at last broken down her strength; and hence he found her pale and wan, and death clutching at her precious life. He called in twenty Elders, who prayed for her; she was anointed with oil, hands were laid upon her, and, in fulfillment of God's promise, the prayer of faith healed the sick—the Lord raised her up.

It was shortly after the return of the Twelve from England that the Prophet Joseph made known to them the doctrine of celestial marriage—the marriage system that obtains in the celestial worlds where the Gods dwell,—marriage that is to endure for time and for eternity, the ceremony being performed by one holding that power which binds on earth and binds in heaven. Celestial marriage also includes a plurality of wives.

This system of marriage had been revealed to the Prophet a number of years before, but he had kept the matter in his own heart. The time had come, however, when the principles of this marriage system must be made known to others and the practice thereof entered into by the faithful in the Priesthood. Hitherto the Saints, in common with the so-called Christian world, had married until death did them part; but now, through the introduction of celestial marriage, the covenants between men and their wives were to be made for eternity as well as for time. In this marriage system the great truth is revealed that the association of husband and wife, with all its endearing associations is to continue forever; and that—to paraphrase the words of one who spake as if inspired on this theme —as long as there is room in infinite space, or matter in the exhaustless storehouse of nature, or as long as the bosoms of the Gods glow with affection, just so long will new worlds be created and filled with the ever increasing posterity of the righteous, and new kingdoms added to the dominions of the Fathers!

The plurality of wives included in this system of marriage is what gave rise to grave concern in the minds of the faithful men to whom it was revealed. The world never made a greater mistake than when it supposed that plural marriage was hailed with delight by the Elders who were commanded of the Lord to introduce its practice in this generation. They saw clearly that it would bring additional reproach upon them from the world; that it would run counter to the traditions and prejudices of society, as, indeed, it was contrary to their own traditions; that their motives would be misunderstood or misconstrued. All this they saw, and naturally shrank from the undertaking required of them by the revelation of God. How Elder Taylor looked upon this matter and how he received it is best told in his own words:

"Joseph Smith told the Twelve that if this law was not practiced, if they would not enter into this covenant, then the Kingdom of God could not go one step further. Now, we did not feel like preventing the Kingdom of God from going forward. We professed to be the Apostles of the Lord, and did not feel like putting ourselves in a position to retard the progress of the Kingdom of God. The revelation says that 'All those who have this law revealed unto them must obey the same.' Now, that is not my word. I did not make it. It was the Prophet of God who revealed that to us in Nauvoo, and I bear witness of this solemn fact before God, that He did reveal this sacred principle to me and others of the Twelve, and in this revelation it is stated that it is the will and law of God that 'all those who have this law revealed unto them must obey the same.'

"I had always entertained strict ideas of virtue, and I felt as a married man that this was to me, outside of this principle, an appalling thing to do. The idea of going and asking a young lady to be married to me when I had already a wife! It was a thing calculated to stir up feelings from the innermost depths of the human soul. I had always entertained the strictest regard of chastity. I had never in my life seen the time when I have known of a man deceiving a woman—and it is often done in the world, where, notwithstanding the crime, the man is received into society and the poor woman is looked upon as a pariah and an outcast—I have always looked upon such a thing as infamous, and upon such a man as a villain. Hence, with the feelings I had entertained, nothing but a knowledge of God, and the revelations of God, and the truth of them, could have induced me to embrace such a principle as this.

"We [the Twelve] seemed to put off, as far as we could, what might be termed the evil day.

"Some time after these things were made known unto us, I was riding out of Nauvoo on horseback, and met Joseph Smith coming in, he, too, being on horseback. I bowed to Joseph, and having done the same to me, he said: 'Stop;' and he looked at me very intently. 'Look here,' said he, 'those things that have been spoken of must be fulfilled, and if they are not entered into right away the keys will be turned.'

"Well, what did I do? Did I feel to stand in the way of this great, eternal principle, and treat lightly the things of God? No. I replied: 'Brother Joseph, I will try and carry these things out.'"

So indeed he did, for within two years, in Nauvoo, he married Elizabeth Haigham, Jane B. Ballantyne and Mary A. Oakley. Subsequently, in Utah, he married Harriet Whitaker, Sophia Whitaker and Margaret Young.

By tongue and pen, as well as by the force of example, he defended this celestial order of marriage against all who assailed it; and among all who have advocated it in the face of the fierce opposition it provoked, or who spoke out in its defense both at home and abroad, there was not one whose arguments carried more weight than did his.

Meantime Nauvoo had arisen from the bogs of Commerce, and was now an incorporated city, divided into four wards, with a population of nearly five thousand. A glorious temple and other public buildings were in course of construction, a periodical—the *Times and Seasons*—was being published, and there was every prospect of the city becoming a commercial and manufacturing center as well as the headquarters of the Church.

It is scarcely necessary to say that the Twelve were heartily welcomed home by the Prophet. He at once rolled on their shoulders much of the responsibility he had carried during their absence; and called upon them to assist in gathering the people to Nauvoo and to build up the Stakes of Zion.

The Twelve forthwith published a proclamation to the Saints in the British Isles, calling upon them to gather to Zion and to assist in founding manufactories and other enterprises. Another was issued denouncing thieves who began to infest Nauvoo, and whose villainy was charged to the Saints; another calling for aid in the construction of the temple. In all these labors Elder Taylor took a prominent part. He was also elected a member of the City Council, made a member of the Board of Regents for the Nauvoo University, and chosen Judge Advocate with the rank of colonel in the Nauvoo Legion, a position that made him the responsible adviser of the court and also the public prosecutor in affairs military.

These labors, in connection with his private business, occupied his attention after his return from England until February, 1842, when he was chosen associate editor of the *Times and Seasons*, the Prophet Joseph being editor-in-chief. This appointment introduced him into a field of labor for which he was admirably adapted, and in which, during his lifetime—notwithstanding his labors in that sphere were frequently interrupted by the drivings of the Church and calls to other kinds of employments—he accomplished much good, and became well known as a powerful writer.

He occupied the position of associate editor on the *Times and Seasons* for about a year, when the Prophet's increasing cares made it necessary for him to resign his place as editor-in-chief. Elder Taylor was appointed to take his place. He continued to edit and publish that periodical until the Church was driven out of Nauvoo in the spring of 1846.

In addition to his labors on the *Times and Seasons*, within a year he became the editor and proprietor of another paper, the *Nauvoo Neighbor*, a large imperial sheet issued weekly, and devoted "to the dissemination of useful knowledge of every description—the arts, science, religion, literature, agriculture, manufactures, trade, commerce and the general news of the day." In both these periodicals he ably defended the truth against all comers, and did much to stem the flood of falsehood that set in against the character of the Prophet Joseph.

The progress of Nauvoo was now by leaps and bounds, rapidly increasing in trade, commerce and population. The Prophet Joseph's career, too, was approaching its zenith. He was the most prominent man in the State of Illinois, and much courted because of his supposed political influence. Some of the most prominent men in the State sought his friendship, but it too frequently happened that it was for selfish purposes they courted him. No one was more sensitively aware of that fact than Elder Taylor. He knew them to be flatterers of the Prophet, that political thrift might follow fawning. They were heartless parasites, clinging to him in his hour of prosperity, but ready to fall away from and even betray him should the tide of his fortunes begin to ebb, or their interests require his immolation to satisfy the clamor of a prejudiced populace.

It was to remove the Prophet out of the filthy slough of party politics, that he and his people might not be the shuttle-cock for the battledoors of political demagogues—that he and they might not be the subjects of fulsome praise on the one hand, nor of fierce denunciation or unseemly vituperation on the other, that Elder Taylor urged the Prophet's nomination for the presidency of the United States, in February, 1844.

In a long editorial in the *Neighbor*, in which he nominates the Prophet for President, he represents that as Henry Clay—then one of the prominent candidates for President—inclined strongly to the old school of federalists, his political principles were diametrically opposed to those entertained by the people of Nauvoo, and hence they could not conscientiously vote for him; and they had even stronger objections to Mr. Van Buren, who, when the Saints appealed to him to redress the outrages put upon them in Missouri, admitted the justice of their cause, but claimed that he was powerless to assist them; he also held that Congress was powerless to redress their grievances.

"But all these things are tolerable to what we have yet to state," says Elder Taylor. "We have been informed from a respectable source, that there is an understanding between Mr. Benton [Senator], of Missouri, and Mr. Van Buren, and a conditional compact entered into that if Mr. Benton will use his influence to get Mr. Van Buren elected, that Mr. Van Buren, when elected, shall use his executive influence to wipe away the stain from Missouri by a further persecution of the Mormons, wreaking vengeance on their heads, either by extermination or by some other summary process. We could scarcely credit the statement, and we hope yet, for the sake of humanity, that the suggestion is false; but we have too good reason to believe that we are correctly informed."

Then, after enlarging upon the fitness of the Prophet for the high office of President of the United States, he adds:

"One great reason that we have for pursuing our present course is that at every election we have been made a political target for the filthy demagogues in the country to shoot their loathsome arrows at. And every story has been put into circulation to blast our fame, from the old fabrication of 'walk on the water' down to the 'murder of Governor Boggs.' The journals have teamed with this filthy trash, and even men who ought to have more respect for themselves—men contending for the gubernatorial chair—have made use of terms so degrading, so mean, so humiliating, that a Billingsgate fisherwoman would have considered herself disgraced with. We refuse any longer to be thus bedaubed for either party; we tell all such to let their filth flow in its own legitimate channel, for we are sick of the loathsome smell.

Under existing circumstances we have no other alternative [than that of withdrawing from both political parties,] and if we can accomplish our object, well; if not we shall have the satisfaction of knowing we have acted conscientiously and have used our best judgment; and if we have to throw away our votes, we had better do so upon a worthy, rather than upon an unworthy individual, who might make use of the weapon we put in his hand to destroy us.

Then the Prophet was put before the country for President of the United States. He published his views on the powers and policy of the government, and called upon his friends to support him.

By adopting this policy there was a candidate in the field the Saints could vote for conscientiously; and if their candidate from the beginning was sure of defeat, they had at least removed themselves and their religion from the filthy vortex of political controversy.

CHAPTER 12 - TROUBLE BREWING

Thus far I have spoken only of those prosperous events which befell the Saints at Nauvoo from the return of the Twelve from England, in July, 1841, to the nomination of the Prophet Joseph for president of the United States, February, 1843. It now becomes necessary to note some of those unfortunate events which befell them during the same period, with all of which Elder Taylor had more or less to do.

Missouri was not satisfied with robbing the Saints wholesale and expelling them from her borders, her hatred followed them to Illinois. Of course the Prophet Joseph was the chief object of their fury. In the fall of 1841 he was arrested upon a requisition from the Governor of Missouri on the old charge of "theft, arson and murder," assumed to have been committed in Caldwell and Daviess Counties, in the autumn of 1838. He obtained a writ of *habeas corpus* and the case came up before Judge Stephen A. Douglass, at Monmouth, who found the writ on which he was held illegal, and discharged the prisoner.

In the spring of 1842 an attempt was made to assassinate ex-Governor Boggs of Missouri, and as soon as he recovered from the injuries received, he charged Joseph Smith with being accessory before the fact to the attempted murder. Again the Prophet was arrested under a requisition from the Governor of Missouri, and again he obtained a writ of *habeas corpus* and went before the circuit court of the United States, Judge Pope of Springfield, Illinois, presiding. Elder Taylor and a few others accompanied him. The

Prophet was anxious to have the case tried on its merits, but this Judge Pope held to be unnecessary as he was entitled to be discharged because of defects in the affidavit on which the demand for his surrender to Missouri was made.

As the state legislature at the time was in session, there were gathered in Springfield the principal men of the state; and as they were all anxious to learn something of "Mormonism," the Representatives' Hall was tendered the brethren for holding religious service, on Sunday, and Elder Taylor and Orson Hyde were appointed by the Prophet to preach, the latter in the forenoon, the former in the afternoon.

In all these vexatious prosecutions Elder Taylor stood very near the Prophet, and ably defended him through the editorial columns of the *Times and Seasons* and the*Neighbor*.

In the meantime the phenomenal growth of the Church, the prosperity of the Saints in Nauvoo, and the rapid progress of the city, while very gratifying to the founders of both Church and city, attracted to the body religious and municipal a class of men that were very undesirable. Adventurers seeking for place and power and wealth; demagogues who by fulsome flattery of the people hoped to attain through their political influence a realization of their ambitious dreams; knaves who by falsely professing conversion, thought to cover up corrupt, licentious lives, and thrive by villainy; thieves and counterfeiters who saw their opportunity to live by roguery, and steal on the credit of the Mormons, of whom the people of Illinois were too ready to believe anything that savored of evil, because prejudiced against their religion—all these characters were attracted to Nauvoo by the prosperity that reigned there; and their ungodly conduct hastened the evil day of the city's destruction.

Chief among these reckless adventurers was John C. Bennett, a man of learning and intellectual ability but a moral leper. He was guilty of the most infamous, licentious practices, and seduced several women by representing that promiscuous intercourse of the sexes was a doctrine believed in by the Latter-day Saints and that there was no harm in it. He also said that Joseph Smith and other Church leaders both sanctioned and practiced such wickedness; that

Joseph only denounced such things in public so vehemently because of the prejudice of the people, and the trouble that might arise in his own house.

For this conduct he was excommunicated from the Church, compelled to resign the Mayorship of the city, expelled from the Masonic Lodge, chastised by the Legion, and his infamy published to the world and denounced.

This filled him with bitterness against the Saints, and especially against the Prophet. He at once set on foot measures that he hoped would bring him a terrible revenge. He succeeded in getting the Missourians to issue a new warrant for his arrest on the old charge of "theft, arson and murder," and a new requisition for his arrest was granted by Governor Ford, of Illinois.

The warrants were served on the Prophet in Lee County, some two hundred miles from Nauvoo. The officers who arrested him sought to drag him immediately into Missouri, but in this they failed, as Joseph through some friends obtained a writ of *habeas corpus*, and the legality of the warrant was enquired into by the municipal court of Nauvoo. The court also went behind the writ and tried the case *exparte* on its merits, and discharged the accused for want of subsistence in the warrant on which he was arrested, as well as upon the merits of the case.

Elder Taylor in an editorial in the *Neighbor* of July 5th 1843, thus deals with the course pursued by Missouri in these several instances of persecution against the Prophet:

"It has fallen to our lot of late years to keep an account of any remarkable circumstances that might transpire in and about this and adjoining states; as well as of distant provinces and nations. Among the many robberies, earthquakes, volcanic eruptions, tornadoes, fires, mobs, wars, etc., which we have had to record, there is one circumstance of annual occurrence which it has always fallen to our lot to chronicle. We allude not to the yearly inundation of the Nile, nor the frequent eruptions of Vesuvius or Ætna, but to the boiling over of Tophet, *alias* the annual overflow of the excrescence of Missouri. Not indeed, like the Nile, over-flowing its parched banks, invigorating its alluvial soil and causing vegetation to teem forth in its richest attire; but like the sulphurous flame that burns unnoticed in the bowels of a volcano; kept alive by the combustion of its own native element, until it can contain itself no longer within the limits of its crater; it bursts beyond its natural bounds; spreads its sulphurous lava all around, leaving naught but desolation in its path,—destroying alike the cot of the husbandman, and the palace of the noble, in one grand sweep; covering vegetation with its fiery lava, and turning the garden into a bed of cinders. So Missouri has her annual ebulitions, and must belch forth her sulphurous lava and seek to overwhelm others; and as it happens that we are so unfortunate as to live near the borders of this monster, we must ever and anon, be smutted with the soot that flies off from her burning crater.

"Without entering here into the particulars of the bloody deeds, the high-handed oppression, the unconstitutional acts, the deadly and malicious hate, the numerous murders and the wholesale robberies of that people, we will proceed to notice one of the late acts of Missouri, or of the governor of that state, towards us. We allude to the late arrest of Joseph Smith."

Then follows an account of the arrests of the Prophet and the manner in which he was released from the officers as already briefly stated in this chapter; he dwells at some length on the events of the last arrest made near Dixon, detailing the cruelty and brutality of the officers. He then concludes:

"Why Governor Ford should lend his assistance in a vexatious prosecution of this kind we are at a loss to determine. He possesses a discretionary power in such cases, and has a right to use his judgment, as the chief magistrate of this state; and knowing, as he does, that the whole proceedings connected with this affair are illegal, we think that in justice he ought to have leaned to the side of the oppressed and innocent, particularly when the persecuted and prosecuted were citizens of his own state who had a right to his sympathies and to be shielded by his paternal care, as the father of this state. Does not his excellency know, and do not all the citizens of the state know, that the Mormons have been robbed, pillaged and plundered in Missouri without any redress? That the Mormons *en masse* were exterminated from that state without any legal pretext whatever? How, then, could they have any legal claim upon Joseph Smith or any Mormon? Have the Mormons ever obtained any redress for injuries received in Missouri? No. Is there any prospect of their receiving any remuneration for their loss, or redress for their grievances? No. When a demand was make upon the governor of Missouri, by Governor Carlin of this state for the persons who kidnapped several Mormons, were they given up by that state? No. Why then should our executive feel so tenacious in fulfilling all the nice punctillios of law, when the very state that is making these demands has robbed, murdered and exterminated by wholesale, without law, and is merely making use of it at present as a cat's paw to destroy the innocent and murder those that they have already persecuted nearly to the death.

"It is impossible that the State of Missouri should do justice with her coffers groaning with the spoils of the oppressed, and her hands yet reeking with the blood of the innocent. Shall she yet gorge her bloody maw with other victims? Shall Joseph Smith be given into her hands illegally? Never! *No, never!!* No, NEVER!!!"

He afterwards published in the *Neighbor* full details of this *exparte* trial with the affidavits of the several witnesses given *in extenso*. Those affidavits make up an indictment against the State of Missouri which brings the hot blush of shame to the cheek of every lover of his country's institutions. In their treatment of the Latter-day Saints the leading officials of Missouri were guilty not only of high-handed oppression, but of such high crimes and misdemeanors as would have hung them had they met the just penalty of their misdeeds. But as those who suffered were members of an unpopular Church, the atrocious and bloody deeds of that state were passed by and no one felt called upon to demand justice in behalf of the oppressed; and those powers that were appealed to for redress of grievances—the President and congress of the United States—claimed to have no power to interfere. Mobocracy had triumphed in Missouri, and there was no power in the government to call Missouri to an account for her wrong doing.

At the time of the Prophet's arrest at Dixon there was an exciting political campaign in progress in that part of Illinois where Nauvoo was located, for representative to congress, and also for county officers. Two parties were in the field, Whigs and Democrats; each anxious to obtain the Mormon vote. The Democrats accused the Whigs of being the instigators of this last arrest of Joseph Smith, at that particular juncture, that Governor Ford, a Democrat, might be compelled to issue a warrant for his arrest and thus influence the Saints against the Democrats; and in proof of this referred to the fact that John C. Bennett, at whose instance, doubtless, this last warrant for the arrest of the Prophet was gotten up in Missouri, was the special pet of what was called the "Whig junto" in Springfield; that a special session of the circuit court was called in Daviess County, Missouri, in order to have the warrant act at the proper juncture; that Cyrus Walker, the Whig candidate for Congress, was within six miles of Dixon when the Prophet was arrested; that he refused to act as council for him only on the condition that he pledged him his vote (that pledge Walker was pleased to consider as binding to his interest the entire Mormon vote); that on this pledge being given he cancelled all his appointments to speak in that part of the state and repaired to Nauvoo where the validity of the arrest and warrants on which it was made were investigated.

This charge the Whigs vehemently denied and in turn accused the Democrats with having made it to influence the Mormon vote in favor of themselves. Thus crimination and recrimination went on, and whichever party the people of Nauvoo voted for, they were sure to incur the wrath of the other.

The Prophet Joseph kept his pledge with Cyrus Walker and voted for him, but the Democratic ticket was overwhelmingly successful in Nauvoo, and in the county and district. As soon as the result was made known the disappointed candidates and their friends were enraged. They began plotting against the people of Nauvoo, and started an agitation that had for its object the expulsion of the Saints from the state. Public meetings were called and committees appointed to correspond with surrounding counties to ascertain how much assistance they would render in expelling the Mormons from the state.

No effort whatever was made to conceal their intentions. The banishment of the citizens of Nauvoo from the state was openly discussed and advocated in public meetings and through the press. Bitter fruit, this, to be found growing on the tree of liberty, in the land of the free—in the asylum for the oppressed of all nations!

CHAPTER 13 - THE GOVERNOR'S ORDER

We have now reached the eventful year of 1844, the year of the great tragedy, the martyrdom of the Prophets Joseph and Hyrum Smith—a martyrdom which Elder Taylor shared.

The situation of the Saints at that time was, to say the least, remarkable. Besides the arch fiend Bennett, the Church had warmed within her bosom a number of other snakes that turned and stung her. Among these was William Law, Counselor to the Prophet Joseph, and yet his most bitter maligner and enemy. A smooth, dissembling villain! The kind that can look like the innocent flower and yet be the serpent under it. Not only was he guilty of the grossest immorality, but he conspired with assassins from Missouri, to take the life of the Prophet; and even conducted them himself to the house of Joseph. They were only prevented from accomplishing the foul murder that was in their hearts, by the faithfulness of two guards, Josiah Arnold and David Garn, who refused to admit them to the Prophet's presence.

Second to him in treachery and villainy was his natural brother, Wilson Law, a general in the Nauvoo Legion. Dr. R. D. Foster, a man not only inclined to profligacy, but one who had the means to indulge his inclination to the top of his bent, as he was wealthy. Besides these men there were the two Higbees, Francis and Chauncy, the latter a young lawyer. They were both sons of Judge Elias Higbee, a man highly respected by the Church for his upright life and sterling integrity. All the above named apostates were excommunicated from the Church for their wickedness, chiefly for seduction and adultery; and so abandoned and shameful were their crimes that the High Council which tried them had to sit with closed doors. Besides these leaders in wickedness there were a large number of apostates in Nauvoo and vicinity that had been expelled from the Church. They were recreant to every principle of righteousness, and full of bitterness. Fitful anger rankled in their breasts. They seemed to have lost the power to repent, and even the desire for forgiveness. They were possessed wholly with a fierce determination to destroy the structure—the Church—where in the days of their righteousness they were wont to find spiritual repose.

In addition to these enemies, the sectarian religionists, maddened to frenzy because unable to cope successfully with Mormonism, stood ready to persecute to the death those whom they could not convert. Then there were the two political parties, Whigs and Democrats, so equally balanced that whichever party the Saints voted with gained the victory. It often happened that candidates for office made an issue of the Mormon question—promising to exterminate them, or lend their influence to that end if elected. As often as this was done the Saints were compelled in self-defense to vote against them, and their opponents were generally defeated. But whichever party the Saints voted with the other was sure to be offended, and would heap unstinted abuse on their uncovered heads, filling their press with accounts of "the enormities of Nauvoo, and of the awful wickedness of a party which would consent to receive the support of such miscreants."

There was also another class of people that did no end of mischief to the character of the Saints at Nauvoo. They were counterfeiters, horse-thieves, cut-throats and all-round scoundrels, which not only infested Nauvoo and vicinity, but the whole western country. "In some districts", says Elder Taylor, "their influence was so great as to control important state and county offices." Of these Governor Ford bears witness, saying—

"Then again, the northern part of the state was not destitute of its organized bands of rogues, engaged in murders, robberies, horse-stealing, and in making and passing counterfeit money. These rogues were scattered all over the north, but most of them were located in the counties of Ogle, Winnebago, Lee and DeKalb."

They extended into other counties, however, and even judges, sheriffs, constables, jailors and professional men were privy to their deeds and sharers in the fruits of their robberies. "Their object in persecuting the Mormons," says Elder Taylor—and these characters did persecute them—"was in part to cover their own rascality, and in part to prevent the people of Nauvoo from exposing and prosecuting them; but the principal reason was plunder, believing if the Saints could be removed or driven they would be made fat on Mormon spoils, besides having in the deserted city a good asylum for the prosecution of their diabolical pursuits."

All these elements found it convenient to combine against the Church for its destruction, the overthrow of the Prophet and those who stood near him. A regular system of agitation was began, having for its avowed object the extermination of the Saints from the city founded by their industry. Meetings were held in various parts of Hancock and surrounding counties, at which speeches the most intemperate, resolutions the most inflammatory, and accusations the most vile and false were fulminated against Nauvoo and her inhabitants. The press supported the actions of these meetings, publishing their proceedings, and encouraging them by commendatory comments. Especially was this the case with the *Warsaw Signal*, edited by one Thomas Sharp, whom Elder Taylor alludes to as "a violent, unprincipled man, who shrunk not at any enormity."

Such were the elements that combined against the peace of Nauvoo and the destruction of her leading citizens. Seeing mischief afoot and an ever growing popular sentiment against the Mormons and in favor of the reckless, not to say lawless, course of the anti-Mormon agitators, the apostates in Nauvoo ventured to publish the most infamous sheet ever issued from the press—the *Nauvoo Expositor.* Its mendacious slanders were aimed at the most prominent and virtuous of Nauvoo's citizens. No sooner did it appear than a storm of indignation passed through the city; and the people threatened to annihilate it. Wishing to avoid any unlawful procedure, the city council was convened to consider what steps should be taken to suppress the unclean and untruthful thing.

The *Expositor* was produced and read in the council. It was held by some that the purpose for which it was published was to provoke the people to some overt act which would make them amenable to the law, and increase the bitterness of the outside prejudice against them. This was doubtless the case. Such it seems was the understanding of the council. In relation to this circumstance Elder Taylor remarks:

"With a perfect knowledge, therefore, of the designs of these infernal scoundrels who were in our midst, as well as those who surrounded us, the city council entered upon an investigation of the matter. They felt that they were in a critical position, and that any move made for the abating of that press would be looked upon, or at least represented, as a direct attack upon the liberty of speech, and that, so far from displeasing our enemies, it would be looked upon by them as one of the best circumstances that could transpire to assist them in their nefarious and bloody designs."

After spending nearly a whole night in considering the best plan to pursue, it was finally decided to declare the *Expositor* a nuisance, and order its abatement. Elder Taylor made the motion and it was carried unanimously, with the exception of one
that person acknowledged the righteousness of the move
feared it would afford the enemies of the city too great an
by giving some ground for the cry that would be raised
freedom of the press had been overthrown in Nauvoo.
certain, however, that if the city council had not taken this
suppressing the *Expositor*, the citizens would have
masse and a mob would have destroyed it: and that w
given the enemies of the Saints as good ground for agitati
Nauvoo and her people as the action of the city council di
Taylor's motion prevailed.

The *Expositor* Press was destroyed by the city mar
P. Green, and a small *posse* of men he called to his assist
type was pied in the streets and the papers in the office
and burned. The whole proceeding was done qu

Administering to the Sick

Only men who hold the Melchizedek Priesthood may administer to the sick or afflicted. Normally, two or more administer togethe
consecrated oil is not available, a man who holds the Melchizedek Priesthood may give a blessing by the authority of the priesth
A father who holds the Melchizedek Priesthood should administer to sick members of his family. He may ask another man who h
Priesthood to assist him.

Administering to the sick has two parts: (1) anointing with oil and (2) sealing the anointing.

Anointing with Oil

1. Puts a drop of consecrated oil on the person's head.
2. Places his hands lightly on the person's head and calls the person by his or her full name.
3. States that he is anointing the person by the authority of the Melchizedek Priesthood.
4. States that he is anointing with oil that has been consecrated for anointing and blessing the sick and afflicted.
5. Closes in the name of Jesus Christ.

Sealing the Anointing

1. Calls the person by his or her full name.
2. States that he is sealing the anointing by the authority of the Melchizedek Priesthood.
3. Gives a blessing as the Spirit directs.
4. Closes in the name of Jesus Christ.

Father's Blessings and Other Blessings of Comfort and Counsel

1. Calls the person by his or her full name.
2. States that he is giving the blessing by the authority of the Melchizedek Priesthood.
3. Gives a blessing as the Spirit directs.
4. Closes in the name of Jesus Christ.

Dedicating Graves

1. Addresses Heavenly Father.
2. States that he is dedicating the grave by the authority of the Melchizedek Priesthood.
3. Dedicates and consecrates the burial plot as the resting place for the body of the deceased.
4. Where appropriate, prays that the place will be hallowed and protected until the Resurrection.
5. Asks the Lord to comfort the family and expresses other thoughts as the Spirit directs.
6. Closes in the name of Jesus Christ.

Dedicating Homes

Church members may dedicate their homes as sacred edifices where the Holy Spirit can reside and where family members can w
world, grow spiritually, and prepare for eternal family relationships. Homes need not be free of debt to be dedicated. Unlike Chu
consecrated to the Lord. A Melchizedek Priesthood holder may dedicate a home by the power of the priesthood. If there is not a
holder in the home, a family might invite a close relative, a home teacher, or another Melchizedek Priesthood holder to dedicate
gather and offer a prayer that includes the elements mentioned in the preceding paragraph and other words as the Spirit directs

determinedly. The only force employed was the breaking in of the doors to the*Expositor* office when admittance was denied. Some of the leading apostates set fire to their houses and fled to Carthage, the county seat of Hancock County, with the lie on their lips that their lives were in danger. Fortunately the police in Nauvoo discovered the houses of these men on fire and extinguished the flames before any material harm was done, so that they had no blackened ruins to point to as a witness of Mormon atrocity.

All the mischief anticipated from suppressing the *Expositor* nuisance came to pass. "The Mormons had laid unhallowed hands upon the press!" "They opposed the freedom of speech!" "The laws were no longer a protection to life and property in Nauvoo!" "A mob at Nauvoo under a city ordinance had violated the highest privilege in the government!" Such were the sentences that flew as if on the wings of the wind to all parts of Illinois.

A mass meeting was held at Warsaw, the prevailing sentiment of which was that "to seek redress in the ordinary mode would be utterly ineffectual." The meeting therefore adopted resolutions announcing that those present were at all times ready to co-operate with their fellow citizens in Missouri and Iowa to exterminate—*utterly exterminate*—the Mormon leaders—the authors their troubles. Another mass meeting was held at Carthage at which the Warsaw resolutions were adopted.

The anti-Mormon press teemed with intemperate articles, outrageously false accusations and frantic appeals to the very worst passions of human nature. The citizens of Nauvoo were represented as a horde of lawless ruffians and brigands; anti-American and anti-republican; steeped in crime and iniquity; opposed to freedom of speech and to progress; among whom neither persons nor property were secure. They were accused also of having designs upon the citizens of Illinois and of the United States; and for these things the people were called upon to rise *en masse* and utterly exterminate them.

While these falsehoods were being extensively circulated through Illinois and the surrounding states, it was the most difficult thing, almost impossible to get a true statement of the case before the country. True accounts of the proceedings of the city council in the *Expositor* affair were published in the *Times and Seasons* and also in the *Neighbor*; but it was impossible to circulate them in Hancock and surrounding counties, as they were destroyed at the post offices. To get them abroad Elder Taylor had to send them a distance of thirty or forty miles from Nauvoo before posting them. In some instances they had to be taken to St. Louis, a distance of two hundred miles, to ensure their reaching their destination.

The systematic circulation of falsehood on the one hand, and the suppression of the truth on the other, resulted in a tremendous storm of indignation against the Saints—especially against the leading Elders—that threatened to overwhelm them.

In the midst of this excitement, complaint was made by Francis M. Higbee, and a warrant issued against the members of the city council for riot in destroying the*Expositor* press and fixtures. The warrant was issued by Mr. Morrison, a justice of the peace in Carthage, and required the constable, Mr. Bettisworth, to bring the parties named in it before him, "or some other justice of the peace," to be dealt with according to law. When the writ was served on the members of the council they expressed a perfect willingness to submit to an investigation of their proceedings; but as the law of the state made it the privilege of the accused to "appear before the issuer of the writ or any other justice of the peace," they desired to avail themselves of this privilege, and go before some other magistrate than Justice Morrison, alleging as their reason for this that it was unsafe for them to go to Carthage. The constable refused to grant their request, whereupon they sued for a writ of *habeas corpus* before the municipal court of Nauvoo, and on a hearing of the case they were dismissed.

This was declared to be resistance to the law, and made use of to further influence the public mind against the Mormons. Mobs were therefore assembled and the work of violence inaugurated by kidnapping, whipping and otherwise abusing the Saints living in out-lying districts of Nauvoo. For protection the people thus abused fled to Nauvoo, and this was heralded abroad as the massing of the Mormon forces.

Governor Ford was kept informed of all that was transpiring in Nauvoo by the city authorities, and in answer to the question, "What course shall we pursue in the event of an armed mob coming against the city," he replied that Joseph Smith was Lieutenant-General of the Nauvoo Legion; it was his duty to protect the city and surrounding country, and issued orders to him to that effect. Thus qualified to act, by the Governor of the state, the Legion was called together and measures were taken for the defense of the city: as the mob forces grew bolder every day, Nauvoo was at last placed under martial law.

CHAPTER 14 – CARTHAGE

Meantime the mobocrats were active in making their misrepresentations to the governor. He finally determined to visit the scenes of the difficulty. He went from Springfield to Carthage, the head-quarters of the mob forces, and received them as the militia of the state.

His first move was to send a message to Nauvoo asking that a committee be appointed to represent to him the state of affairs in the county. Elder Taylor and Dr. J. M. Bernhisel were appointed that committee. Armed with affidavits and duplicates of documents which had been sent to the Governor at Springfield—he had missed the messengers bearing them by starting for Carthage—they left on the evening of the 21st of June, to wait upon the Governor, arriving in Carthage about eleven o'clock at night. The town was filled with a rabble more or less under the influence of liquor. The yelling and swearing would justify them in the belief that they had arrived in pandemonium.

Elder Taylor and companion put up at the Hamilton House; the Governor also had his rooms there. On retiring they had to pass through another bed-room to get to their own, and stretched out on the bed was one Jackson, a vicious cut-throat and desperado, one of the chief enemies of the Saints. On reaching the chamber assigned them, Elder Taylor hinted to his companion that things looked suspicious, and took the precaution to see that his weapons were in order.

No sooner had they retired than the young apostate Chauncy Higbee came to their door, and stated that Daniel Garn was under arrest and was about to be committed to prison; that as he believed him to be an honest man, one who had done wrong only through the instigation of others, he thought it a pity for him to be committed to prison, and he had come to ask Dr. Bernhisel to be his bail. Touched by this appeal the doctor said he would go, and Higbee left him while he dressed, saying he would call for him in a few minutes.

After the departure of Higbee, Elder Taylor expressed his fear that this was but a ruse to separate them. They had important documents to submit to the Governor, and it was his opinion that the object was to separate them and get possession of those papers, and perhaps murder one or both of them. The doctor admitted the probability of this and informed Higbee that Elder Taylor and himself would wait upon the justice in the morning. That night Elder Taylor laid awake with his pistols under his pillow, ready for any emergency.

The light of morning came at last, and with the darkness fled their apprehensions. They waited upon the justice who held Daniel Garn in custody, and offered to be his bail. The justice answered that he doubted if property in Nauvoo would be worth anything in a few days, and therefore refused to accept them as bondsmen. They both had property outside of Nauvoo which they offered as security. The justice then told them that such was the nature of the accusation against Mr. Garn, that he would not feel justified in admitting him to bail. This confirmed Elder Taylor's suspicion that the request for them to be his bail the night before was only a ruse to separate them.

That morning they had an interview with the Governor. "And such an interview!" exclaimed Elder Taylor. He was surrounded by the very vilest of apostate Mormons and desperadoes, bent on the destruction of the Saints. As he opened and read aloud some of the documents submitted to him, he was frequently interrupted with such expressions as, "that's a lie!" "that's a G—d d——d lie!" "that's an infernal falsehood!" etc.

After the whole case was stated to the Governor, and all the documents submitted, he insisted that in order to prove to the people that they were willing to submit to the law, it would be best for Joseph Smith and all concerned in the destruction of the *Expositor* press to come to Carthage for examination. Elder Taylor represented that they had already been examined before two competent courts on that charge, the municipal court of Nauvoo and before Squire Wells, a justice of the peace, and each time acquitted; that they had fulfilled the law in every particular and that their enemies had murderous designs and were only making use of this matter to get Joseph Smith and other leading men into their power. The Governor, however, insisted that the proper thing for them to do would be to come to Carthage.

Elder Taylor then stated that in consequence of the excitement prevailing, it would be extremely unsafe for Joseph to come to Carthage; that they had men and arms to defend themselves, but if their forces and those of their enemies should be brought into close proximity the most probable result would be a collision. In reply to this the Governor "strenuously advised us," says Elder Taylor, "not to bring our arms, and *pledged his faith as Governor, and the faith of the state, that we should be protected, and that he would guarantee our perfect safety*."

After waiting until evening for a communication which the Governor prepared for Joseph, Elder Taylor and companion started for Nauvoo in company with Captain Gates and a squad of mounted men sent by the Governor to escort the Prophet to Carthage, should he conclude to act on his advice. They reached Nauvoo about nine o'clock, and at once delivered the Governor's message to Joseph with a report of their labors. Joseph was much displeased with the spirit manifested in the Governor's letter and with his whole course. The little group of friends that met in council were much perplexed as to what course to pursue, and various plans of action were discussed. Among others the feasibility of Joseph going to Washington to lay the case before President Tyler. At this juncture the council was interrupted by the withdrawal of Joseph to give an interview to two gentlemen,—one of whom was a son of John C. Calhoun,—who had arrived at the mansion and were anxious to meet with the Prophet. He was detained sometime, and between two and three o'clock in the morning, having had no rest the night before, and thinking that Joseph would not return, Elder Taylor left the mansion for his home, to rest.

Shortly after he retired, however, the Prophet returned and the informal council meeting was resumed. The project of laying the case before President Tyler was abandoned. Joseph had received an inspiration to go west, and all would be well. He said: "The way is open. It is clear to my mind what to do. All they want is Hyrum and myself; then tell everybody to go about their business, and not collect in groups, but scatter about. There is no danger; they will come here and search for us. Let them search; they will not harm you in person or in property, and not even a hair of your head. We will cross the river tonight and go away to the west."

The Prophet and his brother Hyrum at once crossed the river and their friends were instructed to procure horses for them and make all necessary preparations to start for "the Great Basin of the Rocky Mountains."

The next morning a Mrs. Thompson entered Elder Taylor's house about seven o'clock.

"What, you here!" she exclaimed, very much surprised, "the brethren have crossed the river some time since."

"What brethren?"

"Brother Joseph and Hyrum, and Brother Richards."

Elder Taylor at once concluded that those brethren had determined finally to leave for the East for a season, as had been talked of the night before, instead of going to Carthage. He knew what a storm of rage and disappointment that would arouse in the breasts of the mob militia at Carthage, who were waiting with ill-concealed impatience for the coming of their prey. Being satisfied that if the mob forces which Governor Ford had exalted to the dignity of "state militia" should come to Nauvoo, and find their victims gone, the first thing they would do would be to destroy the printing office. He therefore called to his assistance a few brethren in whom he had confidence and removed the type, the stereotyped plates of the Book of Mormon and the fixtures that were the most valuable.

This done he made arrangements for the adjustment of his accounts, having determined, in the event of not finding Joseph and his companions, to go to Upper Canada for a season. In caring for the valuables in the printing office, and in making his preparations to leave Nauvoo, he had been materially assisted by Cyrus H. Wheelock. He was an active, enterprising man, just such a man as Elder Taylor would need if he went to Canada, so he said to him:

"Brother Wheelock, can you go with me ten or fifteen hundred miles?

"Yes."

"Can you start in half an hour?

"Yes."

Those were times and circumstances that required prompt action, and Brother Wheelock had evidently drunk deeply into the spirit of the times. Brother Wheelock lived on the Montrose side of the river; and Elder Taylor told him to go and visit his family, procure horses and the necessary equipage for the journey, and if they heard nothing from Joseph they would start by night fall. He also arranged for Brother Wheelock and a Brother Bell to row him across the river during the afternoon. That he might not be recognized while leaving Nauvoo, he went to the house of a Brother Eddy on the banks of the river, and there disguised himself as an old man. He went down to the boat while the brethren were sauntering along on the banks just below it. Brother Bell did not recognize him and at last remarked to Brother Wheelock—"I wish that old gentleman would go away; he has been pottering around that boat for some time, and I am afraid that Elder Taylor will be coming." His mistake, when discovered, afforded them considerable merriment.

At Montrose he was taken by the brethren to a house surrounded by timber, and there made arrangements to take the stereotyped plates of the Book of Mormon and Doctrine and Covenants with him, thinking he could supply the publishing company at Nauvoo subsistence money through the sale of these books in the east.

Meantime Elias Smith, cousin to the Prophet, had procured him some money for his journey; his horses were reported ready, the friendly night which would cover him from the eyes of his enemies was approaching, when word was brought to him from Joseph to meet him in Montrose. The Prophet had suddenly changed his mind and had determined on going to Carthage to give himself up; and he wished Elder Taylor to accompany him.

"I must confess that I felt a good deal disappointed at the news," says Elder Taylor, "but I immediately made preparations to go."

The facts in the case were that some of Joseph's friends, learning that he was intending to leave Nauvoo, instead of rendering him all possible assistance to escape from his enemies, complained of his conduct as most cowardly, and entreated him to return to the city and not leave them like a false shepherd leaves his flock when the wolves attack it. The parties most forward in making this charge of cowardice were, Reynolds Cahoon, L. D. Wasson and Hiram Kimball. His wife Emma also sent a letter by the hand of Reynolds Cahoon, entreating him to return and give himself up, trusting to the pledges of the governor for a fair trial. Influenced by these entreaties to return, and stung by the taunts of cowardice from those who should have been his friends, the Prophet said: "If my life is of no value to my friends, it is of none to myself." And against his better judgment, and with the conviction fixed in his soul that he would be killed, he resolved to return. He crossed over the river to Nauvoo, and sent a message to Governor Ford that night that he would be in Carthage the next day.

Early the following morning Elder Taylor started in company with the Prophet and others for Carthage. Within four miles of that place they met Captain Dunn *en route* to Nauvoo, with a requisition from the Governor for the state arms. At the solicitation of Captain Dunn and his command, the party from Nauvoo returned with him to assist by their influence to obtain the arms belonging to the state. This accomplished, the whole party again started for Carthage.

It was midnight when they entered the town, but a militia company encamped on the public square—the Carthage Greys—

were aroused and gave vent to profane threats as the company passed, of which the following is a specimen: "Where's the d——d prophet? Stand away you McDonough boys and let us shoot the d——d Mormons! G——d d——n you, old Joe, we've got you now! Clear the way, and let us have a view of Joe Smith, the prophet of God! He has seen the last of Nauvoo! We'll use him up now."

A crowd followed the party from the public square, and hung round the Hamilton House yelling and cursing like demons. Governor Ford pushed up a window and thus addressed them: "Gentlemen, I know your anxiety to see Mr. Smith, which is natural enough, but it is quite too late tonight for you to have that opportunity; but I assure you, gentlemen, you shall have that privilege tomorrow morning, as I will cause him to pass before the troops upon the square, and I now wish you, with this assurance, quietly and peaceably to return to your quarters." There was a faint "Hurrah for Tom Ford," and the crowd withdrew.

CHAPTER 15 - THE MARTYRDOM

The next morning—the 25th of June—the city au

thorities of Nauvoo and some persons who had assisted the marshal to remove the *Expositor* press, appeared before Robert F. Smith, a justice of the peace, to answer again to the charge of riot. Owing to the excitement prevailing, the aforesaid parties consented to be bound over to appear before the circuit court at its next session; and became security for each other in $500 bonds each.

No sooner was this matter thus disposed of than one Henry O. Norton and Augustine Spencer—two worthless scoundrels whose words were utterly unreliable, went before the justice of the peace who had just dismissed the brethren, and charged Joseph and Hyrum Smith with having committed the crime of treason. The warrant for their arrest was placed in the hands of Constable Bettisworth, an over-bearing, insolent officer. He went to the Hamilton House, where the Messrs. Smith and their friends were staying: he arrested them and was for dragging them off to jail. They demanded to see the mittimus committing them to prison, a request which at first was denied, but finally the instrument was produced.

Carthage Jail

It recited that the parties under arrest had been before the justice for trial, but that said trial had been necessarily postponed because of the absence of material witnesses. That was an infamously false statement, unless the accused could have appeared before the justice without being present in person or by counsel. It afforded Constable Bettisworth an excuse, however, to drag these men off to jail, and this he was determined to do, their vigorous protest to the contrary notwithstanding.

Seeing his friends thus illegally and brutally dealt with aroused the righteous indignation of Elder Taylor. He sought out the governor, informed him of what was going on, and the character of the men who had made the charge. The governor regretted that the thing had occurred, he did not believe the charges, but thought the best thing to do was to let the law take its course. All this was unsatisfactory to Elder Taylor. He reminded the governor that they had all come to Carthage at his instance, not to satisfy the law, for that had no claim upon them; but to manifest a willingness to meet their action in relation to the *Expositor* affair; that at his suggestion they had given bonds to appear before the circuit court; that they had come without arms at his request, and relied upon him to shield them from insult; that after his solemn pledge to Doctor Bernhisel and himself he thought they had a right to expect protection from him: but if in his very presence they were to be subject to mob rule, and, contrary to law, be dragged into prison at the instance of every infernal scoundrel whose oath could be bought for a dram of whiskey, his protection did not amount to much and they had miscalculated his promises.

Leaving the presence of the governor he hurried back to his friends. A great rabble, a mixture of soldiers and citizens and partly under the influence of liquor, had gathered in the street about the hotel, and rowdyism and excitement were running high. Fearing a design was on foot to kill the prisoners on the way to the jail, Elder Taylor hailed a soldier and said: "I am afraid there is a design against the lives of the Messrs. Smith; will you go immediately and bring your captain, and if not convenient, any other captain of a company, and I will pay you well for your trouble."

The man departed and soon returned with his captain, who, when Elder Taylor told him of his fears, went after his company and brought them up just as the constable was hurrying off his victims to jail; this company of militia guarded them to the prison.

The next day—the 26th of June—there was a long interview between Governor Ford and the Prophet, at which Elder Taylor was present. All the difficulties that had arisen were related by the Prophet and the action of himself and associates explained and defended. In concluding that conversation the Prophet said: "Governor Ford, I ask nothing but what is legal; I have a right to expect protection, at least from you; for independent of law, you have pledged your faith and that of the state for my protection, and I wish to go to Nauvoo."

"And you shall have protection, General Smith," replied the governor. "I did not make this promise without consulting my officers, who all pledged their honor to its fulfillment. I do not know that I shall go tomorrow to Nauvoo, but if I do, I will take you along."

In the afternoon of the same day Joseph and Hyrum were as illegally dragged out of prison as they had been unlawfully thrust into it; for the justice having committed them to prison, "there to remain until discharged by due process of law," had no more power over them. But notwithstanding this fact, he ordered the constable to bring them from jail into his court; and when the prisoners refused to go at the bidding of this autocratic justice, the constable, under instructions from the magistrate, called to his assistance a detachment of the Carthage Greys under Frank Worrell, and again presented himself at the jail, and in spite of the protests of the prisoners and the jailer, they forced them to go before Justice Smith.

On arraignment before the justice, counsel for the accused asked for a continuation until the next day to procure witnesses. This was granted; a new mittimus was made out and they were again committed to prison. After the departure of the accused, and without consulting them or their counsel, the time for the hearing of the case was further postponed until the 29th.

The following day—the ever-memorable 27th of June—the governor broke the promise he had made to Joseph Smith the day previous, viz.: that if he went to Nauvoo he would take him along. He disbanded the mob militia except a small company he detailed to accompany him to Nauvoo, and the Carthage Greys, a company of the very worst enemies the Smiths and their friends had—these he left to guard the prisoners!

The mob-militia, after receiving their discharge, before leaving the public square in Carthage, publicly boasted that they would only go a short distance from town, and after the governor left they would return and kill the Smiths and their friends if they had "to tear down the jail to do it." Captain Dan Jones, one of the brethren, heard this threat and informed the governor of it. The only answer he received was that he was too anxious for the safety of his friends.

Later in the day Captain Jones was dispatched to Hon. O.H. Browning, a prominent lawyer of Quincy, to secure his professional services in the pending trial. Cyrus Wheelock left for Nauvoo a little after noon to obtain witnesses. Before going he left a six-shooting revolver belonging to Elder Taylor with the Prophet. Stephen Markham being seen on the street was captured, put on his horse and compelled to leave town at the point of the bayonet. The departure of these brethren left only John Taylor and Willard Richards with the Prophet and his brother Hyrum.

The afternoon drew its slow length along. The four friends carried on a desultory conversation, in which Elder Richards remarked: "Brother Joseph, if it is necessary that you die in this matter, and if they will take me in your stead, I will suffer for you."

Other thoughts were passing through the mind of Elder Taylor. He regarded the whole thing as an outrage on their liberties and rights; and the mob proceedings under the forms of law a legal farce. As he contemplated these acts of injustice he broke out with—"Brother Joseph, if you will permit it, and say the word, I will have you out of this prison in five hours, if the jail has to come down to do it." His idea was to go to Nauvoo, collect a sufficient force of the brethren to liberate his friends. Joseph refused to sanction such a course.

The four friends were sitting in a large, square room in the prison, usually occupied by men imprisoned for the lighter offenses. The afternoon was warm and the spirits of the brethren extremely dull and depressed—did the shadow of their impending fate begin to fall upon them? Elder Taylor sang the following song, which had recently been introduced into Nauvoo. The tune is the one to which he sang it on that melancholy occasion:

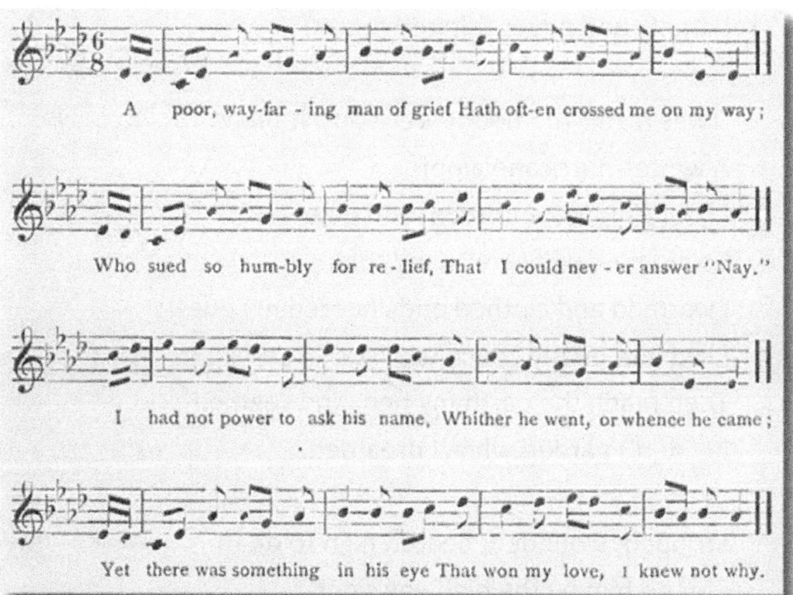

A Poor Way-faring Man of Grief

Once when my scanty meal was spread,
He entered—not a word he spake!
Just perishing for want of bread;
I gave him all; he blessed it, brake,
And ate, but gave me part again;
Mine was an angel's portion then;
For while I fed with eager haste
The crust was manna to my taste.

I spied him where a fountain burst
Clear from the rock; his strength was gone;
The heedless water mocked his thirst;
He heard it, saw it hurrying on—
I ran and raised the sufferer up;
Thrice from the stream he drained my cup;
Dipped, and returned it running o'er;

I drank, and never thirsted more.

'Twas night; the floods were out; it blew
A winter-hurricane aloof;
I heard his voice abroad, and flew
To bid him welcome to my roof.
I warmed and clothed and cheered my guest;
I laid him on my couch to rest;
Then made the earth my bed, and seemed
In Eden's garden while I dreamed.

Stripped, wounded, beaten nigh to death,
I found him by the highway side;
I roused his pulse, brought back his breath,
Revived his spirit and supplied
Wine, oil, refreshment—he was healed;
I had myself a wound concealed;
But from that hour forgot the smart,
And peace bound up my broken heart.

In prison I saw him next,—condemned
To meet a traitor's doom at morn;
The tide of lying tongues I stemmed,
And honored him 'mid shame and scorn.
My friendship's utmost zeal to try,
He asked if I for him would die;
The flesh was weak, my blood ran chill
But the free spirit cried, "I will."

Then in a moment to my view,
The stranger darted from disguise;

The tokens in his hands I knew;
The Savior stood before mine eyes.
He spake, and my poor name he named—
"Of me thou hast not been ashamed;
These deeds shall my memorial be;
Fear not, thou didst them unto me."

Shortly Hyrum asked him to sing the song again, to which he replied:

"Brother Hyrum, I do not feel like singing."

"Oh, never mind; commence singing and you will get the spirit of it."

Soon after finishing the song the second time, as he was sitting at one of the front windows of the jail, he saw a number of men, with painted faces, rushing round the corner towards the stairs. The brethren must have seen this mob simultaneously, for as Elder Taylor started for the door to secure it, he found Hyrum Smith and Doctor Richards leaning against it to prevent its being opened, as the lock and latch were of little use. The mob reaching the landing in front of the door, and thinking it was locked, fired a shot through the key hole. Hyrum and Doctor Richards sprang back, when instantly another ball crashed through the panel of the door and struck Hyrum in the face; at the same instant a ball from the window facing the public square where the main body of the Carthage Greys was stationed, entered his back, and he fell exclaiming, "I am a dead man!" With an expression of deep sympathy in his face, Joseph bent over the prostrate body of the murdered man and exclaimed, "Oh! my poor, dear brother Hyrum!" Then instantly rising to his feet he drew the pistol Cyrus Wheelock had left, and with a quick, firm step, and a determined expression in his face he advanced to the door and snapped the pistol six successive times; only three of the loads, however, were discharged.

While Joseph was firing the pistol Elder Taylor stood close behind him, and as soon as he discharged it and stepped back, Elder Taylor took his place next the door, and with a heavy walking stick—

left there by Brother Markham—parried the guns as they were thrust through the doorway and discharged.

The firing from within made the mob pause, but it was only for an instant, and then the attack was more furious than ever. The scene was terrible! Streams of fire as thick as a man's arm belched forth from the ever increasing number of guns in the door-way, yet calm, energetic and determined, Elder Taylor beat down the muzzles of those murderous guns.

"That's right, Brother Taylor, parry them off as well as you can," said Joseph, as he stood behind him. Those were the last words he heard the Prophet speak on earth in the flesh.

Meantime the crowd on the landing grew more dense and were forced to the door by the pressure of those below crowding their way up the stairs. The guns of the assailants were pushed further and further into the room—the firing was more rapid and accompanied with demoniac yells and horrid oaths and execrations. Certain that they would be overpowered in a moment if he remained longer at the door, and thinking that they might have some friends outside, Elder Taylor sprang for the open window directly in front of the prison door, and also exposed to the fire of the Carthage Greys from the public square. As he was in the act of leaping from the window, a ball fired from the door-way struck him about midway of his left thigh. He fell helpless on the window sill and would have dropped on the outside of the jail—when another shot from the outside, striking the watch in his vest pocket, threw him back into the room. As soon as he struck the floor his animation returned, and, in order to avoid the range of fire from the door way, he drew himself as rapidly as possible in his crippled condition under the bedstead that stood near the window.

While on his way three other bullets struck him; one a little below the left knee—it was never extracted; another tore away the flesh to the size of a man's hand from his left hip and spattered the wall with blood and the mangled fragments; another entered the forepart of his left arm, a little above the wrist, and, passing down by the joint, lodged in the palm of his left hand.

As he laid there weltering in his blood, he heard the mob at the door shout: "He has leaped from the window!" There was a cessation of the firing, and a general rush down stairs. At the same instant Dr. Richards crossed the room and looked out of the window.

It would seem that the Prophet Joseph also attempted to leap from the window, but on reaching it he was instantly shot and fell to the ground by the side of an old well-curb. It was this that gave rise to the cry, "He has leaped from the window!" which attracted the attention of Elder Taylor.

Brother Richards remained but a moment at the window; and then started for the inner prison, the door of which opened on the landing in front of the door to the room the brethren had occupied. As he passed him Elder Taylor said:

"Stop, doctor, and take me along."

Ascertaining that the iron door to the criminals' cell was open, he returned and dragged his wounded companion into it. Inside the cell he exclaimed:

"Oh! Brother Taylor, is it possible that they have killed Brothers Joseph and Hyrum? It cannot surely be, and yet I saw them shoot them! Oh Lord, my God, spare Thy servants!" he exclaimed several times, raising his hands to heaven with each exclamation. "Brother Taylor, this is a terrible event," he went on; and then dragged him still further into the cell.

Taking up an old filthy mattress he threw it over the wounded man saying: "I am sorry I cannot do better for you; but that may hide you, and you may yet live to tell the tale, but I expect they will kill me in a few moments."

The doctor then went out to learn for certain the fate which had befallen the Prophet. While he was gone Elder Taylor suffered the most excruciating pain. Dr. Richards returned in a few minutes, and confirmed his worst fears—the Prophet was dead!

"I felt," says Elder Taylor, "a dull, lonely, sickening sensation at the news."

"When I reflected that our noble chieftain, the Prophet of the living God, had fallen, and that I had seen his brother in the cold embrace of death, it seemed as though there was a void or vacuum in the great field of human existence to me, and a dark, gloomy chasm in the kingdom, and that we were left alone. Oh, how lonely was that feeling! How cold, barren and desolate! In the midst of difficulties he was always the first in motion; in critical positions his counsel was always sought. As our Prophet he approached our God, and obtained for us His will; but now our Prophet, our counselor, our general, our leader was gone, and amid the fiery ordeal that we then had to pass through, we were left alone without his aid, and as our future guide for things spiritual or temporal, and for all things pertaining to this world or the next, he had spoken for the last time on earth!"

Scene at Carthage

"These reflections and a thousand others flashed upon my mind. I thought, Why must the good perish, and the virtuous be destroyed? Why must God's nobility, the salt of the earth, the most exalted of the human family, and the most perfect types of all excellence, fall victims to the cruel, fiendish hate of incarnate devils?"

Ah, why?

CHAPTER 16 - WITH THE GREATEST

Immediately after the terrible tragedy was ended, fear seized upon the perpetrators of it, and they precipitately fled. A number of the inhabitants of Carthage gathered about the jail, and some of these went to the head of the stairs to see the work that had been done.

Elder Taylor was brought out of the cell to the landing at the head of the stairs. Through the open door leading into the room that he and his friends had occupied when the assault was made, he had a full view of Hyrum Smith.

"There he lay as I had left him," he writes. "He had not moved a limb; he lay placid and calm, a monument of greatness even in death: but his noble spirit had left its tenement and had gone to dwell in regions more congenial to its exalted nature. Poor Hyrum! he was a great and good man, and my soul was cemented to his. If ever there was an exemplary, honest and virtuous man, an embodiment of all that is noble in the human form, Hyrum Smith was its representative." Such were his thoughts on the character of his friend, even while suffering excruciating pains from his wounds.

Among those who stood about him on the landing was a doctor, and feeling the ball that had lodged in the palm of Elder Taylor's left hand, he took a pen knife, made an incision and then with a pair of carpenter's compasses pried out the half-ounce ball. The alternate sawing with a dull pen knife and prying with the compasses was simply surgical butchery. The doctor afterwards said that Elder Taylor had nerves "like the devil" to stand that operation.

The crowd now urged him to consent to be removed to Hamilton's hotel, where he could be cared for, to which he replied: "I don't know you. Who am I among? I am surrounded by assassins and murderers; witness your deeds! Don't talk to me of kindness and comfort; look at your murdered victims! Look at me! I want none of your counsel nor comfort. There may be some safety here; I can be assured of none anywhere."

They protested that he was safe with them; it was a shame that he and his friends had been treated in the manner they had; they swore by all the oaths known to the damned that they would stand by him to the death. "In half an hour every one of them had fled from the town," says Elder Taylor.

Meantime a coroner's inquest was being held over the bodies of Joseph and Hyrum. Robert F. Smith, the justice of the peace who had issued the warrant for the arrest of the murdered men on the charge of treason, who without a hearing had illegally committed them to prison and then in a few hours as unlawfully dragged them out to appear before his court, who was captain of the Carthage Greys and who had helped to murder them, was the coroner! During the investigation the name of Francis Higbee was mentioned as being in the vicinity.

"Captain Smith, you are a justice of the peace—I want to swear my life against that man," said Elder Taylor. Word was immediately sent to Higbee and he left Carthage.

Through the persuasions of Doctor Richards Elder Taylor was at last removed to Hamilton's hotel, though it was difficult to obtain sufficient help to move him, as a great fear fell upon the people and they had fled the place as though a plague had fallen upon it. It was feared that the Mormons being incensed at the murder of Joseph and Hyrum would call out the Legion and take summary vengeance on the people of Carthage. It was only by earnest entreaty that Doctor Richards could prevail upon the Hamiltons to remain.

All the inhabitants of Carthage knew that a terrible outrage had been perpetrated; that the pledged faith of the state had been broken; that the martyrs had voluntarily gone to Carthage and placed themselves in the power of their enemies at a time when they were amply able to protect themselves against the mob thrice told, and against the governor's troops besides. No wonder the people of Carthage expected that the Mormons would take a terrible vengeance.

Doctor Richards was also afraid that he Saints in their just indignation would rise in their wrath and take vengeance into their own hands. He took counsel with Elder Taylor and concluded to send a note to Nauvoo. "Brother Richards, say that I am *slightly* wounded," said Elder Taylor. And when the note making the awful announcement of the murder of the prophets to the Saints was brought to him, he signed his name as quickly as possible lest the tremor of his hand should be noticed, and the fears of his family aroused.

This note was entrusted to George D. Grant, who at once started for Nauvoo. He was met within three miles of the city by the governor and his escort, who, on hearing a cannon fired in the direction of Carthage, had immediately left Nauvoo. Governor Ford had gone to Nauvoo that morning, and during the day delivered a speech to the people. In it he had insulted them by assuming that all their enemies had said of them was true. At this, according to his own account of the matter, the people manifested some impatience and anger, as well they might, for baser slanders were never circulated of any community, nor a grosser insult ever offered to one than for the governor to assume, without investigation, that all that had been said against them was true.

The governor compelled George D. Grant to return to Carthage with him, that he might have time to remove the county records from the court house and give the citizens a chance to escape before the people of Nauvoo should learn of the murder; for he, too, expected the Mormons would wreak a terrible vengeance. He reached Carthage about midnight, and having conferred with Dr. Richards, and promising that all things should be inquired into, and telling what few people remained in Carthage to flee for their lives, Governor Ford listened to the voice of his own fears and with his posse fled in the direction of Quincy.

It was morning before Elder Taylor's wounds could be dressed and he made in any way comfortable. The day following, the 29th, his wife Leonora came to him, and also his father and mother, as well as a number of the brethren who had come to render assistance in removing the remains of the martyrs to Nauvoo.

General Demming of the Hancock County militia and also Colonel Jones, treated Elder Taylor with marked courtesy, and seemed solicitous for his welfare. There were also a number of gentlemen from Quincy and other places, among them Judge Ralston, who called to inquire after his welfare. Among them was a doctor who extracted a ball that was giving him great pain from his thigh.

"Will you be tied during the operation, Mr. Taylor?"

"Oh, no; I shall endure the cutting all right," was the reply, and he did.

The ball was buried in the flesh, and flattened against the bone to the size of a 25 cent piece, and the thigh was badly swollen; but the cutting was a relief from the pain he had endured.

During the performance of the operation Sister Taylor retired to another room to pray for him, that he might have strength to endure it and be restored to her and her family. While thus engaged an old Methodist lady of the name of Bedell entered the room and seeing Sister Taylor on her knees, approvingly patted her on the back, saying, "There's a good lady, pray for God to forgive your sins; pray that you may be converted, and the Lord may have mercy on your soul!"

While in that house, where the inmates talked of praying for the forgiveness of sins and for mercy, Sister Taylor had heard the murder of the prophets approved of, at least by the old gentleman Hamilton, father of the one who kept the house, and she expressed her belief that the other branches of the family approved of it.

"These were the associates of the old lady referred to," says Elder Taylor, "and yet she could talk of conversion and saving souls in the midst of blood and murder: such is man and such consistency!"

Some of the brethren had considerable anxiety for the safety of Elder Taylor. They by no means thought him secure from the attack of the mob, some of whom hung about Carthage, and others who began to return there when they saw the Mormons did not rise *en masse* and destroy their neighbors. A brother of the name of Alexander Williams feared his enemies had some motive in keeping Elder Taylor in Carthage, and one day he remarked to him that he had fifty men at a given point in some woods adjacent, and he would soon raise another fifty and take him to Nauvoo if he would go. Elder Taylor thanked Brother Williams but thought there was no need of his going.

He did seem to be in some danger, however, for the before mentioned Colonel Jones when compelled to be absent from his room would leave a pair of pistols on the table, in case an attack should be made. Some time after his recovery, too, when publishing an account of the assault upon the jail, a lawyer of the name of Backman stated that he prevented the desperado Jackson, before mentioned, from ascending the stairs of the jail and dispatching him while he lay there unable to move. Backman at the time of making the statement expressed his regrets at having prevented the deed. There were others also who said that he ought to be killed; but that it "was too d—d cowardly to shoot a wounded man." "And thus," remarks the Elder, "by the chivalry of murderers, I was prevented from being a second time mutilated or killed."

The motive prompting such a deed, apart from the murderous spirit of the wretches who contemplated it, would be found in the fact that Elder Taylor had been a witness of their damning deed, and it was uncertain how many and whom among them he had recognized. It was important to the mob that such a witness should be silenced.

How many days Elder Taylor remained in Carthage after he was wounded is not certain, but it was not many; from three to five only. The people at Carthage were anxious for him to remain, since they looked upon him as a sort of hostage; and thought his removal would doubtless be the signal for the uprising of the Mormons.

At last Brother Marks, the President of the Nauvoo Stake, Doctor Ellis, a number of brethren on horseback, and James Allred with a wagon, came to Carthage to remove him to Nauvoo. When asked if he could talk, he could but barely whisper, "No;" so weak was he from the loss of blood and the discharge of his wounds. The physicians and people of Carthage protested that it would be his death if he were removed; but his friends were anxious for his removal if possible.

Being unable to ride in a wagon or carriage, a litter was prepared for him, and a number of men living in Carthage, some of whom had been engaged in the mob, assisted in carrying him. Once on the way, word was sent to some of the Saints living along the route, not far from Carthage, to come and meet them. Meantime the men from Carthage made one excuse after another for leaving until all were gone, much to the relief of the wounded man, who expressed himself as glad to get rid of them.

The tramping of those who carried him at last produced violent pain. A sleigh was therefore obtained and hitched to the back of James Allred's wagon. A bed was made on the sleigh, and with Sister Taylor by his side to bathe his wounds with ice-water, the company moved on towards Nauvoo. The sleigh slipped along over the grass of the prairie almost without a jar. Five or six miles from Nauvoo the Saints who had learned of his coming turned out to meet him, and they increased in numbers as the party with the wounded man drew nearer, until soon there were troops of friends about him on every hand.

With what joy the storm-tossed, ship-wrecked sailor enters the port from whence he sailed! How buoyant with delight is the soldier who, after many a hard-fought field, and a thousand dangers past, returns at last, weary and worn perhaps, to his native village! But more grateful, and more joyous than either of these was Elder Taylor to return into the midst of his friends, after passing through the fearful ordeal at Carthage jail.

"Never shall I forget the difference of feeling," he writes, "that I experienced between the place that I had left and the one that I had now arrived at. I had left a lot of reckless, blood-thirsty murderers, and had come to the city of the Saints, the people of the living God; friends of truth and righteousness, all of whom stood there with warm, true hearts to offer their friendship and services, and to welcome my return."

One thing only cast a shadow upon his happiness—the recollection that Joseph and Hyrum were not there—that they were dead!

When Doctor Richards left Carthage with the bodies of the prophets to convey them to Nauvoo, Elder Taylor suggested that he had better take his purse and watch as he feared the people might steal them. At this suggestion the doctor put the purse and watch into one of the owner's pantaloon pockets, then cutting it off tied a string around the top. It was thus returned to him after he reached Nauvoo. On opening the pocket it was found that the crystal to the watch was literally smashed to powder by the ball that had struck it at the time he had felt himself falling from the jail window. Up to that time, however, his being thrown back into the room when he felt himself falling out had been a mystery; but now it was all clear to him. Had he fallen on the outside he would have dropped into the very midst of his enemies and would have been instantly dispatched; but the bullet aimed at his heart was turned by an over-ruling Providence into a messenger of mercy—it saved his life.

"I shall never forget the feelings of gratitude that I then experienced towards my Heavenly Father," he writes in speaking of the discovery of how his life was saved; "the whole scene was vividly portrayed before me, and my heart melted before the Lord. I felt that the Lord had preserved me by a special act of mercy; that my time had not yet come, and that I had still a work to perform upon the earth." The hands of the watch stood at five o'clock, sixteen minutes, and twenty-six seconds, thus marking the moment when its possessor stood between time and eternity.

The trying ordeal through which he had passed with the martyrs, his devotion and faithfulness to them in those fearful scenes in the jail, his undaunted courage, the cruel wounds he himself had received, and the patience with which he endured his suffering—all bound Elder Taylor in still stronger bands of affection to the Saints in Nauvoo and throughout the world.

Shortly after his return to Nauvoo, Eliza R. Snow addressed the following lines to him:

Thou chieftain of Zion, henceforward thy name
Will be classed with the martyrs, and share in their fame;
Thro' ages eternal, of thee 'twill be said,
With the greatest of prophets he suffered and bled.
When the shafts of injustice were pointed at him,
When the cup of his suff'ring was fill'd to the brim,
When his innocent blood was inhumanly shed,
You shar'd his afflictions and with him you bled.
When around you like hailstones, the rifle balls flew,
When the passage of death opened wide to your view,
When the prophet's free'd spirit thro' martyrdom fled,
In your gore you lay welt'ring—with martyrs you bled.
All the scars from your wounds, like the trophies of yore,
Shall be ensigns of HONOR, till you are no more;
And by all generations of thee shall be said,
With the best of the prophets, in prison, he bled.

CHAPTER 17 - GOVERNOR FORD

Relative to Governor Ford's complicity in this awful tragedy, Elder Taylor has the following:

"There had been various opinions about the complicity of the governor in the murder, some supposing that he knew all about it, and assisted or winked at its execution. It is somewhat difficult to form a correct opinion; from the facts presented it is very certain that things looked more than suspicious against him."

"In the first place, he positively knew that we had broken no law.

"Secondly. He knew that the mob had not only passed inflammatory resolutions, threatening extermination to the Mormons, but that they had actually assembled armed mobs and commenced hostilities against us.

"Thirdly. He took those very mobs that had been arrayed against us, and enrolled them as his troops, thus legalizing their acts.

"Fourthly. He disbanded the Nauvoo Legion, which had never violated law, and disarmed them, and had about his person in the shape of militia known mobocrats and violators of the law.

"Fifthly. He requested us to come to Carthage without arms, promising protection, and then refused to interfere in delivering us from prison, although Joseph and Hyrum were put there contrary to law.

"Sixthly. Although he refused to interfere in our behalf, yet, when Captain Smith went to him and informed him that the prisoners refused to come out, he told him that he had a command and knew what to do, thus sanctioning the use of force in the violation of law when opposed to us, whereas he would not for us interpose his executive authority to free us from being incarcerated contrary to law, although he was fully informed of all the facts of the case, as we kept him posted in the affairs all the time.

"Seventhly. He left the prisoners in Carthage jail contrary to his plighted faith.

"Eighthly. Before he went he dismissed all the troops that could be relied upon, as well as many of the mob, and left us in charge of the "Carthage Greys," a company that he knew were mobocratic, our most bitter enemies, and who had passed resolutions to exterminate us, and who had been placed under guard by General Demming only the day before.

"Ninthly. He was informed of the intended murder, both before he left and while on the road, by several different parties.

"Tenthly. When the cannon was fired in Carthage, signifying that the deed was done, he immediately took up his line of march and fled. How did he know this signal portended their death, if he was not in the secret? It may be said some of the party told him. How could he believe what the party said about the gun signal if he could not believe the testimony of several individuals who told him in positive terms about the contemplated murder?

"He has I believe, stated that he left the "Carthage Greys" there because he considered that, as their town was contiguous to ours, and as the responsibility of our safety rested solely upon them, they would not dare suffer any indignity to befall us. This very admission shows that he did really expect danger; and then he knew that these people had published to the world that they would exterminate us, and his leaving us in their hands and taking off their responsibilities was like leaving a lamb in charge of a wolf, and trusting to its humanity and honor for its safe-keeping.

"It is said again that he would not have gone to Nauvoo, and thus placed himself in the hands of the Mormons, if he had anticipated any such event, as he would be exposed to their wrath. To this it may be answered that the Mormons did not know their signals, while he did; and they were also known in Warsaw, as well as in other places; and as soon as a gun was fired, a merchant of Warsaw jumped upon his horse and rode directly to Quincy, and reported 'Joseph and Hyrum killed, and those who were with them in jail.' He reported further that 'they were attempting to break jail, and were all killed by the guard.' This was their story; it was anticipated to kill all, and the gun was to be the signal that the deed was accomplished. This was known in Warsaw. The governor also knew it and fled; and he could really be in no danger in Nauvoo, for the Mormons did not know it, and he had plenty of time to escape, which he did.

"It is said that he made all his officers promise solemnly that they would help him to protect the Smiths; this may or may not be. At any rate, some of these same officers helped to murder them.

"The strongest argument in the governor's favor, and one that would bear more weight with us than all the rest put together, would be that he could not believe them capable of such atrocity; and, thinking that their talk and threatenings were a mere ebullition of feeling, a kind of braggadocio, and that there was enough of good, moral feeling to control the more violent passions, he trusted to their faith. There is, indeed, a degree of plausibility about this, but when we put it in juxtaposition to the amount of evidence that he was in possession of, it weighs very little. He had nothing to inspire confidence in them, and everything to make him mistrust them. Besides, why his broken faith? Why his disregard of what was told him by several parties? Again, if he knew not the plan, how did he understand the signal? Why so oblivious to everything pertaining to the Mormon interest, and so alive and interested about the mobocrats? At any rate, be this as it may, he stands responsible for their blood, and it is dripping on his garments. If it had not been for his promises of protection, they would have protected themselves; it was plighted faith that led them to the slaughter; and, to make the best of it, it was a breach of that faith and a non-fulfillment of that promise, after repeated warning, that led to their death.

"Having said so much, I must leave the governor with my readers and with his God. Justice, I conceive, demanded this much, and truth could not be told with less; as I have said before, my opinion is that the governor would not have planned this murder, but he had not sufficient energy to resist popular opinion, even if that opinion led to blood and death."

Governor Ford admits, in his History of Illinois, that he heard of some threats made against the prisoners. He writes: "I had heard of some threats being made, but none of an attack upon the prisoners whilst in jail. These threats seemed to be made by individuals not acting in concert. They were no more than the bluster which might have been expected, and furnished no indication of numbers combining for this or any other purpose."

The day previous to the assault on the jail, the governor was planning to march all his forces into Nauvoo. This military expedition, not to say semi-military invasion, was expected to accomplish two purposes: first, it would gratify the clamors of the anti-Mormons; second, it was intended to strike terror to the hearts of the citizens of Nauvoo. Speaking of this intended military display the governor remarks:

"I observed that some of the people became more and more excited and inflammatory the further the preparations were advanced. Occasional threats came to my ears of destroying the city and murdering or expelling the inhabitants. I had no objection to ease the terrors of the people by this display of force, and was most anxious also to search for the alleged apparatus for making counterfeit money; and, in fact, to inquire into all the charges made against that people, if I could have been assured of my command against mutiny and insubordination. But I gradually learned to my entire satisfaction that there was a plan to get the troops into Nauvoo, and there to begin the war, probably by some of our own party, or some of the seceding Mormons, taking advantage of the night to fire on our own force, and then lay it on the Mormons. I was satisfied that there were those amongst us fully capable of such an act, hoping that in the alarm, bustle and confusion of a militia camp, the truth would not be discovered, and that it might lead to the desired collision."

Such are the reasons assigned by Governor Ford for abandoning his plan of marching all his forces into Nauvoo. If he could persuade himself to believe that he had those under his command who would resort to the means he himself alludes to in the foregoing, to bring about a collision with the citizens of Nauvoo, and that he was fearful that his whole command would mutiny when once in the city of the Saints, it is unfortunate for the fame of Governor Ford that his fears could not be aroused for the safety of his prisoners, who were left at the mercy of those same militia forces of which he himself was distrustful, especially since the only barrier between them and the fury of this mob militia was a guard made up of their bitterest enemies—the Carthage Greys.

CHAPTER 18 - THE TWELVE CHOSEN

Soon after the return of Elder Taylor to Nauvoo, he, in connection with Willard Richards and W. W. Phelps, issued an address to the Saints, beseeching them to hold fast to the faith and to be peaceable citizens, doing the works of righteousness. The address also stated that as soon as the Twelve and other authorities could assemble, or a majority of them, the onward course for the great gathering of Israel, and the final consummation of the Dispensation of the Fullness of Times, would be pointed out.

Elders Taylor and Richards were the only members of the quorum of the Twelve in Nauvoo at the time, the others all being absent in the East on Missions.

In a few days Parley P. Pratt arrived and united with these brethren in directing the affairs of the Church. The council meetings of these apostles were held at the house of Elder Taylor, in order that he might take part in them, being still confined to his room by his wounds.

About the time Elder Pratt reached Nauvoo Sidney Rigdon, one of the counselors to the martyred Prophet, arrived from Pennsylvania. He was invited to join them in their movements, but this he declined, as he had his own selfish ambition to gratify. He was determined to become the leader of the Church; and to accomplish this, he began in an underhanded way to work up a feeling in his own favor.

Afraid to put in a claim to be made President outright, he sought to be appointed "guardian" to the Church, to build it up to

Joseph. He held secret meetings among those favorable to his plans, circulated wonderful "revelations" among them, and ordained men to offices heretofore unheard of in the Church; and at last appointed a day for the Church to assemble and select a "guardian." The day appointed was the 8th of August.

By that time President Young and a majority of the Twelve had arrived. Elder Rigdon had full opportunity to present his claims to the people, but they rejected him, and almost unanimously chose the apostles to preside over the whole Church.

Disappointed in his ambitious designs, Elder Rigdon sought to divide the people; but as his influence in Nauvoo was limited, he did not succeed further than to induce a very few to accompany him to Pittsburg, Pennsylvania, where he gathered about him a few other followers. He was shortly afterwards excommunicated from the Church, as he manifested no disposition to repent of his course.

Other restless, ambitious characters, among them James J. Strang and James Emmet sought to divide the Church, since they could not preside over it, and did lead some away; their vaulting ambition overleaped itself, however, and they miserably failed.

The Twelve being sustained as the presiding authority, they took the direction of affairs and issued a general epistle to the Church, in which they expressed a determination to carry on the work so well begun by the Prophet Joseph. Nauvoo must be enlarged, the temple completed and the gathering of Israel go on. "The gospel in its fullness must now roll forth," said they, "through every neighborhood of this wide-spread country, and to all the world, until the kingdoms of this world become the kingdom of our Lord and of His Christ."

Capitalists were invited to Nauvoo to establish manufactories, and were assured that the people there had sufficient skill and ingenuity among them to carry on nearly all kinds of industry. Elder Taylor took a prominent part in these temporal affairs as well as in things spiritual. On his recommendation and under his supervision a "Trades Union" was formed, an organization having for its object the establishment of industries that would produce, as far as possible, everything needed by the people of Nauvoo, and a surplus for exportation.

Suggestions were made to secure a charter for the association, but as there was every prospect that the city and other charters granted to the people of Nauvoo would be repealed by the state legislature, Elder Taylor proposed a plan of organization that was at once novel and not likely to be interfered with by the state:

First, Twelve men to be appointed, forming a *Living Constitution*, with a president, secretary, etc., to take the lead in all the affairs of the association.

Second. Separate trustees to organize themselves and have their own laws, but to be subject to the living constitution.

These movements gave an impetus to industry, and an era of prosperity dawned upon Nauvoo such as she had never before witnessed. Immigration rapidly increased her population, factories of various kinds sprang into existence, and the diversity of industries thus created, made an exchange of home productions possible and very profitable.

After the ruthless murder of the prophets there was a cessation of active hostilities against the Saints, and even a reaction of popular sentiment in their favor. This, however, was but momentary. It grew out of the awe inspired by the dastardly murder committed at Carthage, sufficient in atrocity to make hell itself stand aghast and tremble. It was sufficient, also, to silence the tongue of slander in Illinois for the moment; and even fired some with boldness enough to denounce the deed and call for the enforcement of the law against the murderers.

Brave souls! Kind hearts, to weep over the wounded honor of the state! Their tears were gracious drops! But at the first cry of "*thieves, thieves, thieves* in Nauvoo!" a cry raised by the men whose hands were red with the innocent blood of God's servants—Illinois forgot her horror at the atrocious murder of innocent men while under her protection; and clapped her hands with joy at the prospect of finding even the slightest shadow of palliation for the monstrous crime which dragged her honor in the dust, and stamped the brand of infamy forever on her brow.

The murderers of the prophets were so industrious in crying "thieves" and charging the Mormons with crimes which were never committed, that soon they not only made Illinois forget her shame in permitting the prophets of God to be murdered, but had her applauding the deed. So bold were the mob in their determination not to be brought to justice, that they threatened Governor Ford, and said if he insisted on pushing the investigation they would make him an accessory to the crime. Nine of the mob, however were finally brought to trial; and such trial! it was but a travesty on the term. The testimony of the chief witnesses for the prosecution was thrown out of evidence; and though the accused were notoriously guilty, they were acquitted.

Made bold by the impunity with which scoundrels had preyed upon the Saints, there was a further gathering of thieves, blacklegs and counterfeiters into Hancock County, and all their desperate crimes were credited to the Mormon people, together with many which had no existence, except as they were coined by the lying tongues of men bent on the destruction of the Saints. The city council of Nauvoo took up the matter, investigated it, and defied the world to substantiate a single instance where they had screened criminals from the law. The citizens in mass meeting assembled denied the slanderous allegations; the deputy sheriff of Hancock County denied them over his signature; Governor Ford investigated them, and in his annual message to the legislature, said: "I have investigated the charge of promiscuous stealing and find it to be greatly exaggerated. I could not ascertain that there were a greater proportion of thieves in that community than in any other of the same number of inhabitants, and perhaps it the city of Nauvoo were compared with St. Louis, or any other western city, the proportion would not be so great."

Regardless of these denials the charges of thieving, counterfeiting and shielding criminals were repeated until popular prejudice was thoroughly aroused against the inhabitants of Nauvoo, and began to demand their extermination. Made utterly reckless by the success of their misrepresentations, the anti-Mormons held a meeting to devise means for getting rid of the

Saints. A number of their own crowd fired upon the house where the meeting was being held. This was charged to the Mormons, and made a pretext for burning the houses and stacks of grain belonging to the Saints in Morley settlement, near which the aforesaid meeting was held.

This outrage was not avenged by the citizens of Nauvoo, though their means of doing so were ample. They laid the matter before the authorities and there let it rest. Meantime the mob was making similar assaults on all the out-lying settlements. Houses and stacks of grain were burned, the sick and helpless driven from their homes to the open prairie. Mr. Backenstos, sheriff of Hancock County, called for a posse of the law-abiding citizens outside to put down mob violence. He thought it best to call upon citizens outside of Nauvoo to quell the disturbance lest the operations of a posse from Nauvoo should be made a pretext for the opening of civil war. There was no response to the sheriff's call, and house-burning and other acts of violence went on unchecked.

In the midst of these exciting scenes a mass meeting in Quincy resolved that the only hope for peace was in the removal of the Mormons from the state, and they appointed a committee to wait upon the Church authorities to lay these conclusions before them, and request them to leave. Weary with being continually harassed with illegal prosecutions and mob violence, the Saints agreed to leave the state in the spring, providing the citizens in Hancock and surrounding counties would use their influence in assisting them to rent or sell their property, that they might have means with which to remove; and further that they would cease vexatious lawsuits against them, as they had violated no law. This proposition was accepted by the people of Quincy and also by the anti-Mormons in Hancock County. The civil authorities were largely superceded by the military, Major Warren being sent into Hancock County with a company of militia to keep the peace.

These events occurred in the fall of 1845; and the Saints the winter following began extensive and active preparations for their departure in the spring. Meantime the anti-Mormons were breaking their part of the treaty almost daily. Illegal writs were issued for the arrest of the Twelve, and efforts made to serve them. House-burning and even murder went right on under the very eyes of Major Warren. At last, being exasperated beyond endurance, Elder Taylor declared he would submit no longer to the injustice being heaped upon himself and the people. President Young made a similar declaration. This led Major Warren to seek an interview with the authorities in which he upbraided them for their declared "resistance to law." In the course of that interview Elder Taylor made the following answer to the remarks of the major:

"Major Warren, I stand before you as a man who has received deep injury from the citizens of this state, and consequently have some feelings. You talk, sir, about 'the majesty of the law, and maintaining the law:' why, sir, the law to us is a mere farce. For years past the law has been made use of only as an engine of oppression. We have received no protection from it. I have suffered under its cruel influence. You talk about your troops being efficient, supporting law and preserving peace. This tale may do to tell some, but it fails to charm us. I stand before you as a victim of such protection. I went from this place some time ago in a time of difficulty like the present, as one of a committee by the special request of Governor Ford, who solemnly pledged his honor for my protection; but how was I protected? I was shot nearly to pieces, and two of the best men in the world were shot dead at my side. This is a specimen of your protection!"

Warren doubtless saw the storm that was coming and at this point interrupted to say that he did not wish to enter upon this exciting subject, but wished to speak relative to the present.

Elder Taylor: "I will touch upon the things of the present in a moment.—You may think this outrage was an outbreak—a sudden ebullition of feeling that the governor could not control; but who was it that did this deed? The governor's troops, sir, were among the foremost of that bloody gang. And where, sir—tell me where is our redress? You talk about the majesty of the law! What has become of those murderers? Have they been hung or shot, or in any way punished? No, sir, you know they have not. With their hands yet reeking in blood, having become hardened in their deeds of infamy, knowing that they will not be punished, they are now applying the torch to the houses of those they have already so deeply injured. What has been done to them under your administration? Have they been brought to justice, have they been punished for their infamous proceedings? No, sir; not one of them. They are still burning houses under your supervision; and you have either been unwilling or unable to stop them. Houses have been burned since your arrival here; men have been kidnapped, cattle stolen, our brethren abused and robbed when going after their corn. Are we to stand still and let marauders and house-burners come into our city under the real or assumed name of "governor's troops," and yet offer no resistance to their nefarious deeds? Are we to be held still by you, sir, while they thrust the hot iron into us? I tell you plainly for one I will not do it. I speak now on my own responsibility, and I tell you, sir, I will not stand it. I care nothing for your decrees, your martial law or any other law, I mean to protect myself; and if my brethren are to be insulted and abused in going after their own corn, and pursuing their lawful business—if nobody else will go to protect them I will. They shall not be abused under pretext of law or anything else; and there is not a patriot in the world but what would bear me out in it.

"Where is the spirit of '76? Where is the fire that burned in the bosoms of those who fought and bled for liberty? Is there no one who will stand up in defense of the oppressed? If a man had the least spark of humanity burning in his bosom—if he were not hardened and desperate, he would be ashamed to oppress a people already goaded by a yoke too intolerable to be borne, and that, too, in a boasted land of liberty. Talk about law! Sir, I stand before you as a victim of law. I feel warm on this subject—who would not? I have seen my best friends shot down while under legal protection. What is our governor? These scenes have been enacted under his supervision. What are our generals and judges? They have aided in these matters. If an honorable jury is legally selected, a house-burner or perhaps a murderer makes affidavit that he has reason to believe they are partial and the judge will order a mobocratic sheriff and jury for the purpose of acquitting the guilty and condemning the innocent. What are all these legal men but a pack of scoundrels? And you will talk to us of law and order, and threaten us with punishment for disobeying your commands and protecting our rights! What are we? Are we beasts? I tell you for one, sir, I shall protect myself, law or no law, judge or no judge, governor or no governor. I will not stand such infernal rascality, and if I have to fight it out, I will sell my life as dearly as I can."

A few days after this, Major Warren again rode into Nauvoo with his troops. It was reported that he had writs for the Twelve, but he sent word that he wanted an interview with them and pledged his word that no writs should be served. In the interview which followed he read a letter from Mr. Brayman, attorney general of the state *Pro tem.*, asking if the statement made by Mr. Young and Mr. Taylor to the effect that they would not be subject to any law and would resist all civil process, was to be looked upon as sincere.

They denied having made such statement. What they complained of was mal-administration and illegal prosecution. They had always been subject to law. They had always sustained it and still felt disposed to do so. "But I wish to make a few remarks concerning my own individual feelings," said Elder Taylor. "I have endured as much as I feel willing to endure under this government. I feel myself oppressed and wronged. I have never violated any law in the United States, and to be vexed and annoyed continually with vexatious lawsuits and illegal prosecutions I do not feel disposed tamely to submit to. If it is not enough for me to be deprived of my rights and my liberty; if it is not enough for me to sacrifice my property and to become an exile; if I cannot have the short space of six months to dispose of my effects and to leave the state—if the governor will only tell me, I will leave now; but I cannot and will not endure a continuation of these wrongs. I do not mean to be taken by any unjust requisition and thrust into prison; if I am, I must go there dead; for they shall not take me there alive. I have no personal feelings against you, Major Warren, but I will not put up with these accumulated wrongs."

The *Warsaw Signal* in speaking of this affair said that the troops had writs to serve on the Twelve, and although Major Warren had pledged his honor to the Twelve that no writs should be served, yet he was under promise to assist those holding them the day following; but after hearing the remarks of Elder Taylor fear seized upon them and they were afraid to make any attempt at serving them. Judge Purple also advised them not to serve them as he had no doubt there would be bloodshed. Warren accordingly left with his troops.

"I had felt surprised at myself at the manner in which I had spoken," remarks Elder Taylor, "but I have no doubt I was directed by the Spirit of the Lord."

CHAPTER 19 - THE DEPARTURE

All through the winter of 1845-6 the Saints in Nauvoo were busy making their preparations for the contemplated exodus. Early dawn and the latest twilight saw them hurrying to and fro gathering together provisions, cattle, carriages, wagons, seeds, farming implements—everything that was likely to be of service to them in the new homes they were going to make somewhere in the wilderness. Nor did their labors end with the light of day. Often it happened that the dingy smithies were illuminated through the night by the blazing forge, and the stillness of midnight was broken by the merry ring of anvils, while others sat in council devising the best methods of traveling and organizing into companies those whose arrangements were nearing completion.

Meantime the temple had been so far completed that endowments could be given to the faithful; and in this work Elder Taylor with others of his quorum was employed during that eventful winter. He also continued to publish the *Times and Seasons* up to the time of his departure for the wilderness. The *Neighbor* was discontinued shortly after the Quincy Committee requested the Saints to leave the state.

While making every effort to fill his part of the agreement with said committee to leave the state in the spring, he was continually harassed by his enemies seeking to arrest him on illegal writs. The whole community, in fact, was frequently threatened with mob violence. Their enemies were as impatient for Nauvoo to fall into their hands as hungry tigers are for their prey. The wheels of time moved altogether too slowly for them. They sought to make the people of other counties believe that the Mormons had no intention of leaving in the spring, and therefore to wait for spring to come before driving them out was only a waste of time, for to that issue it would come at last. Their ingenuity exhausted itself in concocting schemes to justify an invasion of Nauvoo. Finally, that all doubts as to the settled intention of the Saints to leave the United States might be put at rest, a large company, four hundred families all told, including nearly all the leaders of the Church and their families, left Nauvoo on the 11th of February, crossing the Mississippi on the ice. The exodus was not commenced so early, and at such an inclement season of the year because there was anything in the treaty the Saints had entered into that demanded it, but the movement was made to give proof that it was their intention to leave, and to take away from the mob all excuse for violence or bloodshed.

Elder Taylor and his family crossed the river on the 16th of February, and joined the Camp of Israel in the wilderness of the Territory of Iowa. For his own family and those who had lived with him in Nauvoo, he had eight wagons and a carriage, with the necessary force of teams. Snow was on the ground when he left Nauvoo, and shortly after crossing the river a thaw set in, which made travelling difficult. An encampment was made at a place where wood was plentiful, and there the exiles made themselves as comfortable as possible, until traveling should become less disagreeable.

There they lay, exposed to the inclement season, while only a short distance away—almost in view—were their comfortable houses, their beautiful city and magnificent temple! These homes which they had left, and that city were still theirs, for so hurried had been their departure that they had no time to dispose of property.

Elder Taylor had left a large, two-story brick house well furnished, with a brick store on one side and a new brick building that he had erected for a printing office on the other, and a large barn in the rear. This lot and the buildings were worth $10,000. In addition to this property, a short distance east of Nauvoo he had a farm of 106 acres of unimproved land, another of 80 acres, 40 of which was under cultivation and the remaining 40 timber. He also had a corner lot 101 x 85 feet on Main and Water street, opposite the Nauvoo Mansion. All this—to say nothing of breaking up his printing and book-binding establishment—he had been compelled to leave with but small hope of ever receiving anything for it; while he himself was driven forth an exile to wander, perhaps to perish, in the wilderness, a victim of religious intolerance.

This was in an age of boasted enlightenment—in the 19th century! In the great American Republic—the vaunted asylum of the oppressed!

To facilitate travel and for the better regulation of the people, the exiles were divided into companies of from seventy to a hundred wagons; but these companies followed each other so closely that they formed an almost unbroken procession across the Territory of Iowa.

To tell in detail the story of that journey from Nauvoo to Council Bluffs—how the Saints struggled on through trackless prairies converted into vast bogs by the spring thaws and rain and sleet which seemed to fall continuously; how the bleak winds from the pitiless northwest were more cruel than the sharpest frosts; how the young and strong left the main companies to go into Missouri and districts in Iowa remote from their line of march to exchange household furniture for corn or flour; how those who had merely enough provisions for themselves—no one had a surplus—divided with those who had none; how heroically they struggled against weakness and disease brought on through exposure; how they laid away their dead in nameless graves—to tell all this would fill a volume of itself, and belongs rather to a history of the whole people than to this biography.

RESIDENCE OF JOHN TAYLOR: NAUVOO, IL 1846

The 5th of June found Elder Taylor with his company at Mount Pisgah, in Iowa, about one hundred and sixty miles from Nauvoo, where the companies under Brigham Young and Heber C. Kimball had encamped and were putting in crops for those who would come on later to harvest.

From Mount Pisgah to the "Bluffs" he met numerous squads of Pottawattomie Indians, all of whom he treated kindly, and generally distributed tobacco among them, a thing with which they were highly pleased. These Indians had been removed from their lands east of the Mississippi some years before, and were themselves exiles. Perhaps it was that fact which led them to treat kindly the exiled Saints. At any rate they gave them permission to pass through their reservation, and finally permitted them to settle for a time upon their lands and use what timber they needed to build temporary abodes.

Elder Taylor brought his company up to the main encampment at Council Bluffs on the 17th of June. Soon afterwards he was busily engaged with his brethren in raising a company of pioneers to go to the Rocky Mountains in advance of the main body of the people. He was going as one of this company and began putting his wagons in order.

It was in the midst of these preparations that Captain Allen of the United States army came to the encampment and called upon the Saints in the name of the United States for five hundred volunteers to march to California. The strained relations which for some time had existed between the United States and Mexico had resulted in a declaration of war, and an actual beginning of hostilities in May. It was part of General Scott's plan of campaign for the "Army of the West" to rendezvous at Fort Leavenworth, invade New Mexico and co-operate with a fleet which was to sweep around Cape Horn and attack the enemy on the Pacific coast of his territory. It was to assist in carrying out this part of the campaign that the exiled Saints were called upon to furnish five hundred men.

In that moment of supreme trial the leaders of the Church did not permit the memory of their wrongs to outweigh their patriotism. They resolved to raise the number of men required. For this purpose meetings were called and the proposition of enlistment made to the brethren. It was not at first received with much enthusiasm by the people. Perhaps they could not forget that the general government had witnessed without protest their expatriation and expulsion from the confines of the United States. They also remembered that their repeated appeals for justice had been met with repeated and increasing indifference, and it required no small amount of persuasion at the first to induce men to enlist.

In this work of arousing the people to trust the government of the United States to deal justly by them, no one was more earnest than Elder Taylor. In a speech he made at a meeting held in George A. Smith's camp, he said:

"Many have felt something like rebelling against the government of the United States. I have myself felt swearing mad at the government for the treatment we have received at the hands of those in authority, although I don't know that I ever swore much. We have had cause to feel as we have, and any man having a spark of the love of liberty in him would have felt likewise. We are now something like Abraham was, wandering about we know not whither, but fleeing from a land of tyranny and oppression."

He then explained that it was the present intention to settle in some part of California, which at that time belonged to Mexico; but to go there they must have a legal pretext else they would be regarded as interlopers. As the United States was at war with Mexico, they had a right, according to the law of nations, to invade her territory; and if they enlisted in the service of the United States they would have a right to go there; and as the stipulations offered by the government provided as the stipulations offered by the government provided for their being disbanded in California, they would be at or near the place of their proposed destination, with a right to remain. There they would be the "old settlers," and bringing in some thirty thousand people, there was a prospect of obtaining a state or territorial government, where they could live in peace. Their children could boast, too, that their fathers had fought and bled for their country. "Although," he remarked, "I do not think you will have much fighting to do. Still, I do not say this to encourage cowards to go on this expedition.

"A great many seem to distrust the government," he continued, "and are afraid they will not be carried to California, but be sent to Texas or somewhere else. They will not be—they need not fear. Who cannot trust the United States? Her flag floats over every ocean, and her ministry are in every nation. I know it is a great journey for a man to undertake and leave his family; but Captain Allen says he will give absolute permission for the families to remain here. He has also obtained a writing from the Pottawatamie sub-agency, signed by the chiefs and braves to that effect, so that everything is straightforward."

He concluded by making a motion that a body of five hundred men be raised, and make Captain Allen Lieutenant-Colonel, a promotion he had been promised providing he raised the battalion. That motion was carried.

It was the 30th of June that Captain Allen arrived at Council Bluffs and asked for the battalion, and by the 16th of July the men were organized and placed under his command, ready to start for Fort Leavenworth.

About the time the battalion was made up, the men Elder Taylor had sent out form his company to trade for corn and flour and to swap horses for cattle returned without having met with any success. "I now found myself in the wilderness without the means of procuring the necessary provisions for a year and a half;" and then he adds, half reflectively, "Twelve months prior to this time, I had ten thousand dollars' worth of property at my disposal!"

The day following the return of his men, however, a brother named Stewart called upon him for counsel; and before leaving loaned him a sum of money sufficient to relieve him of his embarrassments, and we have him saying joyfully, "I felt thankful to the Lord that He had opened my way, as He always does in time of need."

Meantime from England reports of transgression, wild financial schemes, chicanery and fraud reached the authorities—reports which were confirmed by manifestations of the Spirit to President Young.

After the Twelve took the direction of the affairs of the Church, in August, 1844, they sent Wilford Woodruff to preside over the British Mission, a post he filled until called away to join the Saints in their exodus from the United States. On his departure Reuben Hedlock was appointed to preside over the mission with Thomas Ward and John Banks for counselors. Soon after the departure of Apostle Woodruff an agitation was set on foot to found what was called "The British and American Joint Stock Company." The ostensible purposes for which this company was organized were to engage in commercial enterprises with a view of enriching the Church, emigrating the poor Saints to America, shipping machinery, etc., and founding manufactures in the new gathering place in the wilderness, and to operate in building up the kingdom of God generally.

Announcing these as the objects to be accomplished, it was not difficult to induce the Saints to take stock in the concern, and hundreds of pounds were subscribed and paid to Hedlock and his coadjutors. Much of this means was squandered by Hedlock and his associates instead of being used for the purposes for which the company had been organized.

Upon hearing these reports Elder Taylor, in connection with Orson Hyde and Parley P. Pratt, was sent to England to correct these abuses and set in order all the affairs of the Church in that land. He left his family in the wilderness with the other exiled Saints, and with his companions took passage in an open flat boat that was passing down the Missouri River about the time they were ready to start. This boat was owned by a party of Presbyterian missionaries who had been laboring among the Pawnee Indians, and were now returning, with their families, to St. Joseph, Missouri.

At St. Joseph the brethren purchased the boat and continued their journey, rowing all day and tying up the boat and sleeping on shore at night. They reached Fort Leavenworth before the departure of the Battalion for the west and from those brethren—just then drawing their bounty of forty dollars each from the government—received some assistance to help them on their journey. The brethren of the Battalion were also desirous of sending some means to their families in the wilderness, and Parley P. Pratt was chosen to carry it to them. While he returned to the encampment of the Saints, Elder Taylor and Orson Hyde continued their journey to England, arriving in Liverpool on the 3rd of October.

CHAPTER 20 - WORK ACCOMPLISHED

The very day of arrival in Liverpool Elders Hyde and Taylor issued a circular to the Saints in which they stated that the Joint Stock Company was an institution wholly independent of the Church. The circular also appointed a conference to convene at Manchester, on the 17th of the month—October.

By that time Elder Pratt had arrived. The unfaithful stewards were called to account, severely reproved and the chief offenders, excepting Hedlock, disfellowshipped until they could appear before the authorities in the camp of Israel to be further dealt with. Hedlock would not meet the American deputation of Elders; but fled to London where he lived in obscurity in company with a dissolute woman. He was excommunicated at once. On the fall of this man Elder Taylor wrote the following reflections:

"Elder Hedlock might have occupied a high and exalted situation in the Church, both in time and in eternity; but he has cast from his head the crown—he has dashed from him the cup of mercy, and has bartered the hope of eternal life with crowns, principalities, powers, thrones and dominions, for the gratification of his own sensual appetite; to feed on husks and straw—to wallow in filth and mire!"

It was arranged that Elder Hyde should take charge of the *Star* and the office at Liverpool, while Elders Taylor and Pratt visited the various conferences and branches of the Church. Everywhere they were received with demonstrations of joy. Elder Taylor traveled sometimes alone and sometimes in company with

Elder Pratt; but whether alone or with his companion, he was always made welcome by the Saints. He labored in season and out of season, and God worked with him and his associates.

Through their promptness in dealing with the unfaithful stewards, and the power which attended their administrations, confidence was restored, the Saints were re-baptized, many new members were added to the Church, and it was a general time of refreshing from the presence of the Lord. Social gatherings were frequent, and while he fed the Saints the bread of life, they administered to his necessities and made his heart glad with their songs and rejoicing. His reception in Wales was especially enthusiastic,—it amounted to an ovation; indeed the same may be said of his reception throughout the British Mission.

Still in the midst of these busy scenes he found time to write a number of articles for the *Star,* one of which is especially worthy of mention—his *Address to the Saints in Great Britain.* In that address he writes the very best sketches I have yet seen of the evacuation of Nauvoo and the journey of the Saints to Winter Quarters. Its chief value consists in its accuracy and temperate tone—much more temperate than one could reasonable expect it to be from a writer who was a participator in those cruel scenes, and one of the chief sufferers.

He makes prominent the fact that even if the persecution which expelled the Saints from Nauvoo had not arisen, their destiny would have led them to the mountain valleys of the great West. "Many living witnesses," he writes, "can testify that we proposed moving to California, leaving the land of our oppression, preaching the gospel to the Lamanites, building up other temples to the living God, establishing ourselves in the far distant West. The cruel and perfidious persecutions that we endured, tended to hasten our departure, but did *not* dictate it. It jeopardized our lives, property and liberty, but was not the cause of our removal."

"Many a time" he continues, "have I listened to the voice of our beloved Prophet, while in council, dwell on this subject [the removal of the Saints to the Rocky Mountains] with delight; his eyes sparkling with animation, and his soul fired with the inspiration of the Spirit of the living God. It was a theme that caused the bosoms of all who were privileged to listen, to thrill with delight; intimately connected with this, were themes upon which prophets, patriarchs, priests and kings dwelt with pleasure and delight: of them they prophesied, sung, wrote, spoke and desired to see, but died without the sight. My spirit glows with sacred fire while I reflect upon these scenes, and I say, O Lord, hasten the day! Let Zion be established! Let the mountain of the Lord's house be established in the tops of the mountains!"—a thing, I may add,—and which he plainly intimates,—could not have been done had the Saints remained in Nauvoo. The Saints did not come to these mountain valleys because they were compelled to by their enemies, they came here because it was their destiny to come; because the Lord would have them here; and because there were problems to work out in connection with the work of God which could be worked out nowhere else.

While he admits that the Saints had suffered great loss by being driven from Illinois—that they had been obliged to make a great sacrifice—yet, speaking relatively, he held that the Saints were better off than if they had remained in Nauvoo, a remark that then seemed paradoxical, but its truth is now confirmed by history; for the little one has become a great people, occupying an immense area of country, and they have attained a strength they never could have known in Nauvoo.

In this article, while he dwells at some length on the sufferings of the Saints from the fury of the pitiless storm—the drifting snow, the pelting hail and the icy chills of storm and tempest, Elder Taylor does not forget to vindicate God whose part it was to stand very near to His people in such trying times. In continuing his remarks on the exposure of the Saints to cold and storm he says:

"We sustained no injury therefrom; our health and our lives were preserved—we outlived the trying scene—we felt contented and happy—the songs of Zion resounded from wagon to wagon—from tent to tent; the sound reverberated through the woods, and its echo was returned from the distant hills; peace, harmony, and contentment reigned in the habitations of the Saints."

So, too, in speaking of the privations of camp life: "It is true that in our sojourning we do not possess all the luxuries and delicacies of old established countries and cities, but we have an abundance of the staple commodities, such as flour, meal, beef, mutton, pork, milk, butter and in some instances cheese, sugar, coffee, tea, etc., etc. We feel contented and happy in the wilderness. The God of Israel is with us—union and peace prevail; and as we journey, as did Abraham of old, with our flocks and herds to a distant land, we feel that like him, we are doing the will of our Heavenly Father and relying upon His word and promises; and having His blessing, we feel that we are children of the same promise and hope, and that the great Jehovah is our God."

Such remarks as these lighten the rather sombre picture that is usually drawn by writers who relate the story of the evacuation of Nauvoo and the subsequent journey in the wilderness; and who in their anxiety to give a vivid picture of the sufferings of the Saints, forget to vindicate the goodness of God who was with His people in those trying times, and who, by opening the way before them to obtain food and lands to dwell upon, and giving them strength as their day, made their afflictions light as air. These things, Elder Taylor in his sketches does not fail to recognize.

At the time of Elder Taylor's visit, great distress existed among the laboring classes in England, and as the Saints were chiefly of that class, they suffered with the rest. The trouble arose very largely from over-population. This being the case, the queen was memorialized by the Saints to adopt a system of emigration to Oregon, a general name given to an immense but indefinite tract of country in the western part of the British possessions, Vancouver's Island forming part of it. To return the means that government was asked to expend in emigrating the people, it was proposed that in a tract of country divided into sections of six hundred and forty acres, and numbered, that each emigrant be entitled to settle on the sections bearing even numbers, and that government retain the odd sections. The presence of the settlers and their improvements on the even sections would give a value to the odd sections and bring them into market, and through the sale of these lands government would soon be repaid the sum expended for emigration.

In the interest of this scheme, Elder Taylor called upon, and obtained an interview with the Earl of Dartmouth, but the government refused to engage in the business.

Having accomplished the object of his mission to England, Elder Taylor's heart turned to his family in the wilderness. He left the port of Liverpool in the ship *America*, in company with Elder Pratt, and a few Saints—fourteen in all. No ship ever left that port with brighter prospects, but no sooner were they fairly out into the Irish Sea, than they met a heavy gale and for nine days were tempest-tossed and utterly unable to reach the broad Atlantic. At last they were compelled to return to Liver pool.

"I had strange presentiments," says Elder Taylor, "before we went on board, of danger or ship-wreck—the spirit did not manifest which; and I was glad when we safely returned to Liverpool."

A second start was made on the seventh of February, and after a pleasant voyage of thirty-six days, the vessel made the port of New Orleans. Here Elder Taylor wrote to the editor of the *Star*, his farewell address to the Saints, which virtually is a review of his brief mission among them. Following are extracts from it:

"As I had no time before I left England, I now wish to say a few words to the Saints. When I was there, in consequence of having so many places to visit, and to travel so extensively, my stay was necessarily short at the various branches; and it made it impossible for me to visit so many places, to form so extensive an acquaintance with the Saints as I should gladly have done had time permitted. If my stay had been longer, I should gladly have spent two, three, or six months more, in order to have visited all the branches and seen the Saints at their homes, for I love the people of God, and delight in the habitations of the righteous. There peace reigns—there reigns the spirit of God—and there is my home. And here I wish to say, that although very much pressed and hurried, I have seldom enjoyed myself better than I did on my late visit to the British churches. I saw an honesty and simplicity which I admired. The Saints seemed to vie with each other in many little acts of kindness and charity which were duly appreciated by me, and which I have taken pleasure in acknowledging. They were esteemed not so much on account of their intrinsic value as for the feelings of those who administered them.

"Our arrival in England was very opportune. Before we left [Council Bluffs], it was revealed to the authorities that the presidency in England was in transgression, and that it was necessary that some of the Twelve should proceed immediately to England. When Elder Hyde and myself were in New York, and Elder Pratt in Boston, we thought it expedient, rather than to wait two or three days for him, to proceed immediately to Liverpool. We found on our arrival that we had not come any too soon. The teachers of the people were under transgression; they were corrupt: they were acting dishonorably, and dishonestly; stripping the poor of their last pittance, and yet those wanton profligates professed that they were doing the will of God, while they, under a cloak of religion, were reveling in debauchery, drunkenness and fraud! But they have their reward.

"Many of the Elders were at a loss what to do. They saw that things were out of order, but how to regulate them they knew not. They felt a disposition to hope for the best, but it seemed to be hoping against hope; in fact the whole head was sick and the whole heart faint; and had it not been that the Saints were in possession of the eternal principles of truth, and had the testimony of the Spirit, giving them assurance of the truth and verity of this work, they might all have made ship-wreck of faith.

"As Elder Pratt and myself journeyed among the churches, we found them generally doing well, rejoiced to see us, and expressing a willingness to follow our advice in all things. I would here say a word or two to the Saints by way of caution. Because you have been deceived by your former leaders, do not mistrust those you have now, but let them have your confidence and your prayers. I say again have confidence in your presidency; neither condemn one man for what another has done, neither be afraid of him. Give all good men your confidence; if they betray it, judge them according to that which they have done—not what they may or may not do. It is a devilish principle to be jealous of men who have done no wrong, and to withhold our confidence from those who ought to have our support, merely because it is possible they may abuse it.

"Now brethren, as I had not time before I left, I must take the liberty from this side of the ocean, of saying farewell—farewell! And God bless you for ever and ever, worlds without end. Amen. It is a long distance to salute you from, as I am now six thousand miles from you, but I know it will be welcome, for I came more than six thousand miles to see you, and I had to salute my family from your homes. We have yet two thousand miles to go to see our families, and part of that through mobbers, black-legs and murderers, who would gladly take our lives, but we trust in the God of Israel, that He will take us safely through, and that we shall arrive in the camp of Israel in peace, and rejoice in once more meeting our families and friends.

COUNCIL BLUFFS FERRY

"I left the camp in company with my brethren, July 3rd, 1846, and when I return shall have traveled upwards of seventeen thousand miles, three thousand of this was in England, Scotland and Wales. I now feel well in health and spirits, am thankful that so much of my mission is completed, and I bless the name of the God of Israel."

From New Orleans he took passage in the steam-packet, *Patrick Henry*, for St. Louis, where he arrived on the 25th of March. Here he parted company with Elder Pratt, who made his way through the country to the camp; while Elder Taylor in charge of the small company of Saints took steamer up the Missouri for the same point; but on reaching St. Joseph he left the boat and took carriage, as he desired to reach the camp before the pioneer company left for the West, as he had with him some surveying and scientific instruments purchased in England for them. Those instruments consisted of two sextants, two barometers, two artificial horizons, one circular reflector, several thermometers and a telescope.

He arrived in time to meet President Young and deliver these instruments and some money sent from England to aid the Church. The pioneer camp had left Winter Quarters a day or two before, and was then camped on the Elk Horn, some twenty or thirty miles distant, so that he had returned just in time.

The labors of Elder Taylor and companions were highly approved by President Young, and he heartily welcomed them back to their families and the Church.

CHAPTER 21 - THE RENDEZVOUS

The Saints at Winter Quarters had been instructed to organize into companies and follow the pioneers into the mountains as soon as practicable. As Elders Taylor and Pratt did not arrive in time to fit out and accompany the pioneers; and as they were members of the quorum presiding over the Church at the time, Elder Taylor was associated with Elder Pratt in a general superintendency of affairs at Winter Quarters and especially in organizing the companies destined to follow the Pioneers that summer.

The plan of organization for traveling was to divide the people into companies of one hundred wagons, subdivided into companies of fifty wagons, and ten wagons, with captains over each division, the captains of fifties being subordinate to captains of hundreds, and captains of tens being subordinate to captains of fifties—all being subject to the direction of the Apostles. Each fifty had a blacksmith with tools for repairing wagons and shoeing animals. Three hundred pounds of breadstuff were required for each person. Every man had to have a gun with one hundred rounds of ammunition; and each family was expected to take along its proportion of seed grain and agricultural implements.

As fast as individuals and families were found who had the required outfit, or could obtain it, they rendezvoused at a point on the Elk Horn River, where the organization for the journey to the mountains was perfected.

The families who had traveled with Elder Taylor from Nauvoo to Council Bluffs, desired to be again enrolled in the company in which he traveled. That request was granted, and they were chiefly enrolled in the first fifty of the hundred of which Edward Hunter, afterwards Presiding Bishop of the church, was the captain, and Joseph Horne was captain of the fifty.

In preparing for this journey Elder Taylor was kept extremely busy. Wagons had to be overhauled, tires re-set, horses and oxen to be collected and shod, supplies obtained, and only a limited number of hands with which to accomplish it all; for five hundred able-bodied men, it will be remembered, had been taken into the service of the United States, and about one hundred and forty more had gone as pioneers, and those who from their circumstances had to remain at Winter Quarters were busily engaged in putting in crops for supplies for another season.

During the early part of June, however, some six hundred wagons gathered on the Elk Horn ready to start. There were 1553 souls in the company, 2213 oxen, 124 horses, 887 cows, many of which had to do service under the yoke, 358 sheep, 716 chickens and a number of pigs.

On the 21st and 22nd of June this large company began its journey. It was late in the season for starting on such an expedition. It was too late for them to put in crops that season, even if they stopped far short of the eastern base of the Rocky Mountains. They barely had provisions to last them a year and a half, and if their first crop failed, starvation must follow, for they would be from ten to fifteen hundred miles from the nearest point where food could be obtained, and no swifter means of transportation than horse or ox teams!

It was a bold undertaking, this moving over fifteen hundred souls—more than half of whom were women and children—into an unknown country, through hostile tribes of savages. Had it not been for the assurance of the support and protection of Jehovah, it would have been not only a bold but a reckless movement—the action of madmen. But as it was, the undertaking was a sublime evidence of their faith in God and their leaders.

This company differed from the pioneers. The latter was made up of able-bodied men, excepting three women—none were helpless. They had the best of teams, and if they failed in finding a place of settlement they could return to the place of starting. Meantime their families were not endangered. They were secure at Winter Quarters. Not so with the Pratt and Taylor company. They had their all upon the altar, including their wives and children, who must share their hardships and their fate. They knew not their destination, they entrusted all on a single venture, from which there was no chance of retreat. If they should fail to find a suitable location and raise a crop the first season, there was no getting provisions to them, nor them to provisions. They must succeed, or perish in the wilderness to which they had started. With a faith that has never been surpassed, they placed themselves under the guidance and protection of their God, and we shall see in the sequel that they trusted not in vain.

CAMP AT WOOD RIVER

Usually on the journey this great camp traveled in sections of one hundred wagons each. The company in which Apostle Pratt traveled took the lead, and the one in which Elder Taylor traveled followed next, and then the others in their order. Between the hundreds in which Elders Taylor and Pratt traveled was a company of artillery, commanded by Charles C. Rich. When feed for the cattle was scarce, or roads bad, or water not abundant, then they traveled fifty wagons in a section, but always sufficiently near each other to readily unite for protection in case of an assault from the Indians. When the prairies were wide and the ground unbroken, two companies often traveled abreast. Crossing the level plains that now form the state of Nebraska, they came in contact with immense herds of buffalo, which supplied them with plenty of beef. Public prayer was offered up daily in the camps. Sunday was observed as a day of rest, religious services were held in each camp, and the stillness of the great wilderness of the west was broken by Saints singing the songs of Zion.

Thus day after day, week after week, the sections of the great company drew their slow length along, until the wide spreading plains of La Platte are behind them, they enter the Black Hills and at last approach the Rocky Mountains.

On what was known as the Upper Crossing of the Sweetwater, east of the South Pass, between three and four hundred miles east of Salt Lake, Elder Taylor's division met the returning pioneers. That band of men had entered the Salt Lake Valley, selected a site for a city, commenced the erection of a fort, plowed several acres of land and planted late crops; and having left a few of their number with some members of the Mormon Battalion who had joined them there to continue the work, they were now on their way back to Winter Quarters with the glad news that a gathering place had been selected for Israel.

The morning that Elder Taylor's division met the returning pioneers, there was a flurry of snow. The heavens were darkened, the bright sunshine which they had enjoyed without a cloud to obscure it for weeks together, was now shut out from view, and snow fell two or three inches deep. Snow! and in September, too! Was that the kind of climate they were going to? The hearts of some sank within them, and the prospect looked gloomy enough. But that which produced fears in the breasts of the timid, only provoked laughter from Elder Taylor. He bade them be of good cheer, and laughingly proposed to insure the lives of the whole company at five dollars per head.

Elder Taylor and other leading brethren in his division met in council with the Apostles in the pioneer company. What a weight of responsibility rested upon these men! They had selected a location for a great people in an unknown climate; they had planted seed in an untried soil; they knew they would have to depend upon new methods of agriculture to mature their crops—irrigation—would it succeed? There were tens of thousands of people on the banks of the Missouri waiting for them to return to lead them forth into the wilderness, to the new home; the means of getting them there this body of men in council must devise; they were founding a commonwealth in the wilderness; the whole world was watching their movements and would hold them morally responsible for any disasters that might occur. With this burden upon them, they might well hold council meetings, whenever convenient, in order to discuss their present situation and future prospects.

But while the brethren were in council the clouds cleared away, and before the warm sunshine the snow soon disappeared. There was a nervous activity in the camp, mysterious movements among the sisters. Trunks that had been undisturbed on the journey were opened, their contents investigated and certain articles hurriedly conveyed to a beautiful, natural lawn enclosed by a dense growth of bushes. Several improvised tables of uncommon length, covered with snow-white linen, and fast being burdened with glittering tableware, gave evidence that a surprise was in store for the weary pioneers. The "fatted calf" was killed; game and fish were prepared in abundance; fruits, jellies and relishes reserved for special occasions were brought out until truly it was a royal feast.

Moreover, though the place selected for the spread was adjacent to the camp, it was successful as a surprise. The pioneers knew nothing of what had taken place until they were led by Elder Taylor through a natural opening in the bushes fringing the enclosure, and the grand feast burst upon their astonished vision.

One hundred and thirty sat down at the supper; and if for a moment rising emotions at this manifestation of love choked their utterance and threatened to blunt the edge of appetite, the danger soon passed under the genial influence of the sisters who waited upon the tables and pressed their guests to eat: in the end they paid a full and hearty compliment to the culinary skill of the sisters.

Supper over and cleared away, preparations were made for dancing; and soon was added to the sweet confusion of laughter and cheerful conversation the merry strains of the violin, and the strong, clear voice of the prompter directing the dancers through the mazes of quadrilles, Scotch-reels, French-fours and other figures of harmless dances suitable to the guileless manners and the religious character of the participants. Dancing was interspersed with songs and recitations. "We felt mutually edified and blessed," writes Elder Taylor, "we praised the Lord and blessed one another." So closed a pleasant day, though the morning with its clouds and snow looked very unpromising.

The morning following they separated, the pioneers going towards the rising, the others towards the setting sun.

On the 5th of October, Elder Taylor reached Salt Lake Valley.

After so long and so tedious a journey, a few days' rest would have been the proper thing, but there was no time for that. They must prepare for the winter, of the mildness or severity of which they knew nothing only through report. The pioneers and members of the battalion had made some progress in erecting a square fort, enclosing ten acres of ground; this was known as the Old Fort. On the arrival of the Pratt and Taylor encampment, they commenced the erection of a fort on the south side of it, the same width but twice its length. Each family had its allotment of ground according to the number and necessities of its members. Some built with adobies, others with round logs and others with split logs. Whip-saws were called into requisition for the manufacture of lumber by hand.

THE FIRST RESIDENCE OF UTAH

"Our houses," writes Elder Taylor, "were built on the outside line [of the fort] in shanty form, with the highest wall outside, the roof sloping towards the interior. The windows and doors were placed on the side facing the enclosure, the outside being left solid, excepting loop holes—for protection. Our corrals, hay-stacks and stables were some distance behind and outside the fort.

"About Christmas, I had put up, enclosed and covered about ninety feet of building made of split logs, out of which was taken a four-inch plank. The plank was used for partitions, etc. In addition to this, I had built corrals and stables behind, and enclosed a garden spot in front, with a board-rail fence. I assisted in all this labor of sawing, building, hauling, etc.,—enough for one fall."

In the midst of these busy scenes the spiritual instruction of the people was not neglected. After the arrival of the several divisions of the company that left Winter Quarters in June, they were called upon to repent and renew their covenants in baptism, Elders Taylor and Pratt setting the example. The Saints very generally responded to this requirement and the Spirit of God rested upon them in great power.

A Stake of Zion had been organized by the Apostles of the pioneer company before they returned to Winter Quarters, and John Smith, uncle to the Prophet Joseph, was chosen president. The Saints had no public place for worship, but they met in the private houses of leading elders on the Sabbath, and sometimes in the evenings of week days to be taught in their duties. All through that winter Elder Taylor was diligent in that labor, going from house to house to instruct the Saints. Meetings for his own family were frequently called, and there he taught them how to live in peace, to be courteous, kind and considerate of each other's feelings; and there, doubtless, was laid the foundation of that kindly feeling and courteous deportment toward each other, and that union which today is a characteristic of his large family.

The condition of the Church during that first winter in the valley of Salt Lake was very similar to that of the Nephite Church in the first years of the Nephite Republic, of which the historian says; "when the priests left their labor to impart the word of God unto the people, the people also left their labors to hear the word of God, and when the priest had imparted unto them the word of God, they all returned again diligently unto their labors; and the priest, not esteeming himself above his hearers; for the preacher was no better than the hearer; and thus they were all equal, and they did all labor, every man according to his strength."

So Elder Taylor labored through that winter. His days were spent in the saw-pit, where he manufactured lumber by hand with a whip-saw; his evenings and the Sabbaths were spent in councils with his brethren and in the meetings of the Saints, where he taught them the way of life.

Occasionally a social party broke the monotony of their life in the wilderness, and for several reasons I give Elder Taylor's description of one of these parties held at his own house. It seems there had been an order or agreement entered into by the Saints that they would have no dancing until after their first harvest in the valley—such an agreement was *law* to this primitive community—so originated all their laws; but when new year's came, and with it the recollection of the merriment of former years, they seemed to repent of the strictures they had placed upon themselves, and it was rumored as New Year's day approached that license had been given by the president of the stake for dancing on the evening of that day, but there was to be no more until harvest—so much is necessary to the understanding of the following:

January 1st, 1847:

"As today was New Year's day, several of my family spoke to me about having a party as usual upon that day. The plan they proposed getting it up on was that every one should bring his own provisions. The principle itself was repugnant to me, but still under the circumstances, if we had a party, this must be the principle we must have it on, as I could not possibly spare provisions for so large a company as we must necessarily have; and upon this plan there was one gotten up. We had an excellent supper, sixty-nine sat down and we enjoyed ourselves very much. I gave the presidency to Brother Sherwood. I sat at the head of one table, Brother Hunter at another, Brother Horne and Shurtliff at others. After the tables were cleared, the order was given for dancing. My reasons for indulging in this recreation were that Brother Shurtliff went up and saw Uncle John Smith (the president of the stake) and told him that we had made calculations upon having a dance; but when I heard there was a law against it, I was resolved not to have any unless Uncle John should say I was justified in doing it. He said if he was me he would have the dance as it had been arranged for.

"I sent to Uncle John to see about this, not because I thought there was any harm in dancing, but because I did not wish to encourage law-breaking by my example in this thing. There was an intermission in the dancing when we had some singing and a comic sermon from Brother Sherwood, after which dancing was resumed and continued until a little after eleven o'clock. Brother Sherwood called the house to order and told them the time had come to separate; but before parting he had a few remarks to make. He spoke on a variety of principles and made some very good remarks. Upon his concluding I arose and made some remarks upon the object of our meeting, my object in having dancing, on the principles of power existing in the kingdom, and the active part we are destined to take in the affairs of kingdoms."

In the above appears the large and generous nature of Elder Taylor which shrank with repugnance, even in those days of scarcity, from the idea of having his guests bring their provisions with them to a feast in his house. There is also manifested his respect for law. There was no assumed airs because he was an Apostle, followed by a haughty disregard of a rule established by the president of the stake—but a humble disposition to submit to it.

The conclusion of his description of this party gives us to understand that although he, with the rest of the Saints, had been expatriated, and driven into exile in the wilderness, and well-nigh stripped of all their earthly possessions—he had lost none of his faith in the future high destiny of the people of God,—they were yet to be active in the affairs of kingdoms! Lastly his description of this party enables one to see something of social life in the infant commonwealth of Deseret—the homely joys of the people; their simple, guileless ways; their unfeigned enjoyment of innocent, natural pleasures:

Yes! let the rich deride, the proud disdain
These simple blessings of the lowly train;
To me more dear congenial to my heart,
One native charm than all the gloss of art;
Spontaneous joys, where nature has its play,
The soul adopts and owns their first-born sway!
Far better this than—

The long pomp, the midnight masquerade,
With all the freaks of wanton wealth arrayed,
In these, ere triflers half their wish obtain,
The toiling pleasure sickens into pain;
And e'en while fashion's brightest arts decoy,
The heart, distrusting, asks if this be joy!

CHAPTER 22 - THE CRICKET WAR

So the winter passed away, and the spring came, and with it came frequent rain storms. "We made one mistake in building," remarks Elder Taylor; "having been informed there was no rain, or very little, in the valley, we made our roofs too flat, which, when the spring rains commenced, caused considerable trouble." It was with great difficulty that their beds could be kept dry. But this was not their chief difficulty—food was getting scarce, and a number of the improvident ones were without.

At a public meeting, Elder Taylor proposed that a tax be laid upon the people according to their means to pay it, to supply those who were in need; and that the High Council be authorized to levy it, and have discretionary power to determine who should be taxed, and who should be assisted. The motion was carried unanimously.

Elder Taylor and his family, in common with the whole people, made every effort to get in extensive crops of grain and large gardens. In this they were quite successful; but when early summer brought flattering promises of a bountiful harvest, then from the mountains came myriads of black crickets into their grain fields and threatened to destroy them. The people, even to the women and children, turned out, to stay, if possible, the ravages of the destroyer. They devised various ways to rid themselves of the terrible insect, but in vain they labored; the crickets were rapidly making green fields bare. When it is remembered that the colonists were dependent on that crop for food for the ensuing year, it is not surprising that hope sank within them, or that they became alarmed and talked of sending an express to President Young, begging him not to bring in any more people, as there was a famine in prospect. But in the midst of their calamity a wonderful deliverance was at hand; untold thousands of snow-white sea-gulls came in clouds from the direction of the lake, and settling down upon the fields of grain, began devouring the crickets. Day after day did these white-winged messengers of mercy continue the work of devouring crickets, until the pests were destroyed and the fields of growing grain saved.

In August an abundant harvest was gathered, and a public harvest feast proclaimed. In the midst of the feasting and dancing, singing and rejoicing, the Saints did not forget to thank and praise the Power which had given them the rich fruits of the earth; and expressions of gratitude—soul-felt and universal—in prayer and speech, occurred as frequently as song or dance.

In all these anxieties, labors, fears, hopes and rejoicings, Elder Taylor took part. Many leaned on his strength in those days. When despair settled over the colony he infused it with hope; when the weak faltered, he strengthened them; when the fearful trembled, he encouraged them; those cast down with sorrow, he comforted and cheered. His faith and trust in God, and in His power to preserve and deliver His people were as unshaken in the midst of the difficulties they encountered in settling the desert valleys of Utah, as it had been in the midst of mob violence in Missouri and Illinois; as unmoved as it was amid the confused shouts and curses, groans and shrieking's, and murderous bullets which, all mingled together, made up that scene of hell and death in Carthage jail.

Though much of his time was occupied in teaching and encouraging others, he was also active in farming, gardening, fencing fields, etc.; and during the summer of 1849, constructed a bridge over the Jordan River, the first that ever spanned that stream. With Parley P. Pratt and others he went on several exploring expeditions. In one of these he visited Utah Valley and Lake. He built the first boat that was launched on that beautiful sheet of water, and ascertaining that there was an abundance of fish in the lake he manufactured a seine a hundred feet long, for which his wives spun the material. The fish caught in this manner materially assisted in eking out the scant supplies of the colonists.

In August, 1849, General John Wilson, with a small military escort, visited the colonists. He was on a private mission from the President of the United States, Zachary Taylor, to the Saints. The object of that mission was this:

There was trouble anticipated in the then approaching congress, about the territorial question, involving as it did, at that time, the extension of slavery. General Wilson, therefore, was sent to request the settlers in Salt Lake Valley to unite with California and form a state, which it was proposed to admit into the Union, and thus, for the time being, remove the slavery question from congress. The pro-slavery party had been gaining ground rapidly for a few years previous to this time. Texas had been annexed, and was a slave state. So extensive was its territory, that it was capable of being divided into several states, all of which, of course, would tolerate slavery.

The treaty which closed the war with Mexico had resulted in the United States obtaining an immense area of country, out of which new states and territories would be carved; and of course there was in prospect a terrible struggle between the pro-slavery and anti-slavery parties, the former seeking to establish slavery in, and the latter to exclude it from the states and territories to be made out of this new accession of country. It was thought by the administration, that if a large state extending from the Pacific Ocean eastward to Salt Lake, with slavery prohibited by its constitution, was admitted into the Union, it would offset the then late accession of Texas, and calm the rising storm over that question.

General Wilson stated, that so eager was the President of the United States in regard to the subject, that if he [Wilson] found any difficulty in the way, his instructions were to appeal to the patriotism of the Mormon people.

Elder Taylor, Charles C. Rich and Daniel Spencer were appointed to confer with General Wilson upon the subject of his mission. The result of those deliberations was a proposal by the people of Salt Lake Valley, California agreeing therewith, to form a state unitedly, and continue in that condition two years; after which the eastern part of the state was to be formed into a state by itself.

With this as a basic proposition, General Wilson started for California, to confer with another gentleman who had been sent out on a like mission to that place; but he encountered very severe weather in the mountains, by which he was delayed. After many severe hardships he reached the coast, only to find that his coadjutor had become tired of waiting and had sailed for the East, so that they did not meet to confer upon the matter proposed to the Saints.

Senator Truman Smith, of Connecticut, in a speech he delivered in the United States Senate, July 8th, 1850, after having read some statements furnished him by Dr. John M. Bernhisel, thus alludes to the presence of General Wilson in Salt Lake Valley:

"The statement of Dr. Bernhisel touching the wonderful progress made by the people of Deseret within a space of time incredibly brief, is abundantly confirmed by a letter which I received from General John Wilson, dated at Salt Lake City, September 6th, 1849, from which I submit the following extract:

"A more orderly, earnest, industrious and civil people, I have never been among than these, and it is incredible how much they have done here in the wilderness in so short a time. In this city which contains about from four to five thousand inhabitants, I have not met in a citizen a single idler, or any person who looks like a loafer. Their prospects for crops are fair, and there is a spirit and energy in all that you see that cannot be equaled in any city of any size that I have ever been in, and I will add, not even in old Connecticut."

Elder Taylor having labored for two years in laying the foundation of a future great commonwealth was then called upon to leave that kind of labor and introduce the gospel into France.

What a change is here! from the desert wilds of the Rocky Mountains, in the interior of America, to France—to proud, beautiful France, first in all that pertains to modern civilization! From a city of adobe huts, log cabins and board shanties, to the glittering splendors and sumptuous palaces of splendid Paris! From the saw-pit to the pulpit, and lecture-platform—such is the life of an apostle!

PRIMITIVE SAW MILL

CHAPTER 23 – SUSPENSE

It was at the October conference of 1849 that Elder Taylor was called to go to France, and the 19th of the same month saw him leave his home for that distant land. In the same company were Lorenzo Snow, bound for Italy; Erastus Snow, for Denmark; Franklin D. Richards, for England; besides some eight or ten other Elders for various fields of labor, and a number of brethren for the Eastern States on business.

The journey across the plains was a tedious one; the cold, pitiless winds swept over them from the north-west, which made the traveler think of the pleasant fireside he had left in the Salt Lake Valley.

The Indians, too, especially the Crow tribe, manifested something of a hostile disposition. Between the upper crossing of the Platte and Independence Rock, they met with four men carrying the mail to Fort Hall, whom the Indians had partly robbed, or "tithed" as Elder Taylor put it, of their blankets, clothes and provisions. This circumstance made our travelers more vigilant in guarding their horses—"As we rather preferred to be tithed by our own bishops, whom we had with us, than be subjected to the ordeal by those who officiate without authority"—remarks Elder Taylor.

The circumstance also put a rather serious phase at first, upon the following: Two days after passing Fort Laramie, while our travelers were baiting their horses at noon on the banks of the Platte, they saw a large force of Indians suddenly come over the crest of a hill east of them. From the crest of the hill, or swell of the prairie to the river was about three-quarters of a mile, and down the gentle slope came the troop at break-neck speed, clad in all the paraphernalia of "feathers, paints and brooches," that delights the savage heart. The horses were as gaily ornamented as their riders, and seemed to partake of the same free, wild spirit.

As on they came like a whirlwind, some could be seen shaking out the priming of their fire-arms and priming them afresh; others were putting arrows to bow-strings, and others setting their lances at rest. Did this mean war, or what was more likely a massacre—for the approaching troop numbered two hundred? Our travelers had little time to prepare for either an attack or friendly visit; but they made good use of what they had. As soon as the approaching troop was discovered, several of the brethren were ordered to secure the horses to the wagons, while the rest, seizing their arms, were drawn up into line to receive the shock of conflict.

On came the Indians in silence, their faces betraying no emotion by which it could be determined whether they meant war or peace. Meantime our travelers were in anxious suspense. To fire on them first would, perhaps, turn what was intended for a frolic into a massacre, and yet they must needs do something soon or be run over. Meanwhile they stood their ground undaunted. On came the savage troop, determined apparently, to break their line, but as it stood unmoved they came to a dead halt within a rod and a half of it, setting their horses back on their haunches by a sudden jerk of the rein. Even after this, some of them made a show of preparing their arms.

Presently their chief came up and showed signs of peace. But as the Indians neither understood French nor English, and none of our travelers understood the Indian dialect, communication was difficult. One of the chiefs at last, produced a paper, stating that their tribe, the Cheyennes, was friendly to the whites. This being learned, the scene which looked so much like war a few moments before, was changed to one of feasting, the Indians, to their great delight, being treated to crackers, dried meat and tobacco.

The same evening Elder Taylor, with Lorenzo Snow and Bishop Hunter, visited their encampment, some three or four miles distant. They were informed by a Frenchman living with them that the tribe numbered six hundred warriors, and they were quite wealthy—well armed and mounted. The brethren visited a number of lodges and were well treated, though the Indians seemed a little chagrined at the occurrence of the morning. They undoubtedly intended their semi-warlike demonstration to frighten our travelers, perhaps make them take to the river; but as the rather practical joke failed, it left the jokers subject to ridicule.

On arriving at Kanesville the party were received by the Saints still remaining there with every demonstration of joy; and from thence Elder Taylor and several of the company made their way to St. Louis, where there were several strong branches of the Church, numbering upwards of three thousand members all told.

Here I insert a letter addressed by Elder Taylor from St. Louis to his family, not so much for items of history that it contains, as for the expression of his appreciation of family associations and enjoyments. We so frequently have seen him sacrifice the association of family and the comforts of home to carry the gospel to distant lands, and doing it so cheerfully, that it is just possible that those acquainted only with his public career may regard him as being indifferent to the fond endearments of home life. If such there be, let them read the following letter and learn that Elder Taylor possessed strong native attachments for his home and its holy relationships; and that his love for wives and children was not less intense because he sacrificed their companionship for the gospel's sake. It was not because he loved home and wives and children less, but that he loved the gospel more that he left them for its sake:

"My Dear Family:

"After a long absence I now sit down to write to you. I have been in this city about three weeks, and stayed in Kanesville about as long. I have been going leisurely along for the purpose of studying French, that I might be the better prepared to enter on my mission on my arrival in France. I have made some progress in the language and hope to be able to speak it on my arrival there. The Saints wherever I go treat me with the greatest kindness and hospitality.

"The latter part of our journey over the plains was a cold and dreary one, but the Lord was with us and protected us, and opened out our way before us. The snows fell on our right and left, before and behind, but we never encountered a snow storm until the last day. We arrived safe, however, and all is well.

"At Kanesville we were saluted with the firing of guns on our arrival, and the greatest manifestations of rejoicing, and parties, musical entertainments, etc., were gotten up. This has also been the case in St. Louis. Here the Saints have a magnificent hall and a splendid band and do things up in good style. But these outward tokens of friendship are very little to me, when compared with the heart-felt joy, the kindly feeling, the sympathetic and warm-hearted brotherhood manifested by many of my old friends, hundreds of whom seem anxious in every possible way to promote my happiness, secure my company and have my blessing and friendship. On my arrival both here and in Kanesville the Saints flocked around me like bees; and the greatest trouble I have is that of not being able to fulfill the many engagements that have pressed themselves upon me.

"But,' say you, 'do you not think of us and home? and do you never think of me, and of me?' This is what I have been wanting to get at for some time, and this long, tedious preface has become wearisome to me—let me tell my feelings if I can. Home! Home! Home! What shall I say? can I tell it? No, a thousand times no! Your forms, your countenances, your bodies and your spirits are all portrayed before me as in living characters. You are with me in my imaginations, thoughts, dreams, feelings; true our bodies are separated, but there you live—you dwell in my bosom, in my heart and affections, and will remain there forever. Our covenants, our hopes, our joys are all eternal and will live when our bodies moulder in the dust. Oceans, seas, mountains, deserts and plains may separate us—but in my heart you dwell.

"Do I see an amiable, lovely woman—my feelings are not there, they fly to my home. Do I see a beautiful infant—hear the prattle of lovely innocents, or the symmetry and intelligence of those more advanced in years? My mind flies to my home—there I gaze upon my wives, there I fondle and kiss my children and revel for a time in this mental delight; but I awake from my reverie and find that it is but a dream, and that mountains, deserts and plains separate us! Do I murmur? No! Do you? I hope not—shall I not say for you, No?

"I am engaged in my Master's business; I am a minister of Jehovah to proclaim His will to the nations. I go to unlock the door of life to a mighty nation, to publish to millions the principles of life, light and truth, intelligence and salvation, to burst their fetters, liberate the oppressed, reclaim the wandering, correct their views, improve their morals, save them from degradation, ruin and misery, and lead them to light, life, truth and celestial glory. Do not your spirits co-operate with mine? I know they do. Do you not say, 'Go, my husband, go, my father; fulfill your mission, and let God and angels protect you and restore you safe to our bosoms?' I know you do. Well, our feelings are reciprocal, I love my family and they love me; but shall that love be so contracted, so narrow, so earthly and sensual as to prevent my doing the will of my Father in heaven? No, say I, and you echo, No. No! our thoughts and feelings soar in another atmosphere. We live for time, and we live for eternity; we love here and we will love forever—

While life or thought or being last,
Or immortality endures!

"Our separations here tend to make us more appreciative of each other's society. A few more separations and trials, a few more tears, a few more afflictions, and the victory will be ours! We'll gain the kingdom, possess the crown, inherit eternal glory, associate with the Gods, soar amidst the intelligences of heaven; and with the noble, the great, the intellectual, the virtuous, the amiable, the holy, possess the reward held in reserve for the righteous, and live and love forever. May the spirit of peace be and abide with you forever; and when you bow before the Throne of Grace remember your affectionate husband, father and friend."

From St. Louis to New York the journey was uneventful. In company with Elders Curtis E. Bolton and John Pack he took passage in the *Westervelt*, a splendid vessel of fifteen hundred tons' burden, and arrived in Liverpool on the 27th of May, 1850.

CHAPTER 24 - FLYING THEIR COLORS

After a brief stay in England Elder Taylor sailed for France, arriving in Boulogne-sur-Mer—a fortified seaport town in the North of France—on the 18th of June. He was accompanied by Elder Bolton and William Howell, from Wales. The latter had preached the gospel in various places in the Jersey Islands and on the coast of France, and had baptized a few into the Church.

Elder Taylor's first step was to call upon the mayor of the city and find out the extent of his privileges in preaching. He explained to that officer that the object of his visit to France was religious not political; that he wished to preach the gospel, and that his principles taught him to uphold the laws and government wherever his lot might be cast; and that he might not infringe upon the laws of France or of that city, he called upon him as the chief officer in the place for information.

Monsieur le Maire was all politeness and attention. He first inquired if Monsieur Taylor had any papers, and upon having placed in his hand a letter of recommendation from the Governor of Deseret, signed by the Secretary of State, he expressed himself as satisfied; and informed the Elder that if he preached in a consecrated church nothing more would be required; but if he preached in a hall not consecrated, it would be necessary to address a note to him, specifying his intention and the doctrines he would preach; naming the hall and his place of residence, and he would then give him the necessary liberty. Such was the law at the time, that if this routine was not observed, the person attempting to hold the public meeting was liable to be imprisoned or banished from the country.

At first the conversation was carried on by Elder Bolton acting as interpreter; but the mayor either wishing to display his learning or accommodate Monsieur Taylor, undertook to make his replies in English. Elder Taylor observing the mayor's imperfect English, and not to be outdone in politeness, was soon trying to answer his grace in equally bad French.

Elder Pack joined the little party in Boulogne on the 26th of June, and the same evening they walked down on the sea-shore, and as the friendly shades of night shut them out from the rest of the world, they bowed down in prayer, in which Elder Taylor was mouth. He thanked the Lord for preserving them in their travels over mountains, deserts, plains, oceans and seas; and solemnly dedicated himself and his brethren to the labors to which they had been called by His own voice through His servants. He prayed for wisdom, for intelligence—in short, for the co-operation of God in their efforts to introduce the gospel in that land.

His next step was to secure a hall for preaching, near the center of the city, and announce a course of lectures on the principles of the gospel. He also wrote a number of letters to the editor of the *Interpreter Anglais et Francais*, in which he explained the object of his mission, and gave a brief account of the restoration of the gospel, with an explanation of its leading principles. These letters were published both in French and English.

The lectures were not very largely attended. The French people are notoriously indifferent to religion. They are lovers of pleasure more than lovers of God; are gay, volatile, careless, happy, intelligent. Anything in fact but religious. Therefore the announcement of these religious lectures did not create much interest.

There were a number of Protestant ministers in the town and they not only attended his lectures, but made themselves particularly obnoxious by their impudence. The evening of his first lecture a Mr. Robertson, an Independent minister, arose in the meeting and wanted the privilege of asking a few questions. Fearing, however, that to grant such a request might lead to disorder, and the mayor under those circumstances might withdraw his permission for holding the meetings, Elder Taylor told the reverend gentleman that he would answer as many questions as he might think proper to ask at his lodgings, or he would call on the gentleman at his house and answer them there, but could not admit of anything that might lead to a disturbance. Mr. Robertson pleaded that it was for the good of the public, and his friends who were there, that he wished to ask the questions. Elder Taylor replied that he might bring his friends with him, or he would meet them at his house.

Not satisfied with this, Mr. Robertson followed him out into the street and being joined by a Baptist minister, began to abuse "Joe Smith," calling him an impostor, etc.

"Whom do you speak of," said Elder Taylor, "I was personally acquainted with Mr. Joseph Smith; he was a gentleman, and would not treat a stranger as you do me." They still followed him, but he paid no more attention to them.

A few days after this occurrence, he received a challenge to a public discussion from the *Revs*. C. W. Cleeve, James Robertson and Philip Cater. This challenge he enclosed to the mayor, with a note, asking if there would be any objection to such a meeting. Being informed there would be no objection, the challenge was accepted, and the preliminaries arranged.

The questions for discussion were stated as follows: First, the late Joseph Smith; his public and pretended religious career. Second, the Book of Mormon; is it a revelation from God? Third, are the ministers of that people [the Mormons] sent of God by direct appointment? The fourth article of the agreement stated that "Mr. Taylor will have the privilege of discussing the validity of the faith and calling of his opponents."

The discussion began on the evening of the 11th of July, and continued three nights, from seven until ten, each party having thirty minutes alternately. The first two nights, and one hour of the third evening were taken up on the first three questions, leaving Elder Taylor only an hour in which to enquire into the doctrines and callings of his opponents; yet, as we shall see, that was sufficient.

In discussing the character of Joseph Smith, Elder Taylor's opponents introduced the infamous statements of Doctor Bennett, the Rev. Henry Caswell and others, charging Joseph with a number of crimes and immoralities. Elder Taylor had no documentary evidence to rebut these slanders, but he offered his own testimony to the character of the Prophet: and as Elders Bolton and Pack both knew him personally, he called upon them to testify, which they did. Elder Taylor's own testimony was especially strong. Burning with just indignation at the slanders against his friend, repeated by these priests of a dead theology, he said:

"I testify that I was acquainted with Joseph Smith for years. I have traveled with him; I have been with him in private and in public; I have associated with him in councils of all kinds; I have listened hundreds of times to his public teachings, and his advice to his friends and associates of a more private nature. I have been at his house and seen his deportment in his family. I have seen him arraigned before the courts of his country, and seen him honorably acquitted, and delivered from the pernicious breath of slander, and the machinations and falsehoods of wicked and corrupt men. I was with him living, and with him when he died; when he was murdered in Carthage jail by a ruthless mob with their faces painted, and headed by a Methodist minister, named Williams—I was there, and was myself wounded. I, at that time, received four balls in my body. I have seen him, then, under these various circumstances, and I testify before God, angels and men, that he was a good, honorable, virtuous man—that his doctrines were good, scriptural and wholesome—that his percepts were such as became a man of God—that his private and public character was unimpeachable—and that he lived and died as a man of God and a gentleman. This is my testimony; if it is disputed bring me a person authorized to receive an affidavit, and I will make one to this effect."

In another part of the debate, he remarked on the testimony of himself and brethren: "We have heard from our opponents about testimony that would be received in a court. The testimony of three living witnesses against a criminal, if his crime was murder, would hang him."

Chairman: Oh, no! oh, no!

A gentleman in the audience: (a barrister) "It would."

Elder Taylor: "I say Mr. Chairman, that it would. Let three respectable men make affidavit before a court, that they had seen one man murder another, and if their testimony was unimpeached the man would hang—their testimony would be conclusive."

Replying to his opponents remarks about not coming prepared with documents to answer their scurrilous charges, and about his testimony being that of an interested party, or of a particular friend, Elder Taylor said:

"Mr. Cleeve thinks I ought to bring documents to be accredited, as if it were necessary for us to bring replies to all the trash ever published against us! Now, what testimony had St. Paul when he preached at Athens, at Rome or at Antioch? He said that he had seen a vision, the people, of course, could believe him or not, as they thought proper. The wicked Jews were sent after him and his colleagues to testify evil. How could he rebutt it? Where were his documents? The Jews could state that he had been found guilty in several places, and whipped and imprisoned. Could he deny it? Assuredly not. They could testify that Jesus whom he preached, was crucified, as a blasphemer and an impostor, by the Jews, his own people. Could he say that this was not a legal decision? It seems to me that these gentlemen have never studied their Bibles, or they would have known more about such things; they must see that they are taking the same stand that the Pharisees and chief priests did formerly."

He then showed his opponents what position they would be in providing they were transplanted to a nation that did not believe in Jesus or the Bible. As the passage is both instructive and amusing, I quote it in full:—

"Now, I will speak a little about the position of my opponents. I suppose they are considered gentlemen here; their doctrines are believed, at least, by their respective flocks, if they have any. The Bible is believed by all. Suppose we transplant them to Hindostan or China. What evidence would they have to present before the people? They present the scriptures, and tell the people they are true. But how are we to know it, say the people. We tell you so. That is all very well, but we want some proof. Well, say you, they speak of Jesus coming to atone for the sins of the world.

"Yes, but the Jews tell us he was an impostor and a wicked man."

"But we believe Him to be a good man, and the son of God."

"Did you ever see Him?"

"No."

"Did you ever see anybody that had seen him?"

"No."

"How do you know anything about Him then?"

"We believe Him to be good."

"Who wrote this book?"

"His apostles."

"Oh, his particular friends!"

"Yes."

"Did you ever see them?"

"No."

"Did you ever see anybody that did?"

"No."

"Well, we don't put much confidence in your remarks; but we will read your book."

Having read it they say:

"Oh, I perceive that certain signs are to follow them that believe—the sick are to be healed, devils cast out, they are to speak in other tongues, have the gift of prophecy, etc. Do these signs follow you?

"Oh, no!"

"But you say you are believers, and your Bible says these signs shall follow them that believe."

"Oh, they are done away with and not necessary."

"But one of your apostles says, 'follow after charity and desire spiritual gifts.'"

"But they are not needed."

"Strange! Your Apostle St. Paul says, 'the eye cannot cay to the ear, I have no need of thee; nor the head to the foot, I have no need of thee.' But shall we not receive these gifts if we believe in Jesus, repent and are baptized?"

"No."

"Oh, you have a friend here, I see who is also a Christian minister. Do you believe in the same book, sir?"

"Yes."

"Do you believe in the same doctrine?"

"No."

"But do you get yours from the same book?"

"Yes."

"And does it teach you differently?"

"We believe differently."

"But you have, we perceive, another friend here; is he also a minister?"

"Yes."

"Which of your doctrines does he believe?"

"Neither."

"Do you all believe the Bible?"

"Yes."

"Do you believe it to be true or false?"

"True."

"Does a true book teach three different ways [of salvation]?"

"Those are our opinions."

"Oh, I thought you had come to teach us truth; if opinions are all, we have plenty of them already and can dispense with your services."

When the discussion turned upon the doctrines and authority of his opponents, he made short work of it. He proved very clearly that they were without authority to act in the name of God; that their doctrines were out of harmony with the scriptures and their religion a mere form of Godliness without the power thereof. To his statements and arguments they refused to reply, but still continued harping on the character of Joseph Smith. Paying no heed to their vain repetition of the slanderous charges against the Prophet, to which he had once made answer, he continued to unmercifully bombard their religious citadels, until, seeing them tumbling about their ears, the reverend gentlemen sought safety in flight.

The following is, in part, the bombardment before which they finally fled:

"What about their calling? Are we to have no answer to this subject? I have positively proved and demonstrated that they have no authority to preach, and they never attempted to disprove it, but have given us another rehearsal of the old ditty [the character of Joseph Smith]. Gentlemen, you sit down very quietly under the appellation of false teachers; of course we must believe that you are such unless you can prove to the contrary. Mr. Robertson, indeed, honestly says that he has no authority. Then God has nothing to do with him or his calling. He, of course, acknowledges that he is administering in the name of one who never sent him. We shall take him at his word, and set him down as a teacher whom God has not sent. In France or England they would punish persons as imposters for committing an act of forgery. But the judgment of those who administer falsely in the name of Jesus has not yet come; but the time will come when some will come and say, we have preached in thy name; and He will answer, depart from me, I never knew you. We shall set Mr. Cater on the stool with Mr. Robertson. Mr. Cleeve will not degrade himself by investigating the matter! Will he tell me why he, as a gentleman, undertook to discuss a subject, and published that engagement, which he is now disgusted with? And why he did not express his feelings of disgust before he heard the argument? I presume a criminal would express his disgust at an executioner for being so impolite as to put a noose round a gentleman's neck. But it is there, and there it will remain, Mr. Cleeve, until it is removed by you. It needs more formidable weapons than disgust or contempt to remove it; and we shall still say you have no authority, that you are a false teacher, and that God has not sent you, unless you can show some reason to the contrary."

Elder Taylor, amid considerable confusion, hastily sketched the outlines of the doctrines of Christ as contained in the New Testament, the organization of the Church and the gifts and powers that attended the primitive Saints, all of which was to be perpetuated in the Church.

"Now let us examine how this doctrine agrees with that of these gentlemen; for be it remembered that St. John says, 'He that transgresseth and abideth not in the doctrines of Christ hath not God, but he that abideth in the doctrines of Christ hath both the Father and the Son.' (II John, 9.) Now, have they apostles? No. They ridicule the idea of them. Have they prophets? No. They tell us there is to be no more prophecy. Have they evangelists, pastors and teachers—inspired men? No. They don't believe in inspiration, and tell us the cause of inspiration has ceased. Do they speak in tongues? No: you have heard in turned into ridicule time and again. Do they have prophets among them who prophesy? This they call a delusion. If any are sick, do they do as St. James says, 'send for the Elders of the Church that they may pray for them, and anoint them with oil in the name of the Lord?' No. That they call fanaticism. Do they baptize in the name of the Lord for the remission of sins? No. Do they lay on hands for the gift of the Holy Ghost? No. What have they got that in the least resembles the gospel? They have not even a clumsy counterfeit. How will they stand the test? 'He that abideth not in the doctrines of Christ hath not God.' I will not, however, call them imposters, that I shall leave, and go on to examine their doctrines more in detail.

"First, I will commence with Mr. Cleeve. He professes to be a Methodist minister. I am somewhat acquainted with their doctrines. Their ministers are not all ordained as Mr. Cleeve is; they have their class leaders, local preachers, exhorters and itinerant preachers, made just at random, according to convenience. But I will here take Mr. Cleeve and Mr. Cater and compare their doctrines. Mr. Cleeve believes in sprinkling; Mr. Cater in immersion; neither of them believing in baptism as Peter did, for remission of sins. But the Methodists have arranged the matter more conveniently, for according to the discipline of the Methodist Episcopal Church in America, they have three different modes of baptism—they will baptize either by sprinkling, pouring or immersion. This is the doctrine of the Episcopal Methodist Church in America; so that after teaching a person what they call the plan of salvation, they do not know as teachers how to baptize, but must apply to the person whom they are teaching. Thus Mr. Cleeve would—"

Mr. Cleeve.—I am not a Methodist, sir.

Elder Taylor.—I certainly understood you were a Wesleyan Methodist.

Mr. Cleeve.—I have nothing to do with the Wesleyan Methodists, either directly or indirectly.

Elder Taylor.—Then I must say that I am laboring under a mistake; this was certainly my understanding. I will therefore turn to Mr. Cater. I understand that he is a Baptist minister.

Mr. Cater.—I am not a member of the Baptist Association.

Elder Taylor.—I was certainly told and understood until now that you were, sir. Pray, gentlemen, what are you? (Great laughter and no answer.)

At this point the Rev. Mr. Long, evidently ashamed of the cowardice of the ministers that were flying from their colors, arose in the audience and exclaimed, "I am not ashamed of my profession, sir; I am a clergyman of the Church of England."

Elder Taylor.—I certainly think the gentlemen have taken a strange position, they seem to be afraid of acknowledging what their profession is. However, I will proceed. I have three different ministers to do with of some persuasion, for they all call themselves *Reverends*. Now, do their doctrines agree with the scriptures? Have they the organization, ordinances, gifts, prophecy, revelations, visions, tongues, apostles, prophets? No. This they cannot deny, for they have all of them opposed these things; yet all of these things were associated with primitive Christianity. Their offices, their doctrines, their calling, their teaching, their ordinances are all incorrect, they are devoid of the blessings, powers, unity, certainty and revelation, and are left struggling in the mazes of confusion, division, strife, uncertainty and error. They know not God nor the power of God. There is scarcely a principle that these gentlemen have that is correct, even the doctrine of baptism for the remission of sins they treat lightly; yet Philip baptized the Ethiopian eunuch—when he believed, he immersed him in water; John baptized in non because there was much water there; St. Paul was told to arise and wash away his sins, and Jesus says that except a man be born of water and of the spirit, he can in no wise enter the kingdom of God.

Chairman.—(to Elder Taylor) Do you wish to continue, the gentlemen on the opposite side are satisfied that it rest here?

Elder Taylor.—I certainly did not anticipate this. I expected to investigate their principles further, according to agreement.

Chairman.—They do not wish to say any more.

Elder Taylor.—If they have no reply to make, of course I must let it rest.

Here the debate closed, and the Champion of Truth was triumphant.

The chairmen of the meetings, Mr. Luddy, Dr. Townley and Mr. Groves made some remarks at the close of the debate, and very unfairly, as Elder Taylor could have no opportunity to reply to them, undertook to rescue the vanquished ministers. In the published report of the discussion, however, he wrote out his replies to their strictures, and very effectually answered them.

There is one item connected with this discussion that should be dealt with, since it is a matter that the enemies of Elder Taylor have sought to make much of in casting reproach upon his veracity and moral courage. In the course of the discussion his opponents rehearsed all the charges of crime and immorality made in the writings and lectures of John C. Bennett after he was excommunicated from the Church; and accused the Saints with practicing the grave immoralities described by this arch apostate. Among the immoralities charged were those of promiscuous sexual intercourse, a community of wives, the keeping of seraglios, polygamy, illicit intercourse by permission of the Prophet, and the keeping of spiritual wives.

To all this Elder Taylor made a general and emphatic denial, and read from an article then published in the Appendix of the Doctrine and Covenants, expressing the belief of the Church on the subject of marriage; and inasmuch as he knew of and had obeyed the law of celestial marriage, including as it does a plurality of wives, he has been accused of falsehood, and of seeking to deceive by denying the charges then brought against the Church.

The polygamy and gross sensuality charged by Bennett and repeated by those ministers in France, had no resemblance to celestial or patriarchal marriage which Elder Taylor knew existed at Nauvoo, and which he had obeyed. Hence in denying the false charges of Bennett he did not deny the existence of that system of marriage that God had revealed; no more than a man would be guilty of denying the legal, genuine currency of his country, by denying the genuineness and denouncing what he knew to be a mere counterfeit of it.

Another illustration: Jesus took Peter, James and John into the mountain and there met with Moses and Elias, and the glory of God shone about them, and these two angels talked with Jesus, and the voice of God was heard proclaiming Him to be the Son of God. After the glorious vision, as Jesus and His companions were descending the mountain, the former said: "Tell the vision to no man, until the Son of Man be risen again from the dead." Suppose one of these apostles had turned from the truth before the Son of Man was risen from the dead; and under the influence of a wicked, lying spirit should charge that Jesus and some of His favorite apostles went up into a mountain, and there met with Moses and Elias,—or some persons pretending to represent them,—together with a group of voluptuous courtesans with whom they spent the day in licentious pleasure. If the other apostles denounce that as an infamous falsehood, would they be untruthful? No; they would not. Or would they be under any obligations when denying the falsehoods of the apostate to break the commandment the Lord had given them by relating just what had happened in the mountain? No; it would have been a breech of the Master's strict commandment for them to do that. So with Elder Taylor. While he was perfectly right and truthful in denying the infamous charges repeated by his opponents, he was under no obligation and had no right to announce to the world, at that time, the doctrine of celestial marriage. It was not then the law of the Church, or even the law to the Priesthood of the Church: the body thereof at the time knew little or nothing of it, though it had been revealed to the Prophet and made known to some of his most trusted followers. But today, now that the revelation on celestial marriage is published to the world, if the slanderous charges contained in the writings of John C. Bennett should be repeated, every Elder in the Church could truthfully and consistently do just what Elder Taylor did in France—he could deny their existence.

That Elder Taylor neither lacked the courage of his convictions on this subject, nor the boldness to proclaim them, nor the skill to defend, was amply proven in subsequent years, when, after the law of celestial marriage was proclaimed to be the law of the Church, he went to the city of New York to publish a paper, and there in the metropolis and center of civilization of America, fearlessly proclaimed that doctrine, and successfully defended it against all comers.

CHAPTER 25 - FRIED FROTH

Shortly after the discussion Elder Taylor left Boulogne for Paris, where he began studying the French language, and teaching the gospel. Among the interesting people whom he met there was M. Krolokoski, a disciple of M. Fourier, the distinguished French socialist. M. Krolokoski was a gentleman of some standing, being the editor of a paper published in Paris in support of Fourier's views. Another thing which makes the visit of this gentleman to Elder Taylor interesting is the fact that it was the society to which he belonged that sent M. Cabet to Nauvoo with the French Icarians, to establish a community on Fourier's principles. At his request Elder Taylor explained to him the leading principles of the gospel. At the conclusion of that explanation the following conversation occurred:

M. Krolokoski.—"Mr. Taylor, do you propose no other plan to ameliorate the condition of mankind than that of baptism for the remission of sins?"

Elder Taylor.—"This is all I propose about the matter."

M. Krolokoski.—"Well, I wish you every success; but I am afraid you will not succeed."

Elder Taylor.—"Monsieur Krolokoski, you sent Monsieur Cabet to Nauvoo, some time ago. He was considered your leader—the most talented man you had. He went to Nauvoo shortly after we had deserted it. Houses and lands could be obtained at a mere nominal sum. Rich farms were deserted, and thousands of us had left our houses and furniture in them, and almost everything calculated to promote the happiness of man was there. Never could a person go to a place under more happy circumstances. Besides all the advantages of having everything made ready to his hand, M. Cabet had a select company of colonists. He and his company went to Nauvoo—what is the result? I read in all your reports from there—published in your own paper here, in Paris, a continued cry for help. The cry is money, money! We want money to help us carry out our designs. While your colony in Nauvoo with all the advantages of our deserted fields and homes—that they had only to move into—have been dragging out a miserable existence, the Latter-day Saints, though stripped of their all and banished from civilized society into the valleys of the Rocky Mountains, to seek that protection among savages—among the *peau rouges* as you call our Indians—which Christian civilization denied us—there our people have built houses, enclosed lands, cultivated gardens, built school-houses, and have organized a government and are prospering in all the blessings of civilized life. Not only this, but they have sent thousands and thousands of dollars over to Europe to assist the suffering poor to go to America, where they might find an asylum.

"The society I represent, M. Krolokoski," he continued, "comes with the fear of God—the worship of the Great Elohim; we offer the simple plan ordained of God, viz: repentance, baptism for the remission of sins, and the laying on of hands for the gift of the Holy Ghost. Our people have not been seeking the influence of the world, nor the power of government, but they have obtained both. Whilst you, with your philosophy, independent of God, have been seeking to build up a system of communism and a government which is, according to your own accounts, the way to introduce the Millennial reign. Now, which is the best, our religion, or your philosophy?"

M. Krolokoski.—"Well, Mr. Taylor, I can say nothing."

"Philosophy" has always been a passion with the French; but Elder Taylor seems not to have had a very high regard for what he saw of it among them. He held it in the same esteem that Paul did the "science" of the Greeks—he considered it a misnomer—philosophy, falsely so called.

One day in walking through the splendid grounds of the *Fardin des Plantes* with a number of friends, one of the party purchased a curious kind of cake, so thin and light, that you could blow it away, and eat all day of it and still not be satisfied. Some one of the company asked Elder Taylor if he knew the name of it. "No," he replied, "I don't know the proper name; but in the absence of one, I can give it a name—I will call it French philosophy, or fried froth, which ever you like."

During his stay in Paris he visited the Palace Vendome, and with a number of friends ascended Napoleon's Column of Victory. His companions scratched their names on the column as thousands had done before them. Seeing that Elder Taylor had not written his name, they asked him to write it with theirs. "*No*," he replied, *"I will not write my name there; but I will yet write it in living, imperishable characters !"*

Having baptized a number of people in Paris, he organized a branch of the Church in that city early in December. During the summer, too, he had made arrangements for translating the Book of Mormon into the French language, and publishing a monthly periodical, also in French, called *Etoile Du Deseret*—The Star of Deseret,—a royal octavo sheet, the first number of which appeared in May, 1851.

In the work of translating the Book of Mormon he was greatly assisted by the patient labors of Elder Curtis E. Bolton, Brother Louis Bertrand and several highly educated gentlemen whom he baptized in Paris, but whose names unfortunately cannot be obtained.

When he announced his intention of publishing the Book of Mormon in French, Elder Franklin D. Richards called upon the conferences of the British Mission to come to his assistance with means; but he made other arrangements to meet his engagements with the publishing house; and wrote the following characteristic letter to Elder Richards:

"I feel very much obliged to you for the remarks you made on the subject of the French mission, a short time ago, wherein you requested the presiding Elders, of the conferences, to raise means for publishing the Book of Mormon in French. In noticing, however, the position of the churches in this country, and the many calls that have been made upon the brethren, I have been seeking to make other arrangements without troubling them, which I am very happy to inform you, I have accomplished, and therefore shall not be necessitated to make any calls upon the conferences. The scriptures say, that, 'it is more blessed to give than to receive,' and if in making the above move, I may have deprived some of an anticipated blessing, I hope they will excuse me; for perhaps there may be an opportunity afforded them of assisting some of my brethren in another way. If not, the world is large, and there is ample opportunity to do good."

A few wealthy members of the Church in England had privately furnished him the means, and he made such arrangements with the publishers that when copies of the book were sold a certain amount of the proceeds was put away for printing another edition. "And thus it can be continued from time to time," writes Elder Taylor, "as necessity shall require, until 200,000 copies are printed without any additional expense."

The translation is said to be a very correct one, the original simplicity of the Nephite writers is retained, and it is as literal as the genius and idiom of the French language will admit.

In addition to these literary labors Elder Taylor applied to the government authorities for permission for himself and the Elders to preach throughout France; and the prospects were fair for obtaining it; but at that juncture, a mob arose against the Saints in Denmark, their meeting house where they assembled was torn down and much excitement created. It was this circumstance which doubtless led the French ministry to prohibit the Elders from preaching altogether, instead of granting them the liberty for which they asked.

The political situation in France at the time was precarious, and did much to prevent Elder Taylor and his companions from spreading the gospel among that people. In 1848 Louis Philippe had been compelled to abdicate the throne of France by an insurrection of the people; the provisional government that succeeded was soon supplanted by the republic which was proclaimed by the voice of the people; of which Louis Napoleon, the nephew of the great Napoleon, was elected president for four years, as provided for in the constitution. This term of office was altogether too brief and too precarious for a Bonaparte, and the newly elected President soon set on foot secret measures for an increase of power and an extension of time in office.

Having won over the army to his views, he boldly seized such members of the National Assembly, and other prominent citizens, who were opposed to his interests and imprisoned them, suppressed the newspapers and proclaimed the dissolution of the assembly and council of state. He hastily sketched a new and more despotic constitution, which was accepted by the people, and had himself elected president for ten years.

These movements were soon followed by even bolder acts of usurpation. He secured the passage of a decree by the new senate, making him hereditary Emperor with the title of Napoleon III. And thus an empire was erected on the ruins of the fallen republic.

Such were the agitations and revolutions going on in France during the time that Elder Taylor was there introducing the gospel; and with such an irreligious and excitable people as the French, it is not to be expected that they will turn away from excited multitudes shouting now *vive la Republique*, and then *vive l'empereur*, with the whole country on the verge of civil war—it is not to be expected, I say, that a people, and especially the French people, are going to turn from all this to listen to a stranger preach on the peaceable things of the kingdom of heaven!

Still, meetings were held in Paris twice a week, and the work spread into Havre, Calais, Boulogne and other places. In the three cities named, as well as in Paris, branches of the Church were organized. In June, 1851, the Channel Islands,—hitherto belonging to the British mission—in which there were several branches of the Church, were added to the French mission and of course considerably increased its strength.

In the latter part of July or about the first of August, 1851, Elder Taylor accompanied by Elder Viet, a German, and a teacher of that language in France, and Elder George P. Dykes, went to the city of Hamburg, Germany. Here, with the aid of Elder Viet, a Mr. Charles

Miller, whom he baptized shortly after his arrival there, and George P. Dykes, he made arrangements for and supervised the translation of the Book of Mormon into the German language. The work was finally completed and stereotyped; and the text so arranged that the French and German would face each other, each page containing the same matter in the same opening, and thus both could be bound together.

In Hamburg as in Paris, he published a monthly periodical, a royal octavo sheet, which was called *Zion's Panier*—Zion's Banner. The first number was issued November 1st, 1851. He also preached the gospel and raised up a branch of the Church in Hamburg; after which he returned to Paris, to attend a conference of the French mission appointed to convene there.

He ran considerable risk in appointing this conference, for the law prohibited more than twenty persons assembling together, and a number of times the meetings of the Saints in Paris were entered by the police, and the number present counted to see if they were violators of the law. Referring to this cramped situation of affairs Elder Taylor remarks: "'Liberty,' 'Equality,' 'Fraternity,' were written upon almost every door. You had liberty to speak, but might be put in prison for doing so. You had liberty to print, but they might burn what you had printed, and put you in confinement for it"—such was French liberty!

Elder Taylor arrived in Paris about the 18th or 19th of December. On the 2nd of the same month Louis Napoleon by his famous *coup d'etat* had overthrown the first republic succeeding the government of Louis Philippe; and in the meantime had sketched the more despotic constitution which was to succeed it, with himself elected President for ten years. Paris was in the hands of the soldiers; her streets had recently been soaked with blood; many of the buildings had been battered down into shapeless ruins; and about five hundred prisoners, untried before any tribunal—even that of a drum-head court martial—had been shipped off to Cayenne.

It happened, too, that the day appointed for the holding of this conference was the very day on which the people were to vote for Napoleon for president—it would evidently be a day of excitement; and altogether the circumstances would have been considered sufficient, by ordinary men, to have postponed the conference indefinitely. Not so with Elder Taylor. A French revolution was not to hinder him in his work. The revolution would give the authorities of Paris something else to do than to look after him. So the conference was held.

There were about four hundred represented at the conference. A number of elders, priests and teachers were ordained; a conference was regularly organized and a presidency appointed over the Church in France. "At the very time they [the French people] were voting for their president," Elder Taylor remarks, "we were voting for our president; and building up the kingdom of God; and I prophesied that our cause would stand when theirs is crushed to pieces; and the kingdom of God will roll on and spread from nation to nation, and from kingdom to kingdom."

It scarcely need be said that the prophecy has been, or is being fulfilled. The work the French people did that day was undone in less than a year by the usurping "Prince President" becoming Emperor, and crushing out the life of the republic by founding a despotism as absolute as any kingdom of the middle ages; and which in its turn was violently overthrown, a few years afterwards, by another revolution. Meantime the kingdom of God goes steadily forward—slowly, perhaps, but none the less surely on that account. The Almighty is not anxious to reap results today from promises He laid down yesterday. The oak grows slowly; but every year adds something to its size; the winds which beat upon it only fix its mighty roots deeper in the earth and increase the strength of its fiber; and at last, in spite of slowness of growth, in spite of howling tempest and the thunder-bolt, the grand oak stands monarch of the forest. So shall it be with the kingdom of God among the nations of the earth.

Elder Taylor's mission in France and Germany was now completed; and he began making his arrangements for returning home. It was the day after the conference in Paris that he started for England, intending to call at the Channel Islands *en route*.

It was not more than ten minutes after he had taken the cab and started to the railway station to take his departure from France, when one of the high police officials came to inquire for him. The gentleman with whom he had stayed in Paris, M. Ducloux, was a very affectionate friend to him, and he, with his sister-in-law, kept the officer in conversation for two hours, speaking very highly of their late guest, maintaining that he was a respectable, high-minded gentleman. In turn the officer told him every place Elder Taylor had been since his arrival in Paris; when he came to France, what hotel he stayed at; when he went to England, and how long he remained; when he went to Germany, and how long he stayed there; what books he had printed, etc. In fact he gave a most minute account of all his movements, all of which were recorded in the police records.

Whether an attempt to intercept Elder Taylor was made or not is unknown. It might have been done by telegraphing their police agents, which were so numerous as to be ubiquitous, but without any design on his part to avoid them, for he did not know they were after him, he turned off the main route to England, to visit a little seashore town where he remained a week, and thus missed what might have been something more serious than a mere annoyance.

CHAPTER 26 - AN OLD FRIEND

Elder Taylor took advantage of his visit to England and Europe, where skill in the fine arts was more perfect than in the United States, to get out the busts of his friends and fellow-martyrs, Joseph and Hyrum Smith. He evidently contemplated this work before leaving home, since he had with him in England casts taken from the faces of the martyrs immediately after their death. He also had with him the various drawings made of them during their lives, to assist the artist in his work. The modeller, Mr. Gahagan, was one of the first artists of England, in proof of which it is only necessary to say that he had taken the busts of the duke of Wellington, Lord Nelson, Sir Robert Peel, the emperor of Russia and a number of the principal nobility and gentry of England. The work was done under the personal direction of Elder Taylor, and he was successful in obtaining for himself and future generations a correct outline of the heads and features of the two martyrs, and as perfect a likeness of them as it was possible to obtain so long after their death.

It was while he was on this French and German mission, too, that he wrote his admirable work "The Government of God," a book of some two hundred pages. The author defines the kingdom of God to be the government of God, on the earth, or in the heavens; and then in his first two chapters proceeds to place the magnificence, harmony, beauty and strength of the government of God, as seen throughout the universe, in contrast with the meanness, confusion and weakness of the government of men.

It is a bold picture he draws in each case; one displaying the intelligence, the light, the glory, the beneficence and power of God; the other the ignorance, the folly, the littleness and imbecility of man. The great evils, both national and individual which He depicts with such vividness, the author maintains are beyond the power of human agency to correct. "They are diseases," he remarks, "that have been generating for centuries; that have entered into the vitals of all institutions, religious and political, that have prostrated the powers and energies of all bodies politic, and left the world to groan under them, for they are evils that exist in church and state, at home and abroad; among Jew and Gentile, Christian, Pagan and Mahometan; king, prince, courtier and peasant; like the deadly simoon, they have paralyzed the energies, broken the spirits, damped the enterprise, corrupted the morals and crushed the hopes of the world. No power on this side of heaven can correct this evil. It is a world that is degenerated, and it requires a God to put it right."

Bust of Joseph Smith

Bust of Hyrum Smith

The author then rather hurriedly reviews the incompetency of the means made use of by man to regenerate the world; showing that neither the Roman Catholic nor Greek churches, though having full sway in some countries, and backed by national and even international power, have been able to make happy, prosperous, unselfish and righteous those countries whose destinies they have directed; and being unable to accomplish these desirable objects in the nations where their power has been supreme, the author argues that they would be unsuccessful in regenerating the world should their dominion be universal.

Nor is our author more hopeful that the reformed churches, the Protestants, would be any more successful than the Greek and Roman churches have been. So far Protestantism has but increased division, and multiplied strife without changing materially the moral and spiritual condition of the world.

Turning from those who would regenerate the world through the medium of Christianity—a false, a corrupted Christianity, for such is the so-called Christian religion of the churches above mentioned—turning from these to those who would take their destiny into their own hands, and who, either denying the existence of God or ignoring His right to direct in the affairs of men, seek by their own wisdom to establish institutions for the amelioration of mankind, our author remarks:

"If skepticism is to be the basis of the happiness of man, we shall be in a poor situation to improve the world. It is practical infidelity that has placed the world in its present condition; how far the unblushing profession of it will lead to restoration and happiness, I must leave my readers to judge. It is our departure from God that has brought upon us all our misery. It is not a very reasonable way to alleviate it by confirming mankind is skepticism."

Neither has man been able to devise any form of government that is a panacea for the numerous ills with which the world is cursed. Poverty, iniquity, crime, injustice, greed, pride, lust, oppression, exist in republics as well as in kingdoms or empires; in limited monarchies as well as in those that are absolute. Our author maintains that neither religion nor philosophy, the church nor the state, nor education nor all of these combined, as they exist among men, are sufficient to regenerate the world; "our past failures," he writes, "make it evident that any future effort, with the same means, would be useless."

The author then proceeds to discuss the questions—What is man? What his destiny and relationship to God? The object of his existence on the earth, his relationship thereto; and his accountability to God. To say that Elder Taylor treats these grave questions with marked ability is unnecessary.

He then deals with God's course in the moral government of the world; and then of the question—"Whose right is it to govern the world?" He clearly proves that it is God's right, basing that right on the fact that God created it—that it is His; and He, and they to whom He delegates His power are the only ones who have legitimate authority to govern it. But men have usurped authority; they have taken the management of affairs, so far as they have the power into their own hands; they have rejected God and his counsels; and, as a consequence, the evils and corruptions of which all nations and peoples are sick follow.

This leads him to the question: Will man always be permitted to usurp authority over his fellow-men, and over the works of God? He answers in the negative. It would be unreasonable, unjust, unscriptural—contrary to the promises of God—and would frustrate His designs in the creation of the world. No, the time must come when the moral world, like the physical universe, shall be under the direction of the Almighty, and God's will be done on earth as it is done in heaven. The manner in which this is to be brought about, the peace, prosperity, happiness and general blessedness which are to follow the establishment of the government of God on earth, are the subjects of his concluding chapters.

Such, in brief, is an outline of this fine work—Elder Taylor's masterpiece! A work which is sufficient at once to establish both his literary ability and his power as a moral philosopher. One can only regret that in the later years of his life he did not find time to enlarge it. The flight is splendid, but one wishes he had remained longer on the wing. He wrote this work, as he tells us in his foot-note on the first page, to believers in the Bible. I regret that he did not so add to it that its sublime truths would appeal with equal force to those who reject the Jewish Scriptures. No writer in the Church of Jesus Christ of Latter-day Saints has yet, in any manner worth mentioning, undertaken to establish the divinity of the Jewish Scriptures, or made answer to the indictments brought against the Bible by infidels; but no one can read the "Government of God" without being convinced that its author was pre-eminently qualified for such an undertaking.

While in France Elder Taylor became somewhat acquainted with the process of manufacturing sugar from the sugar-beet, and being convinced that both climate and soil in Utah were favorable to the production of the beets, he organized a company to found that industry in the distant vales of Deseret. The company was to be known as the "Deseret Manufacturing Company," and while its purposes were not confined to the establishment of one industry alone, sugar was to be its first venture.

The company was composed of four partners with equal shares, of which Elder Taylor was one. The capital stock was put at fifty thousand pounds sterling, equal to a quarter of a million dollars.

Elder Taylor had the machinery for the intended sugar works made in Liverpool by Faucett, Preston & Co., at a cost of twelve thousand five hundred dollars. It was first class machinery, the very best that could be obtained, and such was its weight that it would require fifty-two teams to carry it from Council Bluffs to Salt Lake. It was an immense undertaking.

Having fulfilled his mission and accomplished in addition these miscellaneous but important labors, Elder Taylor set sail from England on the 6th of March, 1852, on board the steamship *Niagara*. There were about twenty emigrating Saints who accompanied him.

The first Sunday out the passengers, composed principally of the English aristocracy, were anxious to have Elder Taylor preach to them in the cabin; but the law, *alias*the captain, a narrow-minded, bigoted man refused to accede to their request.

The *Niagara* reached Boston harbor on the eighteenth of the same month, and Elder Taylor proceeded to Philadelphia, where he visited Colonel Thomas L. Kane, then confined to his bed by sickness. After preaching to the Saints in that city, he proceeded to Washington, where he met his old friend, Dr. John M. Bernhisel, Utah's delegate to Congress. He also met with Senator Stephen A. Douglas and a number of other senators and members of the lower house.

From Washington he went to St. Louis and there remained a week or more, awaiting the arrival of the ship *Rockaway*, at New Orleans, having on board a company of emigrating Saints, and his sugar manufacturing plant. While waiting the arrival of this vessel he was actively engaged in preaching the gospel. The *Rockaway* arrived in port in the latter part of April; and having made arrangements for the shipment of his machinery, Elder Taylor again turned his face homeward.

After a tedious journey across the plains, he arrived in Salt Lake City on the 20th of August, where he was welcomed by his family, and by his brethren of the priesthood, who heartily approved of all his labors, blessed him for his faithfulness, his untiring zeal and the energy he had manifested.

How sweet to the ear! how joyous to the soul! how gratifying to the heart is that grandest of all salutations—"Well done thou good and faithful servant!" and when spoken by those holding the holy priesthood, backed by the warm grasp of the hand, and confirmed by the countenance lit up with unfeigned brotherly love, it certainly is a fore-taste of the joy that shall fill the hearts of the faithful who hear the same salutation from the Master, who will add: "Enter thou into the joy of thy Lord!"

CHAPTER 27 - SPIRITS FROM THE VASTY DEEP

It may well be imagined that after an absence of three years, Elder Taylor found plenty of employment in looking after his own affairs for a season, and putting in motion enterprises that would have for their object the accumulation of wealth. But Elder Taylor's affections were not given to the wealth of this world that perishes with the using. Other things than those that please the children of this world had taken hold of him; and hence it happened that although the state of his finances on his return from this protracted mission to Europe, would have induced most men to devote themselves exclusively to the betterment of their personal affairs, Elder Taylor was to be found taking part in the councils of the Church, and devoting a considerable amount of time to preaching the gospel.

The machinery for the manufacturing of sugar arrived in due time and was put in operation; but owing to a lack of skilled workmen to take charge of the various branches of the business, the production of sugar was unsatisfactory, and at the instance of President Young the enterprise was abandoned.

He took part in the ceremonies connected with laying the corner stones of the Salt Lake Temple, on the 6th of April, 1853; and during that conference, with several other members of his quorum and the First Seven Presidents of Seventies, was called and sustained as a missionary "to preach the gospel of Jesus Christ in the valleys of the mountains." In fulfilling that mission he visited nearly all the settlements of Utah, and everywhere was made welcome by the people, who knew so well his manner of life, his untiring zeal and devotion to the great cause he had espoused.

The Saints, no less than sinners, have a habit of assessing the value of pulpit precepts by the test of personal example; and one of the things which made Elder Taylor a welcome visitor of missionary among them was the fact that in this matter of personal example he did not break down. On the contrary, his daily life reflected the precepts he taught in the pulpit and in private; and hence the people believed in him and respected his counsels.

The year following he was elected a member of the Territorial Legislature; but before the Legislature assembled he was again called upon a mission. This time he was called to preside over the churches in the eastern states, supervise the emigration and publish a paper in the interest of the Church. He promptly resigned his position as a member elect of the Legislature, and in the fall of 1854 started for New York, accompanied by Elder Jeter Clinton, Nathaniel H. Felt, Alexander Robbins, Angus M. Cannon, and his son, George J. Taylor. His being called to publish a paper in New York was but part of a general movement by which Mormonism and the Saints were to be represented by their own accredited agents. Orson Pratt was in Washington publishing the *Seer*; Erastus Snow and Orson Spencer were to publish a paper in St. Louis; and George Q. Cannon one in San Francisco.

The object in starting these publications was to disabuse the public mind, then fast being prejudiced against the Church by the tongue of slander. When the Saints disappeared in the great western wilderness of America there were a variety of opinions as to what would be their fate. Few, however, thought they would survive the terrible ordeal through which they passed in their expulsion from the United States and the subsequent perils and hardships of the great desert. But when the miracle of their preservation was forced upon their attention, and not only their preservation, but the fact, also, that they were more numerous and in possession of more power than when driven from Nauvoo—when it was known that they had laid the foundation of a commonwealth which was soon to be knocking at the gate of the capital for admission into the Union as a sovereign state—when all this was known, their enemies, who flattered themselves that they had seen the last of the hated Mormons, suddenly aroused themselves for a renewal of the suspended conflict.

Meantime the Church had publicly announced as a principle of its faith the doctrine of celestial marriage, including as it does, a plurality of wives.

No sooner was the announcement made than misrepresentation distorted this doctrine into everything that was vile and impure. The old stories of licentious practices among the Saints in Nauvoo, fulminated by John C. Bennett and other apostates—but which had no existence except as these same apostates and a few other corrupt men practiced them, and for which they were expelled from the Church—were revived and believed with avidity by a credulous public, until Utah was looked upon as a hot-bed of impurity, and the Mormon religion as a veil under which was hidden all the ungodliness of man's baser and degrading passions.

It was to stem the constantly increasing tide of prejudice, set in motion by this flood of falsehood, that the movement by the Church to establish publications in the cities I have named, was made.

It was a difficult task that had been assigned Elder Taylor. Both the pulpit and the press were against him; and there could be no question as to what course political parties would take respecting the question. What the populace condemned, they would condemn. Besides, he found himself cramped financially for such an enterprise. The Church in Utah was unable to furnish the necessary means. The people there were having a severe struggle for existence with the unpropitious elements of the wilderness, and money there was none, or, at least, very little.

It is true there were many members of the Church in the eastern states at the time, but they were unorganized, and indifferent to the progress or defense of the work of God. Elder Taylor called upon the Saints to come to his assistance in publishing a paper, but it reminded him of a man, he humorously said, in describing the result to President Young, who said, "I can call spirits from the vasty deep;" "So can I," shouted another, "but they won't come." Still there were a few who responded, and with what they furnished and the money obtained for the teams and wagons he had brought with him from Utah, and a few hundred dollars which he and those with him could borrow, a paper was started, the first number bearing the date of the 17th of February, 1855.

"We commenced our publication," writes Elder Taylor to President Young, "not because we had means to do it, but because we were determined to fulfill our mission, and either make a spoon or spoil a horn. How long we shall be able to continue, I don't know. We are doing as well as we can, and shall continue to do so; but I find it one thing to preach the gospel without purse or scrip, and another thing to publish a paper on the same terms."

CHAPTER 28 - CANKERED GOLD

"The Mormon" was the title which Elder Taylor gave his paper. It was a handsome, well printed, twenty-eight columned weekly. It had a very striking and significant heading, filling up at least one fourth of the first page. It represented an immense American eagle with out-stretched wings poised defiant above a bee-hive, and two American flags. Above the eagle was an all-seeing eye surrounded by a blaze of glory, and the words: "Let there be light; and there was light." On the stripes of the flag on the left was written: "Truth, Intelligence, Virtue and Faith;" signed, "John Taylor;" upon those on the right; "Truth will prevail;" signed, "H. C. Kimball;" while in the blue fields of one of the flags, the star of Utah shone resplendently. Two scrolls on either side of the eagle bore the following inscriptions: "Mormon creed—mind your own business," Brigham Young; and "Constitution of the United States, given by inspiration of God," Joseph Smith.

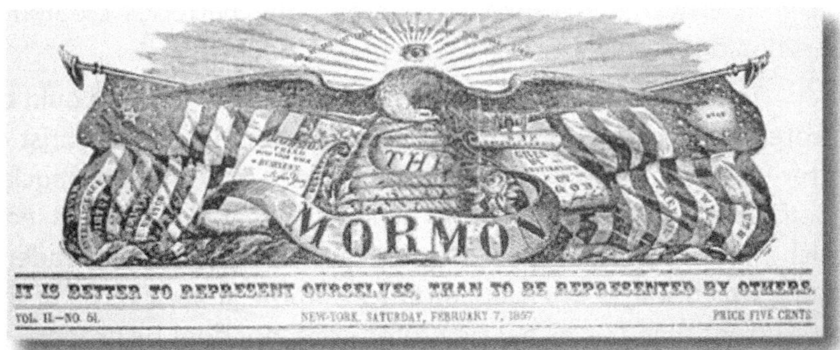

HEADING OF "THE MORMON"

On the inside, at the head of the editorial column was the American eagle standing on a bee-hive with an American flag on either side. Upon the bee-hive, on one side, leaned the Doctrine and Covenants, Book of Mormon and Bible; on the other a tablet on which was written: "Peace and good will to man." The eagle held in its break a scroll on which was written: "Holiness to the Lord."

The Mormon office was situated on the corner of Nassau and Ann streets, with the offices of the New York *Herald* on one side, and those of the *Tribune* on the other. Elder Taylor was thus in the very heart of Gotham's newspaper world. Selecting such a stand is evidence enough that he did not intend to hide his light under a bushel. On the contrary he had taken a prominent position with a determination to keep it. He stationed himself in the front rank, unfurled his colors and we shall see that with the bold, dashing courage of a Henry of Navarre, how well he held his place.

It was the custom at the time to distribute the first issue of newspapers free to the news boys, and let them sell them for what they pleased. Accordingly on the first day of its publication hundreds of news boys filled the lower offices and thronged the stairway leading to the upper rooms, clamoring for *The Mormon*. As they were promptly supplied, the paper with its conspicuous heading was waved in the face of the public and all through the principal thoroughfares the cry of "*Mormon,*" "*Mormon*"—"Here's yer *Mormon*," was heard ringing and echoing on every side.

To say that this first springing of the batteries created a sensation but feebly expresses the effect produced.

The prospectus of *The Mormon* announced that it would be devoted to the cause and interests of the Church of Jesus Christ of Latter-day Saints; "and will be the advocate of its claims, social, moral, political and religious; and will also treat upon all subjects which the editor may deem instructive or edifying to his readers, among which will be science, literature and the general news of the day. Further than this he has no pretensions, nor does he propose to be bound to any particular party or interest."

Subsequently, though in an early number of *The Mormon*, Elder Taylor made a further announcement of his principles, and what he meant to sustain, as follows:

"We believe in good, sound, healthy morals, in matter of fact philosophy, in politics uncorrupted, and that secure the greatest good to all. We believe in the God of heaven and certainly in religion. We believe in a religion that will make a man go down to the grave with a clear conscience, and an unfaltering step, to meet his God as a Father and a Friend without fear."

During the two years and a half that he continued to edit *The Mormon*, he kept free from all entangling alliances in party politics, but criticized all parties and measures with a fearlessness and intelligence that is truly refreshing at a time when party prejudice or venality controlled the utterances of the press.

But it is as a defender of the faith and character of the Saints that Elder Taylor in *The Mormon* is most conspicuous. He leaped into the public arena, threw down his gage of battle and dared the traducers of the Saints of God to take it up. The very name Mormon—which they had derided and made the synonym for all that was absurd in religion, impure in social life, or disloyal to government, he took up and made the title of his paper—wrote it in bold letters and surrounded it with the symbols of liberty, intelligence and truth, and defied its slanderers to pluck from it the emblems in which he enshrined it.

"We are Mormon," he writes in the first number, "inside and outside; at home or abroad, in public and private—everywhere. We are so, however, from principle. We are such, not because we believe it to be the most popular, lucrative, or honorable (as the world has it); but because we believe it to be true, and more reasonable and scriptural, moral and philosophic; because we conscientiously believe it is more calculated to promote the happiness and well-being of humanity, in time and throughout all eternity, than any other system which we have met with."

A short time afterward we have him saying: "We have said before and say now, that we defy all the editors and writers in the United States to prove that Mormonism is less moral, scriptural, philosophical; or that there is less patriotism in Utah than in any other part of the United States. We call for proof; bring on your reasons, gentlemen, if you have any; we shrink not from the investigation, and dare you to the encounter. If you don't do it, and you publish any more of your stuff, we shall brand you as poor, mean, cowardly liars; as men publishing falsehoods knowing them to be so, and shrinking from the light of truth and investigation."

The *New York Mirror*, in calling attention to his presence in the city and the spread of Mormonism, said: "While our public moralists and reformers are making war upon the hotels and taverns and private property of our citizens, a hideous system—an immoral excrescence—is allowed to spring up and overtop the Constitution itself. Why are there no public meetings convened in the tabernacle to denounce Mormonism? The evil has become a notorious fact—its existence cannot be any longer ignored—and it is not therefore prudent that the eyes of the public should be closed to its effects."

To this Elder Taylor replied: "We are ready to meet Mr. Fuller in the tabernacle on this question at any time. We court investigation and have nothing to hide." Mr. Fuller did not accept the challenge; and when, some time afterwards, he repeated his abuse, Elder Taylor taunted him with cowardice and charged him with being guilty of willful falsehood; but the editor of the *Mirror* shrank from the investigation in the tabernacle which he had proposed. His act was truly that of a blustering coward who had raised the cane over the head of his enemy, but was afraid to strike the blow.

The New York *Herald* was as bitter and unfair in its attacks upon the Saints and Mormonism as the *Mirror*; and Elder Taylor was as incisive and fearless in his rejoinders to the former as to the latter. The *Herald* proposed that a meeting be called in Tammany Hall and that the ministers of the several churches should make an expose of the absurdities and wickedness of Mormonism. Elder Taylor promptly announced his willingness to meet those ministers in such a gathering and defend the character and doctrine of the Saints. The meeting was not called. The ministers of the several churches were not fighting Mormonism that way. Slander, vituperation, denunciation, falsehood uttered at times and places where no answer could be made, not discussion open and manly has ever been the methods of Christian ministers against Mormonism.

The New York *Sun* was also in the field against Mormonism, and was behind none of its contemporaries in the bitterness of its attacks. So bitter, indeed, was the press generally, that the *Woman's Advocate*, touched with pity for a people so universally denounced, deplored the lack of charity manifested in the discussion of the Utah question; and when the famine of 1855 threatened the destruction of the Saints in Utah, and the press of the east but ill concealed its rejoicing at the prospect of the solution of the Mormon problem by such a calamity, the same journal lamented the lack of sympathy manifested toward the Mormon people in their trying circumstances, In reply the *Sun* said:

"As to the alleged want of sympathy, it is enough to say that there has yet been no appeal for help from Utah. If an appeal were made in the name of humanity, the degrading and disgusting doctrines of Brigham Young, and others of the priesthood, promulgated as articles of faith, would not hinder the American people from responding to it."

To which Elder Taylor with some warmth answered:

"The *Sun* says there has been no appeal from Utah for help. An appeal for help indeed! They have called for their own, but their rights have been continually withheld, though your statesmen owned their cause was just. And shall they now ask charity of those that robbed and despoiled them of their goods and murdered their best men? We have been robbed of millions and driven from our own firesides into the cold, wintry blasts of the desert, to starve by your charitable institutions, and shall we now crave your paltry sixpences? Talk to us with your hypocritical cant about charity! Pshaw! it's nauseating to everyone not eaten up with your corrupt humbuggery and pharisaical egotism. You forgot you were talking to Americans, born upon the soil of freedom, suckled in liberty, who have inhaled it from their fathers' lips—their ears yet tingling with the tales of a nation's birth—sons of fathers who fought for rights which you, in your bigotry and self-conceit, would fain wrench from them. Intolerance has thrice driven them from their homes, but the wild burst of liberty of '76, now reverberates through the mountain passes of Utah, bidding defiance to mobocracy and its leaders; and hurling mock charity and pretended patriotism back to the fount of corruption from which it issues. The Mormons neither need your sympathy nor your cankered gold. Your malicious slanders only excite contempt for those base enough to utter them. Your contemptible falsehoods fail to ruffle a feather in our caps. The God of Jacob in whom the Mormons trust—He who brought up Israel out of Egypt—He it is who sustained the Mormons in their tedious journeyings over the barren deserts and wild mountain passes of this continent. In the dark hour of trial, amid all their distresses, without friends or home—God upheld and sustained them; He sustains them still, and will cause them to shine forth with the bright radiance of eternal truth over the wide world, long after their malicious slanderers shall have sunk to oblivion in the filth of their own corruptions."

This boldness in rejoinder to all opponents reminds one of the tone of Tertullian's defense of the early Christians. Of him it is said: "His was not the tone of a supplicant pleading for toleration. He demanded justice." So with Elder Taylor.

CHAPTER 29 - A STRANGE SOLUTION

And what of the question of polygamy, which, during the years that *The Mormon* was published, was the slogan of the enemies of the people of Utah—the head and front of Mormon offending? To understand the amount of bitterness infused into the remarks of the press—discussion would be too dignified a term for the denunciation and invectives found in it—the reader must remember that besides being a religious controversy, Mormon plural marriage was also dragged into the politics of the country.

The Democratic party at that period took the ground that the territories were to be free to regulate their domestic institutions in their own way, subject only to the Constitution of the United States. This was the celebrated "Popular Sovereignty" doctrine, which grew up out of the slavery controversy; and was the manner in which certain sections of the pro-slavery party proposed to settle the question of the existence of slavery in the territories—that is by leaving it to the inhabitants of the Territory to establish or reject it on becoming states. The Abolition Party promptly took advantage of their opponents who accepted the "Popular Sovereignty" doctrine, by saying that if the Territories were to be free to regulate their domestic institutions in their own way, then Utah had a right to establish polygamy as well as slavery if she so elected, and thus threw the odium of sustaining polygamy as well as slavery—which they denominated the "Twin relics of barbarism"—upon the popular sovereignty division of the pro-slavery party.

To escape this odium of sustaining a Territory in the right to establish polygamy, if the inhabitants thereof should so desired, the pro-slavery party was more vindictive in its denunciations of Mormon plural marriage than the abolitionists themselves—and thus all parties, with all the bitterness which characterized political discussions in those days were arrayed against Mormonism—especially against plural marriage: and finally, when the Republican Party was organized, in 1856, and adopted the doctrines of the abolitionists, it incorporated in its platform the following:

"*Resolved,* That the Constitution confers upon Congress sovereign power over the Territories of the United States for their government, and that in the exercise of this power it is both the right and the imperative duty of Congress to prohibit in the Territories those twin relics of barbarism, slavery and polygamy."

In the midst of the agitation and bitterness which led up to such a conclusion as this, though unaided and alone—sustained only by his own conviction of the truth of the system of marriage that God had revealed, and conscious of the support and approval of Almighty God—Elder Taylor stood unmoved and fearlessly sustained the rightfulness of Mormon plural marriage against all who opposed it.

In the very first issue of the *Mormon*, under the caption "Polygamy," he said:

"Since this doctrine has been promulgated by us as a part of our religious creed, every variety of opinion has been expressed by men in all classes of society. It has been talked about by religious and irreligious, professors and profane. It has been the theme in the legislative hall, the pulpit, the bar-room and the press. Polygamy and the Mormons, Mormons and polygamy have resounded everywhere. In this our first issue it may be expected that something would be said in relation to this matter. This we undertake as cheerfully as any other task; for we are not ashamed here in this great metropolis of America to declare that we are polygamists. We are not ashamed to proclaim to this great nation, to rulers and people, to the president, senators, legislators, judges; to high and low, rich and poor, priests and people, that we are firm, conscientious believers in polygamy, and that it is part and parcel of our religious creed. We do this calmly, seriously and understandingly, after due deliberation, careful examination and close investigation of its principles and bearings religiously, socially, morally, physically and politically! We unhesitatingly pronounce our full and implicit faith in the principle as emanating from God, and that under His direction it would be a blessing to the human family."

After drawing a vivid picture of the immoral state of the world, and allowing that some who opposed polygamy did so because they considered it as a scheme devised to still further plunge humanity into licentiousness, he continues:

"We are not surprised, then, that men of reflection and virtue, and having a knowledge of the world should feel indignant at polygamy. They look upon it as something pandering to the brutal passions of man; and from the exceedingly low standard of virtue, can scarcely conceive of anything but lasciviousness associated with the sex. We respect the conscientious feelings of such men; for we know that with their ideas of such things, they must be extremely revolting. But we would respectfully ask such persons if they ever seriously reflected upon the matter? And further: Is it prejudice, education and the corrupt state of society that has led them to these conclusions [respecting plural marriage]; or matters of fact deduced from scripture, reason, history or precedence? Did they ever think that Abraham, Jacob, David, Solomon and a host of other good men mentioned in the scriptures were polygamists? That the Twelve Tribes of Israel, to whom belong the covenants and promises, descended from four women, the wives of one man? Did they ever reflect that those men were more virtuous than this generation; and that for such things that are practiced here every day with impunity—adultery—a man would be stoned to death by all Israel? Did they ever reflect that it might be possible for the Lord to be unchangeable? That He had not learned much from man in a few thousand years; and that possibly He was not in error then; and if not then, the same principles might probably be as correct now as they were at that time? It is well for us not to be too hasty."

Referring again to the sexual corruption everywhere prevalent, and the vain endeavors of philanthropists, statesmen, kings and presidents to check it, he concludes by saying: "The Lord's way [plural marriage] as practiced by ancient men of God—the restitution of which has lately taken place—we think will stop it among us."

Upon these lines he continued to defend the marriage system which God revealed; and when the press, for want of better argument, denounced it as immoral, and pretended to be shocked at Mormon wickedness, because they believed it right under certain conditions for a man to have more wives than one; Elder Taylor drew aside the flimsy veil covering the licentious practices of monogamous "Christian" communities, and reminded his opponents that the cities and towns and states in which they themselves lived, were not so immaculate in their purity that ministers, editors and moralists must needs cross the plains and the mountains, in order to find impurity to suppress. He reminded them that the demon of licentiousness stalked abroad unchallenged in their own midst; that he was to be found in their guilded ball-rooms and opera houses; met them upon their streets, mingled in their best society and even sat in their pews.

This was no attempt to justify the practice of one evil by pointing to the existence of another; but to remind them of the fact that even if Mormon polygamy was as bad as they represented it to be, there were evils infinitely worse rotting and festering in their very midst, and which they sought in vain to ignore, as they met them at every street corner, flaunted in their public highways, and were disgustingly placarded on their walls; while the victims thereof filled their poor houses, shrieked out their madness in their asylums, lay slowly rotting in their hospitals or sought relief in self-destruction. He referred to these things to show up the hypocrisy of a generation that could live in the midst of such social corruption, without an effort to check its ravages; and at the same time pretend to be horrified at supposed social evils existing in distant Utah. In this he further resembled Tertullian, of whom it is said, that being arraigned as a criminal at the bar, he accused and condemned his judges.

But while he uncovered for an instant the corruptions of monogamous Christian communities, in order to reprove their hypocrisy, he by no means regarded that exposure as a defense of plural marriage. His defense of that doctrine he based upon the sanction which Almighty God gave to it, as clearly demonstrated in holy writ; upon well known physiological facts; upon moral and social necessities, and his defense was unassailable.

While he was in New York a number of plans were suggested for the overthrow of Mormonism. Among the more humane ones was that of the American Bible Society, which proposed flooding the settlements of Utah with Bibles, being under the impression, doubtless, that the Mormon people did not accept the Bible as the word of God. Hearing of the project Elder Taylor called at the office of the society and offered his assistance in the enterprise, urging them to send well bound books, and gave them the following advice through *The Mormon*:

"Our mountaineers never do things by halves or for appearance; if they carry Bibles they mean to use them; they'll read them frequently and thoroughly, too. We have a Bible that has kept us company many years on our pilgrimage through life; it has dangled in our pockets many a thousand miles, when, for the gospel's sake, we have visited towns, cities and hamlets. We have had to patch it together frequently, and in fact our friend has got so covered over with our own notes and references, that a white spot is scarcely discernible. We would, therefore, respectfully suggest to the managers of the American Bible Society—if they propose doing real good to the inhabitants of Utah in the Bible line—do it, gentlemen, respectably, for the inhabitants of that Territory will probably use them as we have ours."

Whether his visit and these remarks dashed the ardor of the Bible Society in the undertaking or not, or convinced them of its uselessness, I do not know, but certain it is that the project failed.

Shortly afterwards the *Sun*, seized with a sudden spasm of confidence that Christianity could overwhelm Mormonisn, called upon the churches of New York to send out ministers to convert the Mormons from the error of their ways. Elder Taylor approved of the undertaking, and gave assurance that they would be well treated and receive respectful attention; but he at the same time expressed his doubts as to their going, and referred to the failure of the Bible Society, saying:

"The Bible Society got up a report about two months ago, that they were going to send a Bible agent to Utah. We then hastened to offer them our co-operation, but as we advanced to receive the precious gifts, they vanished into their original element—gas!"

But of all the schemes for the suppression of Mormonism, there was one suggested by the New York *Herald*, which for vileness, stood pre-eminent. In August, 1854, Lieutenant-Colonel E. J. Steptoe arrived in Salt Lake, with a detachment of United States troops *en route* for California, but remained in Utah until the following spring. During their stay, it is said, that members of the command prostituted a number of squaws and also seduced and betrayed several white women. The latter, having lost caste among their former associates, followed their betrayers to California. When this item of news reached the East, the New York *Herald* made the following comments and recommendations:

"This is momentous news, and very significant withal. It shows that the Mormon women are ripe for rebellion, and that a detachment of the regular army is a greater terror to the patriarchs of the Mormon Jerusalem than Indians or drouth or grasshoppers. It indicates the way, too, for the abolishment of the peculiar institution of Utah. The astonishing results of the expedition of Colonel Steptoe, in this view, do most distinctly suggest the future policy of the government, touching this nest of Mormons. It is to send out to the Great Salt Lake, a fresh detachment of young, good-looking soldiers, and at the end of two or three months, order them off to California and replace them by a new detachment at Salt Lake City and so on until those Turks of the desert are reduced, by female desertions, to the standard Christian regulation of one wife apiece. Unquestionably, if, with a taking detachment of the army in a new and showy uniform, the President were to send out to Utah at this crisis of impending famine, a corps of regular disciplined woman's rights women, to lay down the law to their sisters among the Mormons, they would soon compel the patriarchal authorities of Salt

Lake to an exodus to some other region beyond the reach of our gallant army, and our heroic warriors in petticoats, who know their rights, and knowing, dare maintain them. The hint should be appropriated by the administration, for, if under the doctrine of squatters' sovereignty, we cannot constitutionally reach this crying evil of polygamy at Salt Lake, we must reach it by stratagem. We recommend, therefore, to the President and Secretary of the Interior, the policy of detailing another detachment of troops for Great Salt Lake City with the auxiliary force of half a dozen regular woman's rights women whatever the cost; and thus even should the grasshoppers fail to conquer the Territory in the expulsion of the Saints, the work may be done by a revolution among the wives of the apostles."

To this shameless gloating over the downfall of innocence, and still more infamous recommendation, Elder Taylor remarked:

"Such then is the *modus operandi* proposed! Gentlemenly debauchee officers are to be sent out—'good looking ones,' that they may be the better able to take away from vice the horrid appearance it would have dressed in another garb. After these shall have performed their work of misery and death, they are to be recruited by others—fine, dashing, young, good-looking fellows, who will be quite competent to deceive and destroy; real Christian gentlemen with 'new, showy uniforms,' who will be able to corrupt the daughters of Utah, and introduce Christianity in all its beauty as practiced in the United States. They are to take with them a number of pals,—'woman's rights women,' who are to assist in their conversion, and to show them their rights, that the inhabitants of Utah may have ocular demonstration of the beautiful workings of monogamous Christianity, and be brought back to the standard Christian regulation of one wife apiece—and as many misses or fast young women as suits our convenience, that a deadly blow may be struck at the virtue of Utah: and that she may be crowded with voluptuaries, and prostitutes like all other good Christian states and cities; that debauchery and corruption may run riot, that we may have our procuresses, pimps, cyprians, hotel accommodations, and houses of assignation; that virtue, chastity and purity may be banished from Utah; that our daughters may be prostituted and our wives debauched; that we may have our *nymphis du pave*, our 'Five points,' our Randall's Island, our infanticides, our *Maisons d'accouchment*, our diseases, doctors and hospitals and all the other appliances of a good Christian community. That when officers, lawyers, judges, soldiers and Gentiles in general go to Utah they can find the same conveniences and accommodations that are to be met with everywhere among the virtuous Gentile monogamous Christians! And all this glory is to be achieved by the gallant officers and soldiers of our army, under the auspices and direction of James Gordon Bennett.

"What are we to think of a man who is publishing a popular journal, and who publicly and unblushingly advocates seduction, and openly proposes the introduction of debased characters into a Territory for the avowed purpose of seduction, prostitution and infamy, for the purpose of corrupting the Mormons and reducing them to our standard previous to their overthrow?"

CHAPTER 30 - INVASION OF UTAH

Besides defending the character of the Saints in Utah and their religion, *The Mormon* raised its voice for the preservation of the Union. In those years disunion sentiments were rife and schemes for splitting up the country into two or more nations were openly discussed. *The Mormon* sounded a warning to those engaged in such discussions, and called upon the degenerate sons of noble sires to cease such wrangling and preserve the nation bequeathed to them by their fathers.

The Mormon also urged the construction of a railroad to the Pacific coast, and, in short, discussed in an intelligent spirit the general questions then agitating the public mind.

Elder Taylor occasionally visited Washington, and assisted in watching over the interests of the inchoate state of Deseret. He was introduced to and had several interviews with Mr. Franklin Pierce, then the President of the United States. The first of these interviews occurred in the spring of 1855, when President Pierce, following a mistaken popular sentiment, rather than acting from any relish he had for the undertaking, was persuaded to remove Brigham Young from the office of Governor of Utah. In this interview President Pierce submitted the proposition to Elder Taylor and spoke very highly of the urbanity, wise conservatism and honor of Colonel Steptoe, the man he had in his mind to appoint as Governor Young's successor.

Elder Taylor expressed his pleasure at learning that Colonel Steptoe was so honorable a gentleman, and took occasion to tell the

President that the people of Utah had been so frequently abused by incompetent men who seemed determined to make a hobby of the Mormon question whereon to ride into power, that they began to think their rights were infringed upon and that they were used as a convenience for unprincipled political aspirants, who frequently not only interfered with their political but with their religious rights.

The President assured him that Colonel Steptoe would not resort to such meanness.

Elder Taylor then referred to the circumstances under which Utah had been settled, in all of which Brigham Young was their trusted leader; that if any man had a claim upon that position it was Governor Young. Besides, accepting the doctrine of popular sovereignty, the people of Utah considered that their wishes as to who should govern them ought to be somewhat consulted, and if that were done, Brigham Young would be the universal choice of the people. Still he assured the President that he need have no anxiety as to any difficulty arising from his appointing another man: for while the people would think it an act going to the extent of his authority, they of course recognized the authority of the President of the United States, and would submit to any legal or constitutional enactment.

Colonel Steptoe during his stay in Utah was tendered the governorship of Utah by the President, but he refused to accept it, and joined in a petition to President Pierce praying for the re-appointment of Brigham Young, both as Governor and Superintendent of Indian Affairs. Governor Young was accordingly re-appointed.

In March, 1856, a Constitutional Convention was held in Salt Lake City, and a constitution, republican in spirit and liberal in its provisions, was adopted. John Taylor and George A. Smith, appointed delegates to present Utah's request for admission into the sisterhood of states. Elder Taylor joined his colleague in Washington during the summer of 1856, and labored among the members of Congress with a view of having a bill introduced for the admission of Utah. The Republican party, however, was already in the field with its platform that denominated polygamy and slavery as "twin relics" of barbarism. This marshaled all the Republicans against the admission of Utah; and so desirous were the Democrats to cast off the odium of befriending a polygamous people, that they were more bitter in their denunciation of the Mormons, if possible, than the Republicans. Even Senator Stephen A. Douglas, who had been a professed friend of the Mormon people, and who had been intimately acquainted with the Prophet Joseph, and in addition to that was recognized as the champion of the Popular Sovereignty doctrine, turned against them, and in a speech delivered in Springfield, Illinois, early in 1856, referred to Mormonism as "the loathsome ulcer of the body politic."

Under such circumstances it would have been folly to have pushed the claims of Utah in Congress; it would only have invited defeat, therefore the delegates decided to withhold any introduction of the matter at that time.

In addition to all these labors, Elder Taylor rendered considerable valuable assistance in looking after the emigration business of the Church, especially in caring for the poor, who, having started from England, could get no further than New York. These he found employment for and watched over them with all the interest of a brother and a friend. He also directed the labors of the brethren who were preaching the gospel in the east and presided over all the churches. When he first went to the east to preside, the branches were disorganized, the Saints were scattered and like sheep without shepherds. But his assuming control of affairs was the signal for activity everywhere, and the work of the Lord revived. In reporting the progress of the work, early in 1856, we have him saying in *The Mormon*:

"It affords me very much pleasure to have to state that since the arrival of myself and brethren in these eastern states, Mormonism assumes quite another aspect: we have large and flourishing churches in different parts of this state, [New York] which are continually increasing, not only by emigration but by baptisms. The Spirit of the Lord rests among the assemblies of the Saints; the inquiries after truth are many; the floods of falsehood with which this country was deluged before our arrival are being dissipated, and the light of eternal truth is bursting forth with resplendence and glory."

The spirit of reformation which in those days moved on in such mighty power among the Saints in Utah, extended its operations among the Saints in the east, and there was a general awakening to a sense of duty and responsibility. President Young in a letter to Elder Taylor under date of October 30th, 1856, urged him to take up the work of reformation. He said:

"Brother Taylor, we are arousing the people of this Territory to a sense of their obligations and their duties; great and thorough reformations are pervading every quorum, every family, neighborhood and settlement. The power of the Highest is resting down upon us, and blessing our exertions. We wish to suggest to you that probably a reformation might transpire in New York among the Saints, and in other states, and in Europe and other places where there are any Saints. Arouse you, then, first getting the Holy Ghost, and be ye filled with it, and pour it out upon the people. Preach evenings, make appointments in the various branches and fill them. Make the Elders feel the fire in you, and make them labor."

With many such words did he urge him forward to this work. But long before the slow mails brought the letter to hand, Elder Taylor had been seized with the spirit that the words of President Young were calculated to arouse within him; and the work of reformation was well advanced on the arrival of the letter. The speed of the Spirit of God out-ran the tardy mails, and communicated the will of the Lord to His servant.

Meantime the adversary was not idle. A number of United States officials that had been sent to Utah turned out to be the vilest of characters. Vain, ambitious, corrupt, revengeful, hypocritical; and evidently regarding the Mormons as their legitimate prey—as a people having no rights which they were under obligations to respect. As the time-serving, villainous Oswald, in King Lear, looked upon the eyeless head of the unfortunate, traitor-proclaimed and yet innocent Gloucester, as being framed to raise his fortunes, so did these impudent, corrupt officials regard the Mormon people; and hoped by opposing their unpopular religion, and social customs—

with which they had, of right, nothing to do—to ride into popular favor and good fortune. Utah was to be a convenient stepping-stone to higher political preferment.

The outrages of these officials reached a climax in the conduct of Associate Judge W. W. Drummond; who, having deserted his wife in Illinois, brought with him a prostitute who sat by him on the judicial bench in open court; and in various ways insulted the people by unwarranted assaults upon institutions religious and social which they held to be most sacred; and even their territorial laws, to which the government at Washington had taken no exceptions whatever, were threatened by this gambler and black-leg, upon whose unworthy shoulders the ermine had been unwisely thrown. To the honor of the Mormon community, he did not long remain in the Territory to disgrace her judiciary, but fled in fear from Utah to California, from which place he wrote his resignation and falsely reported to the Attorney-General that the Mormons were in open rebellion to the government; that the records and papers of the supreme court had been destroyed by order of the Church; that Brigham Young and other leading Church officials were responsible for the murder of a number of U. S. officials who had died in the Territory, and others who had been massacred by Indians.

Upon receiving these statements from Judge Drummond, President Buchanan, without taking the pains to ascertain the truth or falsehood of them, about the latter part of May, 1857, ordered an army into Utah to suppress this imaginary rebellion.

Many criticisms were made upon the evident inconsiderate action of President Buchanan in this affair. Elder Taylor, in a discussion he had some years later on the "Mormon Question" with Vice-President Schuyler Colfax, in referring to this action on the part of the government, says: "Mr. Buchanan had another object in view, [than that of suppressing the "Mormon Rebellion"] and Mr. J. B. Floyd, Secretary of War, had also his ax to grind, and the whole combined was considered a grand*coup d'etat*. It is hardly necessary to inform Mr. Colfax that this army, under pretense of subjugating the Mormons, was intended to coerce the people of Kansas to his views, and that they were not detained, as stated by Mr. Colfax's history, which said: 'The troops necessarily moving slowly were overtaken by the snows of November and wintered at Bridger.' I need not inform Mr Colfax that another part of this grand tableau originated in the desire of Secretary Floyd to scatter the U. S. forces and arms preparatory to the Confederate Rebellion. Such is history and such are facts."

John B. Floyd, Secretary of War in Buchanan's cabinet, was from Virginia, and favored the southern cause, as indeed the whole administration and the party that elected it did; so that Elder Taylor's charge respecting the scattering of United States forces, rests upon the ground of strong probability. Relative to the charge that under pretence of subjugating Utah the President intended to coerce the people of Kansas to an acceptance of his views, it is true that part of the army for Utah left Fort Leavenworth before the last of July; but Brigadier-General Harney, to whom the command of the expedition had been given, remained with several squadrons of the second dragoons in Kansas, until after the elections in that Territory in October; and President Buchanan was involved in an intrigue to defeat the popular will in Kansas.

There is, however, another consideration which I doubt not influenced the action of the administration in sending an army to Utah. The party that supported the administration was anxious to give proof to the country that it was no more favorable to the unpopular Mormons than the Republican party was; and seized upon the false reports of Judge Drummond as a golden opportunity to out-herod Herod, hoping by that movement to throw off the odium its opponents had fastened upon it in charging that its doctrines of popular sovereignty would permit the people of Utah to establish polygamy as well as slavery if they so elected.

It was in May, 1857, that Elder Taylor left New York for the west. Judge William I. Appleby and T. B. H. Stenhouse were left in charge of *The Mormon*, and continued its publication until September 19th, when it was discontinued, principally on account of the threatened "Mormon War."

CHAPTER 31 - LET THE TRIAL COME

Elder Taylor arrived in Salt Lake City from his mission to the eastern states on the 7th of August, 1857. Two days later, in the bowery on the Temple square, he preached a powerful discourse, in which he represented what the spirit of the people of the east was in respect to Mormonism, and dwelt at some length on the grandeur of the mission in which the Saints had engaged.

He was followed by President Young, who took occasion to commend the labors of the committee appointed to present Utah's claims for admission into the Union (Elder Taylor was one of the committee, it will be remembered), and respecting the individual labors of Elder Taylor, expressed himself as follows:

"With regard to the labors of Brother Taylor in editing the paper called *The Mormon*, published in the city of New York, I have heard many remarks concerning the editorials in that paper, not only from the Saints, but from those who do not profess to believe the religion we have embraced; and it is probably one of the strongest edited papers that is now published. I can say, as to its editorials, that it is one of the strongest papers ever published, so far as my information extends; and I have never read one sentence in them but what my heart could bid success to it, and beat a happy response to every sentence that I have read or heard read. Brother Taylor, that is for you; and I believe that these are the feelings and the sentiments of all in this community who have perused that paper."

It was a critical time in Utah when he returned. For several years the crops, through excessive drought and grass-hoppers, had been at least a partial failure; the isolation of the people from manufacturing and commercial centers, with very limited and very slow means of transportation, had left them almost destitute of clothing; an army was *enroute* for the Territory, but as to its mission the governor received no definite information, though there was a general and a fairly accurate understanding that its mission was not one of intended peace and good will to the people of Utah. If its mission was to be judged by the boasts of its officers and men, there was to be a sort of "Mormon conquest," and Mormon houses, gardens, orchards, vineyards, fields, and also Mormon wives and daughters were to be the spoils. The very houses were picked out that certain persons were to inhabit; farms, property and women were to be distributed. "Beauty and booty" were their very watchwords.

It had already been determined by Governor Young and his associates that such an army with such objects in view should not enter the Territory, even if it had to be prevented by force of arms. It had further been determined that before their enemies should again revel in the homes which their industry had built, they would burn them to ashes; cut down every fruit-tree and shrub, burn the fences, and leave the country behind them a ruined, blackened waste, while they fled again to the wilderness. These were bold measures. The "army of Utah," as the invading force was called, marched under the United States flag; it was commanded by United States officers; it had been ordered to Utah by the President of the United States; and to resist it might be construed into rebellion or even treason—that meant hanging, to the leaders, who opposed it. Yet bold as these measures were, and fraught with such serious consequences to the leaders who adopted them, they were fearlessly proclaimed, and would have been as promptly executed on occasion.

Among that brave band of men who had the courage to thus proclaim their rights, and dared to maintain them even against the United States, none were more bold or fearless than John Taylor. In speech and action he went as far as he who went farthest. In the council chamber and in the field he was in the front rank; shoulder to shoulder he stood with President Young and his brethren, and his public discourses in those times glow with a soul-stirring eloquence that reminds one of the spirit of the Revolutionary patriots of '76. In the very discourse delivered two days after his return from the east, he said:

"So far as I am concerned, I say let everything come as God has ordained it. I do not desire trials; I do not desire affliction; I would pray to God to leave me not in temptation; but if the earthquake bellows, the lightnings flash, the thunders roll and the powers of darkness are let loose, and the spirit of evil is permitted to rage and an evil influence is brought to bear on the Saints, and my life with theirs, is put to the test—let it come. I know that President Young and those associated with him are full of the spirit of revelation, and they know what they are doing; I feel to acquiesce and put my shoulder to the work, whatever it is. If it is for peace, let it be peace; if it is for war, let it be to the hilt."

Speaking again in the latter part of the same month, he stated and expounded the principles which justified the resistance of the people of Utah to the proceedings of the administration at Washington. His speech on that occasion was a sound exposition of the rights of the people inhabiting the Territories as against the encroachments of the general government, and should be preserved as a valuable addition to the political literature extant upon that subject. After disclaiming any disposition on his own or on the part of his brethren to commit the act of treason, Elder Taylor said:

"There are thousands of you who are Americans, who have been born in this land, whose fathers fought for the liberties we used to enjoy, but have not enjoyed for some years past. There are thousands of such men here who feel the same spirit that used to burn in their father's bosoms—the spirit of liberty and equal rights—the spirit of according to every man that which belongs to him, and of robbing no man of his rights. Your fathers and grandfathers met the tyrant when he sought to put a yoke on their necks; as men and true patriots, they came forward and fought for their rights and in defense of that liberty which we, as their children, ought to enjoy. You feel the same spirit that inspired them; the same blood that coursed through their veins flows in yours; you feel true patriotism and a strong attachment to the Constitution and institutions bought by the blood of your fathers, and bequeathed to you by them as your richest patrimony. There are others of you that have taken the oath of allegiance to the United States; and some of you not understanding correct principles, may, perhaps, feel qualms of conscience, and think, probably, that if we undertake to resist the powers that are seeking to make aggression upon us, we are doing wrong. No such thing. You let your conscience sleep at ease; let it be quiet; it is not we who are doing wrong; it is others who are committing wrong upon us."

He then referred to the circumstance of the Saints being driven from Missouri, and of their expulsion from Nauvoo—not for any ill that they had done, not that they had interfered with the rights of others; but because there was not virtue enough either in state or general government to protect an innocent, helpless people in the enjoyment of their Constitutional rights; because, for sooth, they were unpopular—friendless. The speaker then asked:

"What did we do when we came here? We framed a Constitution, a provisional government, and reported our doings to the United States. Right on the back of all the insults, robbery and fraud which we had endured, we still went Constitutionally to work. Afterwards they gave us a territorial government. Is there any step that we have taken that is contrary to law? There is not. They have appointed our governor, our secretaries, our judges, our marshals; they have done to us the same in this matter as they have done with other Territories. I do not believe in their right Constitutionally to appoint our officers. Still they have done it, and we have submitted to it. And they have sent some of the worst scoundrels here that ever existed on the earth. Instead of being fathers, they have tried every influence they could bring to bear in order to destroy us. Such have been our protectors! Those have been the men who have been sworn to fulfill their public duties; but they have foresworn themselves in the face of high heaven. We have submitted to their sending officers here; that is all right enough if we have a mind to. We are citizens of the United States, and profess to support the

Constitution of the United States; and wherein that binds us we are bound; wherein it does not, we are not bound. If there is any man in this congregation, or anywhere else, that will show me any principle or authority in the Constitution of the United States that authorizes the President of the United States to send out governors and judges to this Territory, I would like to see it. I cannot find such authority. I will admit that a usage of that kind has obtained—that it is quite customary for the President of the United States, by and with the consent of the senate to appoint governors, judges, marshals, secretaries, and all of those officers that you have had here. But it is a thing that is not authorized by the Constitution,—much less to force them upon us by an armed soldiery. There is no such authority existing.

"I will quote to you from the Constitution—if I had the Constitution here I would read it to you—it is to the effect 'that the powers not delegated to the United States by the Constitution, nor prohibited by it to the states, are reserved to the states respectively, or to the people.' No matter, therefore, whether the people live in the states or territories, they possess constitutional privileges alike. The most that is said in regard to Territories and the authority of the President or Congress is, that 'The Congress shall have power to dispose of and make all needful rules and regulations respecting the territory *or other property* of the United States,' that is speaking of it as land; and some of the most prominent statesmen of the United States have so construed it. It is property as land—territory as land they have a right to interfere with, not territory as regards people. I published this in *The Mormon* long ago, and said the Missouri Compromise was unconstitutional. By and by the United States judges gave the same decision. I gave mine, however, before they gave theirs. It is a true principle—they have not the authority. If they have it at all, it is in the people ceding it to them, and not what they possess by the Constitution of the United States. So far as right is concerned, then, they have no right to appoint officers for this or any other Territory; and I will defy any man to prove that there is any such right in the Constitution.

"I conversed with a judge Black who was coming up to Nebraska Territory on a steam boat—an intelligent man, a Democrat, of course. When talking about these principles to him, which he acceded to, I said: 'Judge, what are you doing here?'

'I am here,' said he, 'according to the usage that has obtained; but if the people do not want me, all they have to do is to express it, and I will go away again.' I wish we had only half such decent men as that sent here.

"We are not lacking for men in the United States, at the present time who want to make it appear that the United States have a right to lord it over the Territories, the same as the British government used to over their colonies. Thousands of you before me were citizens of the United States, where you came from. You had the right of franchise—had a right to say who should be your governor and who should be municipal and state officers. You came out here by thousands or by tens of thousands. *By what right or upon what principle are you disfranchised*? Can anybody tell me? Say some: 'You need not have come out here unless you had a mind to.' Of course not. But we had a mind to; we were American citizens before we came out, and we have transgressed no law in coming; and by what rule are we deprived of our citizenship. If we had a right then to vote for anything, we have a right now; and nobody has a right to crowd this or that man upon us without our consent,—much less have they a right to dragoon us into servility to their unconstitutional exactions.

"In the Declaration of Independence, it is stated [as one of the just causes of complaint against the English government] that the people had rulers placed over them, and they had no voice in their election. Read that instrument. It describes our wrongs as plainly as it did the wrongs the people then labored under and discarded. Our government is doing the very things against us that our fathers complained of—'They send armed mercenaries among us to subjugate us.' What is our government doing? The same thing."

"As American citizens and patriots, and as sons of those venerable sires can we, without disgracing ourselves, our fathers and our nation, submit to these insults, and tamely bow to such tyranny?

We cannot do it, and we will not do it. We will rally round the Constitution, and declare our rights as American citizens; and we will sustain them in the face of high heaven and the world.

"No man need have any qualms of conscience that he is doing wrong. You are patriots, standing by your rights and opposing the wrong which affects all lovers of freedom as well as you; for those acts of aggression have a withering, deadly effect, and are gnawing like a canker worm at the very vitals of civil and religious liberty. You are standing by the Declaration of Independence, and sustaining the Constitution which was given by inspiration of God; and you are the only people in the United States at this time that are doing it. You dare do it, and you feel right about the matter.

"We are not taking any steps contrary to the laws and the Constitution of the United States, but in everything we are upholding and sustaining them. *Gentlemen, hands off*! We are free men; we possess equal rights with other men; and if you send your sealed orders here, we may break the seal, and it shall be the opening of the first seal!"

Such, then, were the principles which justified the resistance of Utah to the encroachments of the general government. The Mormons were not religious enthusiasts—fanatics—rebels—seeking to become a law unto themselves; but patriots demanding their rights—rights based upon the broad principles of liberty as set forth in the Declaration of Independence, and guaranteed in the Constitution of their country. They were contending for the right to regulate their own local affairs in their own way, and to be governed by men of their own choosing—they were but walking in the footsteps of their Revolutionary Fathers.

CHAPTER 32 - SURPRISE AND PERPLEXITY

The advanced companies of the "Army of Utah," having reached Ham's Fork, a tributary of Green River, late in the autumn of 1857, Captain Van Vliet was sent to Salt Lake to purchase forage and lumber and assure the people of Utah that the troops would not harm or molest them. The captain arrived on the 8th of September and was cordially received by the leading Elders of the Church, among others by Elder Taylor.

His mission as to forage and lumber was unsuccessful, neither did he make the people believe the statement that the troops would not harm them. The very natural question was, 'Why are they coming to Utah, then'? An army naturally suggests the idea of war, and war means violence.

The captain's visit, however, was not in vain. He learned that the Mormons had much to justify them in the stand they had taken, and, moreover, that they were very determined in it. He attended service the Sabbath after his arrival, and that day Elder Taylor addressed the assembly. In the course of his remarks he asked the people:

"What would be your feelings if the United States wanted to have the honor of driving us from our homes, and bringing us subject to their depraved standard of moral and religious truth? Would you, if necessary, brethren, put the torch to your buildings and lay them in ashes and wander houseless into these mountains? I know what you would say and what you would do."

President Brigham Young.—"Try the vote."

Elder Taylor.—"All you that are willing to set fire to your property and lay it in ashes rather than submit to their military rule and oppression, manifest it by raising your hands."

The congregation, numbering more than four thousand, unanimously raised their hands.

Elder Taylor.—"I know what your feelings are. We have been persecuted and robbed long enough; and in the name of Israel's God, we will be free!"

Congregation responded "Amen!"

President Young.—"I say amen all the time to that."

Elder Taylor.—"I feel to thank God that I am associated with such men, with such people, where honesty and truth dwell in the heart—where men have a religion that they are not afraid to live by, and that they are not afraid to die by; and I would not give a straw for anything short of that."

Captain Van Vliet's surprise was little short of astonishment. He was not prepared to expect such unanimity of sentiment nor such determination of purpose. He admired their courage, but trembled for their safety in a conflict with the government. He pointed out the fact that if they successfully resisted the army then on their borders, the next year would see an overwhelming force sent to suppress and punish them. His remonstrance was answered:

"We know that will be the case; but when these troops arrive they will find Utah a desert; every house will be burned to the ground; every tree cut down and every field laid waste. We have three years' provisions on hand, which we will cache, and then take to the mountains and bid defiance to all the powers of the government."

The captain returned to the army on Ham's Fork deeply impressed with the seriousness and perhaps with the absurdity of the government's movement against Utah. Moreover he had become the friend of the Mormon people, and his report to the Secretary of War, made at Washington the November following, did much, doubtless, in paving the way for an amicable adjustment of the Utah difficulties.

Shortly after the departure of the captain, Elder Taylor received a letter from Captain Marcy, of the 5th Infantry, camped with the army on Ham's Fork; and as Elder Taylor's reply to that letter is a thoughtful exposition of the causes which led up to the Utah expedition, and a scathing rebuke to the administration that inaugurated it, as well as a fair sample of Elder Taylor's literary style and gentlemanly sensibility, I give the correspondence *in extenso*:

Captain MARCY'S LETTER.

"CAMP OF THE 5TH INFANTRY ON HAM'S FORK,

"October 13th, 1857.

"Herewith I take the liberty of sending you a letter of introduction from our mutual friend, W. J. A. Fuller, of New York City. I also beg leave to trouble you with the accompanying note of introduction to Governor Young from Mr. W. I. Appleby, which I will thank you to read to the governor at your convenience.

"When I left the states I expected to have the honor of delivering these letters in person, but as our movements are so slow, I have thought it better to transmit them by the bearer, hoping that the opportunity may be afforded me of paying my personal respects at some future time.

"In the meantime, suffer me to assure you that within the circle of my observation among the officers of this army, there has not been the slightest disposition to meddle with or in any way interfere with the religious or social customs of your people; on the contrary, there has, from the commencement of our march, been an almost universal manifestation of a desire for a kind and friendly intercourse: and I most sincerely hope that this desirable result may be brought about.

"I verily believe that all the officers entertain the same feelings towards the Mormons as Captain Van Vliet, and I entertain no doubt that an acquaintance with them would satisfy you that such is the fact.

"I am very respectfully and truly yours,

"R. B. MARCY.

"Rev. John Taylor,

"Great Salt Lake City, Utah Territory."

ELDER TAYLOR'S REPLY.

"GREAT SALT LAKE CITY,

"October 21, 1857.

"Captain Marcy.

"MY DEAR SIR: I embrace this the earliest opportunity of answering your communication to me, embracing a letter from Mr. Fuller, New York, to you, an introductory letter to me, and also one from W. I. Appleby to Governor Young; the latter immediately on its receipt I forwarded to His Excellency. And here let me state, sir, that I sincerely regret that circumstances now existing have hitherto prevented a personal interview.

"I can readily believe your statement that it is very far from your feelings and most of the command that are with you to interfere with our social habits or religious views. One must naturally suppose that among gentlemen educated for the army alone, who have been occupied by the study of the art of war, whose pulses have throbbed with pleasure at the contemplation of the deeds of our venerated fathers, whose minds have been elated by the recital of the heroic deeds of other nations, and who have listened almost exclusively to the declamations of patriots and heroes, that there is not much time and less inclination to listen to the low party bickerings of political demagogues, the interested twaddle of sectional declaimers, or the throes and contortions of contracted religious bigots.

You are supposed to stand on elevated ground, representing the power and securing the interests of the whole of a great and mighty nation. That many of you are thus honorable, I am proud as an American citizen to acknowledge, but you must excuse me, my dear sir, if I cannot concede with you that all your officials are so high-toned, disinterested, humane and gentlemanly, as a knowledge of some of their antecedents would expressly demonstrate. However, it is not with the personal character, the amiable qualities, high-toned feelings, or gentlemanly deportment of the officers in your expedition that we at present have to do.

The question that concerns us is one that is independent of your personal, generous, friendly and humane feeling, or any individual predilection of yours; it is one that involves the dearest rights of American citizens, strikes at the root of our social and political existence, if it does not threaten our entire annihilation from the earth. Excuse me, sir, when I say that you are merely the servants of a lamentably corrupt administration, that your primary law is obedience to orders, and that you come here with armed foreigners, with cannons, rifles, bayonets and broadswords, expressly and for the openly avowed purpose of 'cutting out the loathsome ulcer from the body politic.'

"I am aware what our friend Fuller says in relation to this matter, and I entertain no doubt of his generous and humane feelings, nor do I of yours, sir, but I do know that he is mistaken in relation to the rabid tone and false, furious attacks of a venal and corrupt press. I do know that they are merely the mouthpiece, the tools, the barking dogs of a corrupt administration. I do know that Mr. Buchanan was well apprised of the nature of the testimony adduced against us by ex-Judge Drummond and others, for he was informed of it to my knowledge by a member of his own cabinet. And I further know from personal intercourse with members of the Senate and House of Representatives of the United States, that there have been various plans concocted at headquarters for some time past for the overthrow of this people. Captain, Mr. Fuller informs me that you are a politician. If so, you must know that in the last presidential campaign that the Republican party had opposition to slavery and polygamy as two of the principal planks in their platform. You may know, sir, that Utah was picked out, and the only Territory excluded from a participation in pre-emption rights to land. You may also be aware that bills were introduced into Congress for the prosecution of the Mormons, but other business was too pressing at that time for them to receive attention. You may be aware that measures were also set on foot and bills prepared to divide up Utah among the Territories of Nebraska, Kansas, Oregon and New Mexico, (giving a slice to California) for the purpose of bringing us into collision with the people of those Territories.

"I might enumerate injuries by the score—not to say anything about thousands of our letters detained at the post office at Independence—and if these things are not so, why is it that Utah is so *knotty a question?* If people were no more ready to interfere with us and our institutions than we are with them and theirs, these difficulties would vanish into thin air. Why, again I ask, could Drummond and a host of other mean scribblers, palm off their bare-faced lies with such impunity and have their infamous slanders swallowed with such gusto?

Was it not that the administration and their satellites having planned our destruction, were eager to catch at anything to render specious their contemplated acts of blood? Or, in plain terms, the Democrats advocated strongly popular sovereignty. The Republicans tell them that if they join in maintaining inviolate the domestic institutions of the south, they must also swallow polygamy. The Democrats thought this would not do, as it would interfere with the religious scruples of many of their supporters, and they looked about for some means to dispose of the knotty question.

Buchanan, with Douglas, Cass, Thompson and others of his advisers, after failing to devise legal means, hit upon the expedient of an armed force against Utah, and thus thought by the sacrifice of the Mormons to untie the knotty question; do a thousand times worse than the Republicans ever meant,—fairly out-Herod Herod, and by religiously expatriating, destroying or killing a hundred thousand innocent American citizens satisfy the pious, humane, patriotic feeling of their constituents, take the wind out of the sails of the Republicans, and gain to themselves immortal laurels. Captain, I have heard of a pious Presbyterian doctrine that would inculcate thankfulness to the all-wise Creator for the privilege of being damned. Now, as we are not Presbyterians nor believers in this kind of self-abnegation, you will, I am sure, excuse us for finding fault at being thus summarily dealt with, no matter how agreeable the excision or expatriation might be to our political, patriotic, or very pious friends. We have lived long enough in the world to know that we are a portion of the body politic, that we have some rights as well as other people, and that if others do not respect us, we at least have manhood enough to respect ourselves.

"Permit me here to refer to a remark made by our friend, Mr. Fuller, to you viz., 'that he had rendered me certain services in the city of New York, and that he had no doubt that when you had seen and known us as he had, that you would report as favorably as he had unflinchingly done.' Now those favors, to which Mr. Fuller refers, were simply telling a few plain matters of fact, that had come under his own observation during a short sojourn at Salt Lake.

This, of course, I could duly appreciate, for I always admire a man who dare tell the truth. But, Captain, does it not strike you as humiliating to manhood and to the pride of all honorable American citizens, when among the thousands that have passed through and sojourned among us, and know as well as Mr. Fuller did, our true social and moral position, that perhaps only one in ten thousand dare state his honest convictions? and further, that Mr. Fuller with his knowledge of human nature, should look upon you as a *rare avis*, possessing the moral courage and integrity to declare the truth in opposition to the floods of falsehood that have deluged our nation? Surely we have fallen on unlucky times when honesty is avowed to be at so great a premium!

"In regard to our religion, it is perhaps unnecessary to say much, yet whatever others' feelings may be about it, with us it is honestly a matter of conscience. This is a right guaranteed unto us by the Constitution of our country, yet it is on this ground, and this alone, that we have suffered a continued series of persecutions, and that this present crusade is set on foot against us. In regard to this people, I have traveled extensively in the United States, and through Europe, yet have never found so moral, chaste and virtuous a people, nor do I expect to find them. And if let alone, they are the most patriotic and appreciate more fully the blessing of religious, civil, and political freedom than any other portion of the United States. They have, however, discovered the difference between a blind submission to the caprices of political demagogues, and obedience to the Constitution, laws, and institutions of the United States; nor can they in the present instance be hood-winked by the cry of 'treason.' If it be treason to stand up for our Constitutional rights: if it be treason to resist the unconstitutional acts of a vitiated and corrupt administration, who by a mercenary armed force would seek to rob us of the rights of franchise, cut our throats to subserve their own party, and seek to force upon us their corrupt tools, and violently invade the rights of American citizens; if it be treason to maintain inviolate our homes, our firesides, our wives, and our honor, from the corrupting, and withering blight of a debauched soldiery; if it be treason to maintain inviolate the Constitution and institutions of the United States, when nearly all the states are seeking to trample them under their feet—then indeed are we guilty of treason.

We have carefully considered all these matters, and are prepared to meet the 'terrible vengeance' we have been very politely informed will be the result of our acts. It is in vain to hide it from you that the people have suffered so much from every kind of official that they will endure it no longer. It is not with them an idle phantom, but a stern reality. It is not as some suppose the 'voice of Brigham' only, but the universal, deep settled feeling of the whole community. Their cry is 'Give us our Constitutional rights; give us liberty or death.'

A strange cry, indeed, in our boasted model republic, but a truth deeply and indelibly graven on the hearts of 100,000 American citizens by a series of twenty-seven years unmitigated, and unprovoked, yet unrequited wrongs. Having told you of this, you will not be surprised, that when fifty have been called to assist in repelling our aggressors, hundreds have volunteered; and when a hundred have been called, the number has been more than doubled; the only feeling is, 'don't let us be overlooked or forgotten.' And here let me inform you that I have seen thousands of hands raised simultaneously voting to burn our property rather than let it fall into the hands of our enemies.

Our people have been so frequently robbed and despoiled without redress, that they have solemnly decreed that if they cannot enjoy their own property nobody else shall. You will see by this that it would be literally madness for your small force to attempt to come into the settlements. It would only be courting destruction. But say you: have you counted the cost? have you considered the wealth and power of the United States and the fearful odds against you? Yes, and here let me inform you that if necessitated we would as soon meet 100,000 as 1,000, and if driven to the necessity, will burn every house, tree, shrub, rail, every patch of grass, and stack of straw and hay, and flee to the mountains.

You will then obtain a barren, desolate wilderness, but will not have conquered the people, and the same principle in regard to other property will be carried out. If this people have to burn their property to save it from the hands of legalized mobs, they will see to it that their enemies shall be without fuel; they will haunt them by day and by night. Such is in part our plan. The 300,000 dollars worth of our property destroyed already in Green River County is only a faint sample of what will be done throughout the Territory. We have been thrice driven by tamely submitting to the authority of corrupt officials, and left our houses and homes for others to inhabit; but are now determined that if we are again robbed of our possessions, our enemies shall also feel how pleasant it is to be houseless at least for once, and be permitted as they have sought to do to us,—

"'To dig their own dark graves,
Creep into them and die.'

"You see we are not backward in showing our hands. Is it not strange to what lengths the human family may be goaded by a continued series of oppression? The administration may yet find leisure to pause over the consequences of their acts, and it may yet become a question for them to solve whether they have blood and treasure enough to crush out the sacred principles of liberty from the bosoms of one hundred thousand freemen, and make them bow in craven servility to the mendacious acts of a perjured, degraded tyrant.

"You may have learned already that it is anything but pleasant for even a small army to contend with the chilling blasts of this inhospitable climate. How a large army would fare without resources you can picture to yourself. We have weighed those matters; it is for the administration to post their own accounts. It may not be amiss, however, here to state that if they continue to prosecute this inhuman fratricidal war, and our Nero would light the fires, and, sitting complacently in his chair of state, laugh at burning Rome, there is a day of reckoning even for Neroes. There are generally two sides to a question. As I before said we wish for peace, but that we are determined on having if we have to fight for it. We will not have officers forced upon us who are so degraded as to submit to be sustained by the bayonet's point. We cannot be dragooned into servile obedience to any man.

"These things settled, Captain, and all the little preliminaries of etiquette are easily arranged; and permit me here to state that no man would be more courteous and civil than Governor Young, and neither could you find in your capacity of an officer of the United States a more generous and hearty welcome than at the hands of His Excellency. But when, instead of battling with the enemies of our country, you come (though probably reluctantly) to make war upon my family and friends, our civilities are naturally cooled and we instinctively grasp the sword. Minie rifles, Colt's revolvers, sabres and cannon may display very good workmanship and great artistic skill, but we very much object to having their temper and capabilities tried upon us. We may admire the capabilities, gentlemanly deportment, heroism and patriotism of United States officers; but in an official capacity as enemies, we would rather see their backs than their faces. The guillotine may be a very pretty instrument and show great artistic skill, but I don't like to try my neck in it.

"Now, Captain, notwithstanding all this, I shall be very happy to see you if circumstances should so transpire as to make it convenient for you to come, and to extend to you the courtesies of our city, for I am sure you are not our personal enemy. I shall be happy to render you any information in my power in regard to your contemplated explorations.

"I am heartily sorry that things are so unpleasant at the present time, and I cannot but realize the awkwardness of your position and that of your compatriots; and let me here say that anything that lies in my power compatible with the conduct of a gentleman, you can command.

"If you have leisure I should be most happy to hear from you. You will, I am sure, excuse me, if I disclaim the prefix of Rev. to my name. Address: John Taylor, Great Salt Lake City.

"I need not here assure you that personally there can be no feelings of enmity between us and your officers. We regard you as the agents of the administration only, in the discharge of a probably unpleasant duty, and very likely ignorant of the ultimate designs of the administration. As I left the east this summer you will excuse me when I say I am probably better posted in some of these matters than you are, having been one of a delegation from the citizens of this Territory to apply for admission into the Union. I can only regret that it is not our real enemies that are here instead of you. We do not wish to harm you nor any of the command to which you belong, and I can assure you that in any other capacity than the one you now occupy, you would be received as civilly and treated as courteously as in any other portion of our Union.

"On my departure from the states the fluctuating tide of popular opinion against us seemed to be on the wane. By this time there may be quite a reaction in the public mind. If so it may probably affect materially the position of the administration, and tend to more constitutional, pacific and humane measures. In such an event our relative positions would be materially changed, and instead of meeting as enemies we could meet as all Americans should, friends to each other, and united against our legitimate enemies only. Such an issue is devoutly to be desired, and I can assure you that no one could more appreciate so happy a result to our present awkward and unpleasant position than

"Yours Truly,

"John Taylor"

CHAPTER 33 - MARTIAL LAW DECLARED

It was but a few days after the departure of Captain Van Vliet on his return to the army, that Governor Young issued his proclamation forbidding all armed forces from entering the Territory. He called on the territorial militia to enforce the proclamation, and declared martial law to exist throughout Utah. This action was followed by sending a portion of the militia to watch the movements of the army, and prevent its marching into the Territory.

These military movements were under the immediate supervision of Lieutenant-General Daniel H. Wells; but when he went to the front he was accompanied by Elders Taylor and Geo. A. Smith. Elder Taylor remained with the militia at the front until about the middle of December, when he returned to Salt Lake City, as the legislature, to which he had been elected a member from Salt Lake County, convened in the latter part of that month. He was unanimously chosen Speaker of the House.

The most important action of this legislature was the passage of a memorial to the President and Congress of the United States. It called attention to the fact that a previous legislature had memorialized Congress in respect to the situation in Utah, had set forth the grievances of the people and made known their wishes in regard to the appointment of the U. S. officials for the Territory. They had asked that the said officials be selected from the citizens of Utah, whose interests would be identical with those of the people among whom they administered the law.

The present memorialists reminded the President and Congress that no action had been taken, no answer made to this former memorial, "unless," said they, "it is to be understood that the appointment of a full set of officers for this Territory, backed by an army to enforce them upon us is to be deemed an answer." And then, notwithstanding an army was encamped on their borders, with the prospect of being re-enforced and marched into Salt Lake Valley in the spring, the legislature had the spirit to talk to Congress in the following strain:

"We appeal to you as American citizens who have been wronged, insulted, abused and persecuted; driven before our relentless foes from city to city—from state to state—until we were finally expelled from the confines of civilization to seek a shelter in a barren, inhospitable clime, amid the wild, savage tribes of the desert plains. We claim to be a portion of the people, and as such have rights that must be respected, and which we have a right to demand. We claim that in a republican form of government, such as our fathers established, and such as ours still professes to be, the officers are and should be the servants of the people—not their masters, dictators or tyrants.

"To the numerous charges of our enemies we plead not guilty, and challenge the world before any just tribunal to the proof. Try on the plaster of friendly intercourse and honorable dealing instead of foul aggression and war. Treat us as friends—as citizens entitled to and possessing equal rights with our fellows—and not as alien enemies, lest you make us such. All we want is the truth and fair play. The administration have been imposed upon by false, designing men; their acts have been precipitate and hasty, perhaps through lack of due consideration. Please to let us know what you want of us before you prepare your halters to hang, or 'apply the knife to cut out the loathsome, disgusting ulcer.' Do you wish us to deny our God and renounce our religion? That we shall not do. Withdraw your troops, give us our Constitutional rights and we are at home."

This document was signed by Elder Taylor, Speaker of the House; and Heber C. Kimball, President of the council.

During the winter of 1857-8 the "army for Utah" was kept encamped on or near Ham's Fork, and about Fort Bridger, unable to move into Salt Lake Valley, as large numbers of its stock had been run off; and a forced march into the Valley was impracticable as the mountain passes were well fortified and guarded by the Utah militia, determined to resist such a movement. Meantime the favorable report given of the Mormons by Captain Van Vliet at Washington, had produced a change in public sentiment; and President Buchanan found himself with his Utah expedition on his hands without being able to assign any reasonable cause for having inaugurated it.

It was at this juncture that Colonel Thomas L. Kane, of Pennsylvania, offered his services to the perplexed President. Colonel Kane had been a witness of the cruel expulsion of the Mormons from Illinois, and had become their firm and fast friend. It was, therefore, as much the object of the Colonel to render further service to a people to whom he had become attached, as it was to prevent the administration at Washington from making a further blunder, that induced him to offer his services as mediator between the President and the people of Utah.

The Colonel arrived in Salt Lake City in February, 1858, and was heartily welcomed by the Church leaders and the Saints. The result of his mediation was that the people received and acknowledged the President's appointee for Governor of the Territory, Alfred Cumming, of Georgia, provided he would agree to come to Salt Lake City without the army—conditions which Governor Cumming readily accepted.

He was escorted to Salt Lake City by Colonel Kane and several companies of the Utah militia; and everywhere was met with a hearty welcome and acknowledged Governor of Utah. He notified General Albert Sidney Johnston—who had succeeded Harney in the command of the Utah expedition—to this effect; and informed him that the presence of the army was not necessary to maintain his authority.

In his report to the Secretary of State, Governor Cumming denied the charges made against the Mormon people—charges which had been pointed to as justifying the President in sending the army—so that there was left not even the shadow of a justification for this inconsiderate, hostile demonstration. But even before Governor Cumming's report reached Washington, President Buchanan had become so heartily sick of his blunder that he issued a proclamation pardoning the people for their alleged rebellion and treason.

Governor Cumming had entered the Territory, his authority had been acknowledged, he was in the full discharge of his official duties and congratulated himself that all the Utah difficulties were approaching a happy termination. His rejoicing was premature. The difficulties were not ended. The army was within a few days' march of the capital and other thickly settled portions of the Territory, and might rush in at any time to be quartered in Salt Lake City or encamped in close proximity to other settlements to insult, abuse and oppress the people. Furthermore, with the army and its camp followers once settled in or near Salt Lake City, with judges deeply prejudiced against them, and with an idea that they were judges with a mission, it was more than possible, it was quite probable, that juries composed of teamsters and camp followers would be packed to set in judgment on the old settlers of Utah in respect to events which had occurred during the unsettled state of affairs of the past two years. To these things the leaders of the people had determined not to submit; and rather than brook such treatment, an exodus from the Territory was determined upon.

Early spring saw the people in the northern settlements moving *en masse* for the south, leaving only enough men in the deserted settlements to fire them and lay waste the country. Alfred Cumming might be Governor of the Territory, but the people leaving would make his sceptre a barren one. The army might march into the Territory with all the pomp and circumstance of glorious war, but the country would be a blackened waste—not much glory to be reaped on such a field for the army of the great Republic!

By June, Salt Lake City and all the settlements north of Lehi were deserted, save by those left to destroy them. Such was the state of things in Utah when President Buchanan's Peace Commissioners—L. W. Powell, Senator-elect from Kentucky, and ex-

Governor of that state, and Major-General Ben McCullough—arrived. A conference between them and the leaders of the Church, in which Elder Taylor took part, resulted in an adjustment of the Utah difficulties. The past was to be buried. In the language of Commissioner Powell, "Bygones are to be bygones;" and while the army was to be permitted to enter the Territory it was not to be encamped nearer than forty miles of Salt Lake City, and not adjacent to densely settled districts.

The location decided upon for its encampment was in Cedar Valley, south-west of Salt Lake City. The troops marched through the deserted city *en route* for this point, but made no stay in it. Their permanent encampment in Ceder Valley was made at Fairfield, and named Camp Floyd, in honor of the then Secretary of War.

These stipulations carried out on the part of the Governor, the Commission and the army, and assurances given that they should be faithfully observed, the people returned to their deserted homes in time to reap the volunteer harvest with which their fields were spread; and affairs in troubled Utah began to settle to normal conditions.

In all these stirring events Elder Taylor took a prominent part. Having implicit faith in God his glorious hopes for the future, lined the dark and threatening clouds with brightest silver. Confident, as he ever was, that God held the destiny of His people and that of their enemies in His own hands, he was ready for peace or war; or for the abandonment and destruction of his home, if such were the will of God. This spirit of trust and confidence in the Lord he not only possessed himself, but had also the faculty of imbuing others with it. He encouraged the disheartened, cheered the sorrowful, strengthened the weak, reproved the fearful, convinced the unbelieving, counseled even the wise; and throughout those dark and turbulent times, bore himself with dignity, courage and true manliness which intensified the love of the Saints for him, and called forth the admiration of his brethren.

CHAPTER 34 - VICE PRESIDENT

After the close of the "Mormon War," Elder Taylor's public labors were mostly confined to Utah. For a number of years he traveled extensively through all the settlements of the Saints, preaching the gospel, usually accompanying President Brigham Young in his annual preaching tours. He also attended all conferences and councils, and assisted in a general way all public enterprises.

He was a member of the Utah Territorial Legislature from 1857 to 1876; and was elected speaker of the House for five successive sessions, beginning in 1857. As the Speaker of the House he won the esteem of the members by his uniform courtesy and fairness. As a member he sought to promote the interests of his constituents and at the same time to legislate for the welfare of the entire Territory.

In 1868 he was elected Probate Judge of Utah County, and continued in office until the December term of that court in 1870. As the laws of Utah then provided that the probate courts should "have power to exercise original jurisdiction, both civil and criminal, and as well in chancery as in common law," the position was one of considerable importance. Especially in those days when the perverseness of Federal judges led them frequently to close the district courts indefinitely, because, forsooth, the grand juries insisted on indicting men only when the facts before them warranted such action, and petit juries insisted on the right to judge the guilt or innocence of men accused of crime according to the facts proven in open court, instead of finding them guilty or innocent according as the wishes or prejudices of the judge would have them condemned or liberated.

During these years, too, he continued to stand up in defense of the rights and liberties of the Saints, missing no opportunity to speak out in his bold, manly style against those who would wrong them.

In October, 1869, Utah for the second time was visited by the Hon. Schuyler Colfax, then vice-President of the United States. On the 5th of the month he delivered a speech from the portico of the Townsend House, now the Continental Hotel. In that speech, which was extensively published in the east, the vice-president made an attack on the Mormon religion, and justified Congress in the enactment of laws against the practice of plural marriage. To this speech Elder Taylor, then temporarily absent from the Territory, in Boston, replied through the columns of the New York *Tribune*.

In his speech the vice-president took the position that the marriage institution of the Saints did not involve the question of religion; his exact words were: "I do not concede that the institution you have established here, and which is condemned by the law, is a question of religion;" and from that basis argued the question. His main point of argument I quote, observing only in passing that it has been the argument of tyrants and persecutors, acting under the cloak of law, ever since liberty had to struggle against oppression:

"I have no strictures to utter as to your creed on any really religious question. Our land is a land of civil and religious liberty, and the faith of every man is a matter between himself and God alone. You have as much right to worship the Creator through a President and twelve apostles of your church organization, as I have through the ministers and elders and creed of mine. And this right I would defend for you with as much zeal as the right of every other denomination throughout the land.

"But our country is governed by law, and no assumed revelation justifies any one in trampling on the law. If it did, every wrong-doer would use that argument to protect himself in his disobedience to it."

Replying to this part of the Vice-President's argument, Elder Taylor commended the magnanimity and even-handed justice of the first paragraph saying that the sentiments did honor to the author of them and that they ought to be engraven on every American heart. To the second paragraph he replied:

"That our country is governed by law all admit; but when it is said that 'no assumed revelation justifies any one in trampling on the law,' I should respectfully ask, What! not if it interferes with my religious faith, which you state 'is a matter between God and myself alone?' Allow me, sir, here to state that the assumed revelation referred to is one of the most vital parts of our religious faith; it emanated from God and cannot be legislated away; it is part of the 'Everlasting Covenant' which God has given to man. Our marriages are solemnized by proper authority; a woman is sealed unto a man for time and for eternity, by the power of which Jesus speaks, which 'seals on earth and it is sealed in heaven.' With us it is 'Celestial Marriage;' take this from us and you rob us of our hopes and associations in the resurrection of the just. This not our religion? You do not see things as we do. I make these remarks to show that it is considered, by us, a part of our religious faith, which I have no doubt, did you understand it as we do, you would defend, as you state, 'with as much zeal as the right of every other denomination throughout the land.' Permit me here to say, however, that it was the revelation (I will not say assumed) that Joseph and Mary had, which made them look upon Jesus as the Messiah; which made them flee from the wrath of Herod, who was seeking the young child's life. This they did in contravention of law which was his decree. Did they do wrong in protecting Jesus from the law? But Herod was a tyrant. That makes no difference; it was the law of the land, and I have yet to learn the difference between a tyrannical king and a tyrannical Congress. When we talk of executing law in either case, that means force,—force means an army, and an army means death. Now I am not sufficiently versed in metaphysics to discover the difference in its effects, between the asp of Cleopatra, the dagger of Brutus, the chalice of Lucretia Borgia, or the bullet or sabre of an American soldier.

"I have, sir, written the above in consequence of some remarks which follow:

"'I do not concede that the institution you have established here, and which is condemned by the law, is a question of religion.'

"Now, with all due deference, I do think that if Mr. Colfax had carefully examined our religious faith he would have arrived at other conclusions. In the absence of this I might ask, who constituted Mr. Colfax a judge of my religious faith? I think he has stated that 'The faith of every man *is a matter between himself and God alone*.'

"Mr. Colfax has a perfect right to state and feel that he does not believe in the revelation on which my religious faith is based, nor in my faith at all; but has he the right to *dictate* my religious faith? I think not; he does not consider it religion, but it is nevertheless mine.

"If a revelation from God is not a religion, what is?

"His not believing it from God makes no difference; I know it is. The Jews did not believe in Jesus but Mr. Colfax and I do; their unbelief does not alter the revelation."

Commenting more at length on the Vice-President's assumption that the marriage system of the Saints had nothing to do with religion, he said:

"Are we to understand that Mr. Colfax is created an umpire to decide upon what is religion and what is not, upon what is true religion and what is false? If so, by whom and what authority is he created judge? I am sure he has not reflected upon the bearing of this hypothesis, or he would not have made such an utterance.

"According to this theory no persons ever were persecuted for their religion, there never was such a thing known. Could anybody suppose that that erudite, venerable, and profoundly learned body of men,—the great Sanhedrim of the Jews; or that those holy men, the chief priests, scribes and Pharisees, would persecute anybody for religion? Jesus was put to death,—not for His religion,—but because He was a blasphemer; because He had a devil and cast out devils through Beelzebub the prince of devils; because He, being a carpenter's son, and known among them as such, declared Himself the Son of God. So they said, and they were the then judges. Could anybody be more horrified than those Jews at such pretensions? His disciples were persecuted, proscribed and put to death, not for their religion, but because they 'were pestilent fellows and stirrers up of sedition,' and because they believed in an 'assumed revelation' concerning 'one Jesus, who was put to death, and who, they said, had risen again.' It was for false pretensions and a lack of religion that they were persecuted. Their religion was not like that of the Jews; ours, not like that of Mr. Colfax.

"Loyola did not invent and put into use the faggot, the flame, the sword, the thumbscrews, the rack and gibbet to persecute anybody, it was to purify the Church of heretics, as others would purify Utah. His zeal was for the Holy Mother Church. The Nonconformists of England and Holland, the Huguenots of France and the Scottish non-Covenanters were not persecuted or put to death for their religion; it was for being schismatics, turbulent and unbelievers. All of the above claimed that they were persecuted for their religion. All of the persecutors, as Mr. Colfax said about us, did 'not concede that the institution they had established which was condemned by the law, was religion;' or, in other terms, it was an imposture or false religion."

Referring to the injustice and oppression which had been perpetrated on humanity in the name of law, he wrote the following fine vein of sarcasm:

"When Jesus was plotted against by Herod and the infants were put of death, who could complain? *It was law*: we must submit to *law*. The Lord Jehovah, or Jesus, the Savior of the world, has no right to interfere with *law*. Jesus was crucified *according to law*. Who can complain? Daniel was thrown into a den of lions strictly *according to law*. The king would have saved him, if he could; but he could not resist law. The massacre of St. Bartholomew was in accordance with *law*. The guillotine of Robespierre, of France, which cut heads off by the thousand, did it according to *law*. What right had the victims to complain? But these things were done in barbarous ages. Do not let us, then, who boast of our civilization, follow their example; let us be more just, more generous, more forbearing, more magnanimous. We are told that we are living in a more enlightened age. Our morals are more pure, our ideas more refined and enlarged, our institutions more liberal. 'Ours,' says Mr. Colfax, 'is a land of civil and religious liberty, and the faith of every man is a matter between himself and God alone,' providing God don't shock our moral ideas by introducing something we don't believe in. If He does, let Him look out. We won't persecute, very far be that from us; but we will make our platforms, pass Congressional laws and make you submit to them. We may, it is true, have to send out an army, and shed the blood of many; but what of that? It is so much more pleasant to be proscribed and killed according to the laws of the Great Republic, in the 'asylum for the oppressed,' than to perish ignobly by the decrees of kings, through their miserable minions, in the barbaric ages."

The reply of Elder Taylor to the Vice-President's speech brought that gentleman out again in a long article on the Mormon question, published in the New York *Independent*. In addition to repeating the main argument of his speech, Mr. Colfax, undertook to trace out the history of the Mormons and answer the arguments of Elder Taylor. To this second production Elder Taylor made an elaborate and masterly reply that was quite as extensively published in the east as was the Vice-President's article. He followed his opponent through all his meanderings in dealing with the Mormon question; he corrected his errors, reproved his blunders, answered his arguments, laughed at his folly; now belaboring him with the knotty cudgel of unanswerable argument, and now roasting him before the slow fire of his sarcasm; now honoring him for his zeal, which, however mistaken, had the smack of honesty about it; and now pitying him for being led astray on some historical fact.

In the opening of his article the Vice-President made a rather ungenerous effort to belittle the achievements of the Mormon people, in redeeming the desert valleys of Utah. "For this," said he, "they claim great credit: and I would not detract one iota from all they are legitimately entitled to. It *was* a desert when they first emigrated thither. They have made large portions of it fruitful and productive, and their chief city is beautiful in location and attractive in its gardens and shrubbery. But the solution of it all is in one word—

water. What seemed to the eye a desert became fruitful when irrigated; and the mountains whose crests are clothed in perpetual snow, furnished, in the unfailing supplies of their ravines, the necessary fertilizer."

This afforded Elder Taylor a fine opportunity for one of those poetic flights so frequently to be met with both in his writings and sermons. "Water!" he exclaimed. "*Mirabile dictu*! Here I must help Mr. C. out."

"This wonderful little water nymph, after playing with the clouds on our mountain tops, frolicking with the snow and rain in our rugged gorges for generations, coquetting with the sun and dancing to the sheen of the moon, about the time the Mormons came here, took upon herself to perform a great miracle, and descending to the valley with a wave of her magic wand and the mysterious words, 'hiccory, diccory, dock,' cities and streets were laid out, crystal waters flowed in ten thousand rippling streams, fruit trees and shrubbery sprang up, gardens and orchards abounded, cottages and mansions were organized, fruits, flowers and grain in all their elysian glory appeared and the desert blossomed as the rose; and this little frolicking elf, so long confined to the mountains and water courses proved herself far more powerful than Cinderella or Aladdin. Oh! Jealousy, thou green-eyed monster! Can no station in life be protected from the shimmer of thy glamour? must our talented and honorable Vice-President be subjected to thy jaundiced touch? But to be serious, did water tunnel through our mountains, construct dams, canals and ditches, lay out our cities and towns, import and plant choice fruit-trees, shrubs and flowers, cultivate the land and cover it with the cattle on a thousand hills, erect churches, school-houses and factories, and transform a howling wilderness into a fruitful field and a garden? Unfortunately for Mr. Colfax, it was Mormon polygamists who did it. What if a stranger on gazing upon the statuary in Washington and our magnificent Capitol, and after rubbing his eyes were to exclaim, 'Eureka! it is only rock and mortar and wood!' This discoverer would announce that instead of the development of art, intelligence, industry and enterprise, its component parts were simply stone, mortar and wood. Mr. Colfax has discovered that our improvements are attributable to water!"

Replying to the Vice-President's arguments and illustrations that the United States was justified in suppressing what it considered to be immoral, notwithstanding the Mormons claimed it to be part of their religious faith—in the course of which Mr. Colfax referred to the now familiar conduct of the English government in suppressing the suttee in India—Elder Taylor said:

"To present Mr. Colfax's argument fairly, it stands thus: The burning of Hindoo widows was considered a religious rite by the Hindoos. The British were horrified at the practice, and suppressed it. The Mormons believe polygamy to be a religious rite. The American nation consider it a scandal, and that they ought to put it down. Without entering into all the details, I think the above a fair statement of the question. He says 'The claim that religious faith commanded it was powerless, and it went down, as a relic of barbarism.' He says: 'History tells us what a civilized nation, akin to ours, actually did, where they had the power.' I wish to treat this argument with candor:

"The British suppressed the suttee in India, and therefore we must be equally moral and suppress polygamy in the United States. Hold! not so fast; let us state facts as they are and remove the dust. The British suppressed the suttee, but tolerated eighty-three millions of polygamists in India. The suppression of the suttee and that of polygamy are two very different things. If the British are indeed to be our exemplars, Congress had better wait until polygamy is suppressed in India. But it is absurd to compare the suttee to polygamy; one is murder and the destruction of life, the other is national economy and the increase and perpetuation of life. *Suttee* ranks truly with *infanticide*, both of which are destructive of human life. *Polygamy* is salvation compared with either, and tends even more than monogamy to increase and perpetuate the human race."

Elder Taylor closed the discussion with a vivid expose of the loathsome immorality and crime that existed in the villages, towns and cities of the East; and called the attention of the Vice-President to the fact that there was work enough for himself, for Congress and also for the moralists and ministers in the United States nearer home, in suppressing the evils by which they were immediately surrounded, without plunging into the isolated valleys of Utah to legislate away the religion of the Mormons, under the specious plea of suppressing crime.

Taking it all in all, this is doubtless the most important discussion in the history of the Church. The great reputation of Mr. Colfax as a speaker and writer; the fact that he had for many years been a member of Congress and accustomed to debate, together with the high station he occupied at the time of the discussion, gave to it a national importance. It occurred, too, at a critical time in the history of the Church. The Republican party had pledged itself to the accomplishment of two objects: the suppression of slavery and polygamy. Slavery it had abolished; and it was now expected that polygamy would receive its attention.

There was also, just then, an effort being made by prominent and wealthy members of the Church, to destroy the influence of President Brigham Young, or, if that failed, to weaken it by dividing the Church into parties. Of this movement the Vice-President was aware, as was also the President and the members of his Cabinet; and lent their influence as far as they could, to this scheme of disintegration; hoping, by fostering it, to solve the Mormon problem. That it failed miserably is notorious; but these considerations make the discussion between Elder Taylor and the Vice-President all the more important.

The discussion also serves another purpose. It affords an opportunity of comparing Elder Taylor with a man of acknowledged ability, liberal education and wide experience. In that comparison Elder Taylor loses nothing. In fact he gains by it; for, maugre the experience and learning and position of his opponent, he surpassed him not only in the force of argument, but in literary style, in the elegance, ease and beauty of his diction; while for courtesy, fair dealing and frankness, he was not surpassed by the Vice-President, who was noted for possessing these admirable qualities.

CHAPTER 35 - ON THE CRUSADE

The years from 1871 to 1875 are notable in the history of Utah for the judicial reign of terror which prevailed. In the spring of 1871, James B. McKean, of New York, arrived in Salt Lake City and entered upon the duties of his office as Chief Justice of the Territory. He was a man of moderate capacity, a sectarian bigot, fanatical in his opposition to the Mormon people: in a word, he was "a judge with a mission," and utterly reckless in his methods of executing it.

His conception of the work appointed to him to perform as Chief Justice of Utah, is best expressed in what are said to be his own words to Judge Louis Dent, brother-in-law to President Grant:

"Judge Dent, the mission which God has called upon me to perform in Utah, is as much above the duties of other courts and judges as the heavens are above the earth, and whenever or wherever I may find the local or federal laws obstructing or interfering therewith, by God's blessing I shall trample them under my feet."

While it seems too monstrous for belief that a United States judge should make such remarks as these, it is a stubborn fact, borne out by the records of the proceedings of his court, that James B. McKean did all he threatened to do in the above reported conversation.

His first attack was upon the Territorial attorney-general and marshal, both of whom, without the authority of law, were pushed out of office and their duties performed by the United States district attorney and marshal. The next step was to ignore the Territorial statutes providing for the impanelling of grand and petit jurors; and authorizing the United States marshal to select them at his own pleasure. The result was packed juries of pronounced anti-Mormons, chosen to convict the Church leaders. One more step and the machinery of the court was ready for the evidently contemplated judicial crusade; the United States prosecuting attorney having resigned, Judge McKean appointed as his successor R. N. Baskin, a man as bitter in his hatred of the Church of Jesus Christ and its chief officers as the judge himself; and not one whit behind him in recklessness. This appointment was made in violation of law, since only the President of the United States with the consent of the senate, has power to appoint that officer.

The machinery all being ready, a number of indictments were found against men high in authority in the Church, under an old Territorial statute defining and punishing adultery. It was notorious throughout the United States that if these men in their polygamous relations were guilty of any offense at all, it must have been the violation of the anti-polygamy laws of Congress, and not the aforesaid Territorial law enacted by a legislature the members of which were chiefly polygamists.

Among those indicated under this *regime* was President Brigham Young, against whom an indictment with sixteen separate counts was found. Each count constituting a separate offense. He appeared in court to answer to these charges; and the judge in overruling a motion to quash the indictment took occasion to say:

"Courts are bound to take notice of the political and social condition of the country which they judicially rule. It is therefore proper to say, that while the case at bar is called 'The People *versus* Brigham Young,' its other and real name is 'Federal Authority *versus* Polygamous Theocracy.'"

Public sentiment was outraged by the high-handed measures of Judge McKean. Popular excitement ran high. For a time there was a threatened collision between the court and the people. It was at this juncture that Elder Taylor published five letters in the *Deseret News*, reviewing the situation in Utah, and denouncing the Territorial government as un-American in principle and oppressive in its operation; but at the same time warned the people against violent resistance to the court, insolent and oppressive as it was.

He was in court with President Young when Judge McKean made the statement: "It is therefore proper to say that while the case at bar is called 'The People *versus*Brigham Young,' its other and real name is 'Federal Authority *versus* Polygamous Theocracy.' A system is on trial in the person of Brigham Young." This he took for his text in the letters above referred to, and interpreted it to mean, which it did, that war was declared against the Church of Jesus Christ. "Stripped of all its tinsel and wrappings," said he, "it simply resolves itself into this: that the government of the United States is at war with the Church of Jesus Christ of Latter-day Saints."

Elder Taylor then proceeds to show that in making war on a system of religion, the great principle of religious liberty itself is threatened, and that such a crusade as that foreshadowed in the declaration of Judge McKean, could but end in disaster to the liberties of the people.

Giving himself wide latitude in the discussion, he inquired into the principles underlying American institutions, and from that inquiry arrives at the following conclusion:

"The whole foundation and superstructure of American ethics or jurisprudence is based upon the popular will. That its executive, legislative and judicial powers originate with the people, and that the people having granted to the men of their choice, certain powers, agencies and authorities, to act for and in their behalf; limiting all of them by the provisions of the Constitution which all of them take an oath to support, they reserve to themselves, to their state or to 'the people,' all the remainder.

"If indeed the above is a correct exposition of our rights and privileges as American citizens," he writes, "how is it that such infamies can transpire as have lately been exhibited in our courts? I may be here met with the statement that we are only a territory; but we are American citizens, and have never abjured our citizenship nor relinquished our Constitutional guarantees. If the above be true, and the axiom of the declarers of Independence be correct, that governments 'derive their just powers from the consent of the governed,' what becomes of our federal officers? For not one of our citizens invited them here, or had any vote in their coming, nor was their consent asked. If all just powers are derived from the consent of the governed, then the powers exercised by them [the Territorial officials appointed by the President] must be unjust.

"The facts are the people, one hundred thousand American citizens, living in the Territory of Utah, with the full rights of free men, and the protecting guarantees of a written constitution, find in the persons of federal officers 'another government' not of the people, and in violation of Constitutional guarantees and authority; claiming to come from the United States, '*imperium in imperio*,' whose policy and practices are in grave particulars at variance with its own; and I ask by what authority it presumes to set itself up against the legitimately constituted authority of the people of the territory or state; by what authority it ignores its laws; by what authority it over-rides and tears down the safeguards of society, fosters in our midst drunkenness, gambling and whoredoms, those infamous adjuncts and institutions of professed civilization; by what authority it repudiates its officers; by what authority it interferes with the religion of the people, with their social, religious, political and moral rights?"

He then proceeds at some length to show that some of the most eminent statesmen of America held to the view that the people of the territories possessed the right to manage their own municipal, social and domestic affairs in that way which to them seemed best, limited only in the exercise of these powers by the Constitution of the United States.

These letters, however, were most valuable in allaying the excitement of the people, who by the infamous proceedings of the courts were fast approaching that condition of mind when men throw off all restraint, and regardless of consequences avenge their own wrongs. He called the attention of the people to the fact that this was probably the object of the crusade, that a pretext might be found for further oppression and robbery.

"The lamb is drinking below, the wolf is fouling the water above. The big boy is strutting about with a chip on his shoulder, daring you to knock it off. Some pretext is needed. Don't give it to them. Let the same wisdom that has governed your acts hitherto still be continued. They want a cause of quarrel, that they may rob and pillage according to law. Don't give it to them. Let them pack juries fresh from houses of ill-fame to try you on virtue. Never mind, it is their virtue that suffers, not yours. Let them try you for living with and protecting your wives and providing for your children; fidelity and virtue are not crimes in the eyes of the Almighty, only in theirs.

"'But they are accusing some of our best and most honorable men of murder!' What of that? Who have they suborned as their accusers? They themselves call them by the mild name of assassins—these are their fellow-pirates with whom they hob nob and associate. Be quiet!

"'But other aggressions are contemplated; they are bent on provoking a quarrel and mischief.' No matter, it takes two to make a quarrel, don't you be one of them.

"'They offer themselves to be kicked.' Don't do it, have some respect for your boots.

"'But they insult us on every hand.' What! they insult you! Nature has provided for many animals and insects a certain species of aggression and defense. Some snakes crush their victims in their folds; others carry poison in their teeth; the wasp and scorpion sting you; the ant poisons with its bite; the vampire sucks your blood; while the pole-cat protects itself by its insufferable odor—

"'Their power to hurt each little creature feels,
Bulls use their horns and asses use their heels.'

"Now who would consider himself insulted by the hissing of a snake, the attack of the wasp, or the odor of a skunk? You would simply avoid them. It is not in their power to insult you.'

"There is no law they can place us under which we cannot obey. We must live above all law, and nothing can harm us if we are 'followers of that which is good,' so keep quiet!'

"There is something heroic in being able calmly to view with firm nerves and unblanched cheek the acts of your petty tormentors.

Filled with the light of eternal truth, rejoicing in the possession of the favor of God, 'having the promise of the life which now is, and that which is to come," standing on a more elevated platform, you can smile with complacency on their feeble attacks, and"

'Like Moses' bush ascend the higher,

And flourish unconsumed by fire.'

"But independent of this, it is our very best policy to be quiet. The court can proceed, yet the sun will rise and set, the earth will roll on its axis, potatoes and corn will grow irrespective of the decrees of courts. Hitherto you have been subject to the misrepresentations and manufactured lies from the small fry of this coterie—little whelps who lick the hands of their master, and vomit their lies by wholesale, to pervert public opinion; but they are found out. They have run their erratic race. You have no fear from them. Your cause is before the public. The eyes of the great American nation are now upon you, and men of honor, probity and position represent your acts. (And to their honor be it spoken the intelligent press, irrespective of party, denounce your persecutors.) This clique are not representatives of American sentiment. The majority of strangers in our midst repudiate them; and there are hundreds of thousands of honest, high-minded, honorable men throughout the land, who despise as much as you do, these infamous acts. We live in the most liberal and enlightened nation in the world; if there are evils, they can be corrected; but the undercurrent, the vital, strong, living sentiment of America is fair play, justice for all, equal rights, liberty, equality and brotherhood; they are opposed to hypocrisy, fraud, injustice and piracy, and will sustain republicanism, democracy, equity and the inalienable rights of man. Men of standing and position are now noting your acts, and they will report them truly and correctly; therefore keep quiet, and do not play into your enemies' hands. For they war, not only against you, but against the liberal, enlightened sentiment of the nation, against the time-honored principles of republicanism and equal rights."

The wisdom of the policy advised by Elder Taylor was soon vindicated by glorious results. The Supreme Court of the United

States decided that the grand and petit jurors summoned by McKean, were both drawn in violation of law, and as "a legal consequence, all the indictments now pending in the courts of Utah are null and void. Brigham Young and his Mormon brethren must be discharged from confinement, and the records of this judicial conspiracy expunged." McKean had the mortification of setting in the Supreme Court at Washington during the reading of this decision which so utterly condemned his fanatical and illegal proceedings.

But the end was not yet. McKean still had sole control of judicial affairs in Utah, in the district courts; and not being able to prosecute Mormons according to the plan he had first adopted, he determined to follow the policy of "masterly inactivity," by which he hindered and delayed the business of the courts, both civil and criminal, by refusing to empanel either grand or petit juries, hoping by this means to compel Congress to enact such a jury law for Utah as would keep Mormons off all juries, whether they were actual polygamists or only believers in it; and thus enable him to drag the class of men he had singled out as his victims, before their avowed enemies for trial. In these measures he was partially successful for Congress passed the Poland Bill in 1874, which virtually abolished the office of Territorial marshal and Territorial attorney general, by enlarging the duties and powers of the United States marshal and United States prosecuting attorney. The powers of the probate courts were also cut down, being limited by the Poland Bill to jurisdiction in the settlement of the estates of deceased persons and their descendants, guardianship and other like matters; but otherwise they were to have no civil, chancery or criminal jurisdiction whatever. They were permitted to hold concurrent jurisdiction in divorce cases with the United States district courts, but an appeal could be taken from them after appearance, before plea or answer. Thus the courts of the people were practically abolished and others set up in their place. Changes were also made in the manner of selecting juries, so that the Gentile population—at the time but an insignificant minority of the inhabitants of Utah—was given equal representation on the juries with the overwhelming majority of the people.

The conduct of Judge McKean and the measures introduced into Congress respecting Utah affairs, again brought Elder Taylor out in a series of six letters to the press, in which he made a scathing exposure of federal official corruption in our Territory, and a searching criticism of the various measures pending in Congress, previous to the passage of the Poland Bill. In closing one of these letters that reviewed some of the bills in Congress, he made the following stirring appeal to the national legislators:

"With all the reverence and respect due to the rulers of a mighty nation, from the tops of these distant mountains I call upon you to pause in your career, for I also am a teacher, and have a right to be heard. I speak in behalf of one hundred and fifty thousand citizens of Utah. I speak in behalf of forty millions of free American citizens in the United States. I conjure you out of respect for the memory of the dead, as the rightful guardians of the liberties of a vast nation, that stands proudly prominent among the nations of the earth, and in behalf of unborn millions, to pause. I conjure you, in behalf of our honor and integrity, in behalf of republican principles, and the cause of freedom throughout the world. I plead with you in behalf of our common humanity, and the rights of man, to reflect. Would you, to gratify a morbid sentimentality desecrate and tear down one of the most magnificent temples of human liberty, ever erected? Would you wantonly deliver up the sacred principles of liberty, equity and justice, bequeathed by your fathers, to the grim Moloch of party who is crushing, grinding and trampling under foot our God-given rights, and whose sanguinary jaws are extended to gorge and devour the quivering remnants of our feeble, expiring liberty? Have we not had more than enough trouble already with Virginia, North Carolina, Louisana and Utah? Can we ever be satisfied? 'Let us have peace.'"

The opening of the "Black Book," as he called his inquiry into the conduct of federal officials in Utah, revealed a lamentable state of affairs. Men who had come to the Territory for the ostensible purpose of administering the law were found to be among the chief transgressors thereof, and the aiders and abettors of criminals. But I allow Elder Taylor to make his own indictment against them, only adding that he demonstrated the truth of every item charged in it, by publishing the time when, the places where, and the names of the criminals they liberated. Elder Taylor writes:

"While our territorial courts, officers and municipal authorities, have been always foremost in punishing crime, whether committed by Mormons or Gentiles, some of the United States officials have shielded and protected criminals, and for this purpose every subterfuge known to the law has been brought into requisition. Thus, by writs of error, injunctions, *habeas corpus*, pardons, and officious and indecent interference, they have exhibited themselves as the abettors and protectors of crime. They have liberated *felons* and murderers, encouraged drunkenness and riot, protected and shielded brothel-houses, winked at and sustained gambling, and so clogged the wheels of justice, in both civil and criminal cases, that they have brought the judiciary into such contempt that it has become a stink in the nostrils of honest men."

These charges and the facts he published to prove them he prefaced with the following:

"I am not writing under the very questionable shelter of a *nom de plume*, and have nothing but facts to relate, for which I hold myself responsible."

The parties he indicted before the bar of public opinion made no attempt to refute his statements—a tacit admission of the truth of his charges.

Judge McKean and his coadjutors, however, continued their lawless course. The judge entertained a suit for divorce and alimony brought into his court by Ann Eliza Webb, the plural wife of President Brigham Young. The marriage between Ann Eliza Webb and Brigham Young was not recognized by the law of the land. It was illegal, and therefore void from the beginning; consequently there could be neither divorce nor alimony. Still Judge McKean entertained the suit, and ordered the defendant to pay $3,000 attorney's fees to plaintiff's counsel, $9,500 alimony to plaintiff, and also $500 per month to her, pending a decision in the case.

President Young, acting on the advice of his counsel, pending an appeal to the supreme court of the United States, did not obey the orders of the judge; whereupon he was found guilty of contempt of court, fined twenty-five dollars, and sentenced to one day's imprisonment in the penitentiary. In this James B. McKean displayed the petty, personal spite of a small man, instead of the courage of a dignified judge defending the honor of the bench. The rash and illegal act cost the Judge his official head. No sooner did the country become acquainted with the course he had taken than a storm of public indignation arose, and clamored loudly for his removal from office. Four days afterwards he was dismissed from the bench.

The federal officers which followed the McKean ring were a better class of men; and for some years Utah had a period of peace. A circumstance which vindicated the wisdom of Elder Taylor's counsel to "Be quiet."

CHAPTER 36 - THE QUORUM

The interest which Elder Taylor had taken for some years in the educational affairs of Utah, resulted in his election, in 1877, to the office of Territorial Superintendent of district schools. His labor in that department of the public service, however, was considerably interfered with, at least as to details, by his being called to operate in a higher and more important sphere. Still school interests were, by no means, neglected. He called to his assistance the most competent educators in the Territory, and under his direction the work they accomplished, was perfectly satisfactory.

In his bi-annual reports to the Territorial Legislature, in addition to giving the usual general and statistical information from his own Territory, he incorporated a brief summary of important educational statistics for all the states and territories, which led Charles Warren, Esq., acting commissioner of education at Washington, to write him a letter of commendation, in which the following occurs:

"The example thus set is a good one, and only by this means, while Congress limits the circulation of our reports, can the statistics, laboriously collected at this central office, reach the vast body of minor school officers and teachers, for whose benefit they should be spread abroad. It is to be hoped that other superintendents will follow the pattern thus presented, and thus enable all school officers and teachers in their several states or territories, to compare their own statistics with those of others elsewhere."

The circumstances which called Elder Taylor to a higher sphere of labor than that of superintendent of district schools, was the death of President Brigham Young. He died on the afternoon of the 25th of August, 1877. It was a sorrowful event. For thirty-three years Brigham Young had stood as the earthly head of the Church of Jesus Christ of Latter-day Saints, its President, and the Lord's prophet, seer and revelator to it. Under God's direction he delivered the Saints from the oppression of mob rule and violence at Nauvoo, and led them in an unparalleled exodus from civilization through wilderness and desert to the valleys of Utah. He located their settlements, taught them how to build forts for their protection from the savages; how to subdue the desert and make it fruitful; how to become self-sustaining, independent: and by these labors, he laid the foundation of a great commonwealth. He had not only been President of the people, he was, as well, their counselor, friend and brother. He had never betrayed their interests, they could and did trust him implicitly. In times of trial and sorrow they turned to him for comfort; in times of danger they looked to him to direct their action; in times of perplexity they went to him for the word of the Lord; and Brigham Young, full of a heaven-inspired wisdom, never failed them in any of these things. It is not to be wondered at, therefore, that the Saints had come to look upon him as well nigh indispensable to the work of the Lord, or that a cloud of sorrow settled upon all Israel at his death.

But the work the Lord has established in these last days is independent of any man, be he ever so wise, or influential. This has been so frequently demonstrated that it is now accepted as a truism by the faithful. The work, called by the world "Mormonism," is God's work. He is its founder and its Grand Head. Earthly leaders,—Joseph Smith, Brigham Young and others, operate under His directions. They are but instruments in His hands; and as one passes away, He raises up another competent to carry out His purposes. Brigham Young was dead, but the Church of Christ still lived; and its Great Head, the Lord Jesus Christ, though in heaven,—far above the power of death, of mobs or any earthly accident,—was watching over its interests and guiding its destiny. Surely He is able to raise up another earthly leader for Israel! Indeed the man is already at hand. The Saints while weeping for the departure of their late President, recognize him through the mists of their tears. It is the man who in a voice full of power and inspiration that thrills every soul in the vast congregation assembled to pay the last tribute of respect to the remains of Brigham Young—it is the man who is saying:

"We are not alone! God is with us, and He will continue with us from this time henceforth and forever. And while we mourn a good and great man dead, I see thousands of staunch and faithful ones around me, and before me, who are for Israel, for God and His kingdom; men who are desirous to see His will done on earth, as angels do it in heaven."

We are not alone! God is with us! Israel did not doubt it. How could they? He who proclaimed it knew whereof he spake; and the Spirit of God which penetrated the hearts of the Saints as he uttered those words, bore witness that they were true. It was John Taylor who thus spoke.

At the death of President Young, Elder John Taylor was President of the quorum of Twelve Apostles. It is a principle well established now by precedent, that at the death of the President of the Church, the authority of presidency devolves upon the next quorum—the Twelve Apostles: and as Elder Taylor was the President of the Twelve, he became the mouth-piece of the Lord to the people, by virtue of that position so long as that quorum presided over the Church. Not alone by precedent, however, did the Twelve succeed to the presidency of the Church with Elder Taylor at their head, the arrangement was also sanctioned by the spirit of inspiration.

On the 4th of September, 1877, the two counselors of the late President Young and ten of the Twelve Apostles—Orson Pratt and Joseph F. Smith, the other two members, were absent in England—held a meeting and waited upon the Lord. With humble, contrite and saddened hearts they earnestly sought to learn His will concerning themselves and the Church. The Lord blessed them with the spirit of union, and revealed to them what steps should be taken, and the following is what was done: Elder Taylor was unanimously sustained as the President of the Twelve; and with the same unanimity it was voted that the Twelve Apostles should be sustained as the presiding authority in the Church, while the counselors to the late President Young, John W. Young and Daniel H. Wells, were sustained as one with, counselors to and associated in action with the Twelve Apostles. To facilitate the transaction of business it was also voted that for the time being President Taylor should be assisted by John W. Young, Daniel H. Wells and George Q. Cannon, in attending to business connected with the temples, the public works and other financial affairs of the Church. They were a kind of executive committee. These preparations were made for pushing forward the work of the Lord in the earth, without even a halt or jostle.

Here it will be proper to note those circumstances which brought Elder Taylor to the exalted station he now occupied. The position in which the members of the Twelve stand in their quorum is determined by seniority of ordination, not of age. Therefore it is always the senior member by ordination that of right is the president of the quorum.

For a number of years, however, there were three members of the quorum living at the death of President Young whose names stood before President Taylor's: Orson Hyde, Orson Pratt and Wilford Woodruff. Doubtless Wilford Woodruff's name was placed upon the records before the name of John Taylor through some inadvertence, or perhaps through the incorrect idea that seniority of age decided the order in which the members of the quorum stood—Wilford Woodruff was the older man. John Taylor, however, was ordained before Wilford Woodruff, in fact, the former assisted at the ordination of the latter, so there could be no question as to his seniority of ordination. The attention of President Young and his counselors being called to these facts, it was decided—the Twelve also concurring—that John Taylor stood before Wilford Woodruff in the quorum, the names after this were so arranged.

During the troublous times at Far West, Missouri, Orson Hyde became involved in some difficulty, in connection with Thomas B. Marsh, which resulted in his excommunication, so that he lost his place in the quorum.

Orson Pratt was also involved in some difficulty in Nauvoo which led to his being dropped from his quorum, and Amasa Lyman was ordained to fill the vacancy.

Both Brother Hyde and Brother Pratt afterwards repented, were forgiven and received back into the quorum by ordination; and without any particular investigation or arrangement they took the positions formerly occupied by them. But both these brethren had been dropped from the quorum, and when they were received back by ordination, it is evident that all those who had remained in the quorum out-ranked them by seniority of ordination.

It was this consideration, doubtless, which led President Young, several years before his death, to have the name of John Taylor placed at the head of the quorum. Thus he stood in the same position that President Young did at the death of the Prophet Joseph; and like him was upheld "the President of the quorum of the Twelve, as one of the Twelve, and First Presidency of the Church."

But aside from his succeeding to this position by virtue of his standing in his quorum, his long experience in the Church, the love the Saints had for him, their confidence in his fidelity, together with his great abilities as a leader among men, pre-eminently qualified him for the position he was called upon to fill. And in those changes made under the direction of President Young, by which Elder Taylor was assigned his proper place in the quorum of the Apostles, may we not discern the inspiration of God preparing the way for the man whom the Lord designed to succeed to the leadership of His people, when President Brigham Young should be called home?

CHAPTER 37 - A GREAT TESTIMONY MEETING

Great energy characterized President Taylor's administration of affairs in the Church, both in Zion and abroad. He pushed forward with increased zeal the work on the temples, of which three were in course of erection, at the time of his taking control of affairs. He required bishops to hold weekly priesthood meetings in their wards; presidents of stakes to hold general priesthood meetings monthly in their respective stakes; and appointed quarterly conferences in all the stakes of Zion, publishing the dates of holding them for half a year in advance, a custom which has continued until the present.

He personally attended as many of these quarterly conferences as he could, without neglecting the executive branch of his calling, which necessarily occupied much of his time, and kept him at or within easy reach of Salt Lake City. But where he could not go himself, he sent members of his quorum, so that the Saints received much teaching and instruction from the Apostles, more perhaps than at any previous time in the history of the Church. The result was a great spiritual awakening among the Saints.

The work abroad received increased impetus by a greater number of elders being sent to the world. A missionary himself nearly all his life, it was but natural for President Taylor to be interested in the work of preaching the gospel abroad.

Pioneer Day—the 24th of July—1880, was celebrated with unusual grandeur in Salt Lake City. One feature of the splendid procession which marched through the gaily decorated streets of the city was three cars filled with representatives of the various countries where the gospel, as restored through the Prophet Joseph Smith, had been received. A man and a woman, dressed in native costume, represented each country; the women bearing shields with the national colors and the name of the nation represented. In the tabernacle, these nationalities were arranged on a platform in front of the pulpits; and after Apostle Orson Pratt, the Church historian, finished reading a brief account of the introduction of the gospel to the various countries of the earth, the nationalities, twenty-five in number, with their shields and banners, stepped forward in line, facing the congregation. President Taylor then rose behind them and said: "The Lord commanded His servants to go forth to all the world to preach the gospel to every creature. We have not yet been to *all* the world, but here are twenty-five nations represented today, and thus far we have fulfilled our mission; and it is for us to continue our labors until all the world shall hear us, that all who are desirous may obey, and we fulfill the mission given us."

That mission, during the presidency of John Taylor, was faithfully pushed forward among all the nations who would receive it.

At the April conference of 1879, President Taylor was voted the use of the Gardo House as a family residence. The Gardo, located on the corner of South Temple and First East streets, at that time was doubtless the largest and finest residence in Salt Lake City. I call attention to this fact, not because of any petty pride the subject of this writing had in mansions, splendid furnishings, soft carpets, statuary, paintings,—the gewgaws that flatter and engross small minds—but to call attention to a prophecy made by Elder Heber C. Kimball, who, when President Taylor's circumstances were the poorest, boldly prophesied that he would yet live in the largest and best house in Salt Lake City—a prediction that was fulfilled when President Taylor took possession of the Gardo House as his family residence.

It was with considerable reluctance that he accepted the proposition of his brethren. His habits of life were simple; free from ostentation, as were also those of his family; and had he followed the bent of his own inclination he would have remained in his own humbler home. Not until the change was repeatedly urged upon him did he consent to it. The spirit in which he accepted the house as a residence may be best judged from his own words at the conference which voted its use to him:

"I will state that I feel very much obliged to my brethren for the generous feeling manifested to myself. Permit me, however, to say with regard to some of these ideas presented to the conference by Brother George Q. Cannon, and which, as he he has said, he has frequently presented to me and others of the Twelve, that while I duly appreciate the feelings and views of my brethren, and am not ignorant of the proprieties of life, individually I would not wish to change my position. Personally I care nothing about the outside show, the glitter and the appearance of men; but I do care about the great and eternal principles associated with the Church and kingdom of God upon the earth. And as stated it was some time before I could make up my mind to accept a proposition of this kind, and I accept it now simply in the capacity of your servant for Christ's sake, for the benefit of the kingdom of God, and that all things may be conducted in a proper manner."

The general conferences of the Church—those mammoth semi-annual gatherings of the Saints of God, where representatives from all the Stakes of Zion assemble to hear instruction, council, reproof and the word of the Lord—under President Taylor's administration were spirited, valuable and soul-stirring. The one held in April, 1880, known as the Jubilee Conference, was especially so. The Church had just completed the fiftieth year of its existence. Half a century before it had been organized in a log room, possibly fourteen feet square, with six members. During that time a knowledge of the work had spread throughout the civilized world, and among some of the tribes of the heathen.

The Church had survived the ridicule of the worldly-wise, the clamor of bigots, the intrigues of demagogues, the violence of mobs, its banishment from civilization. Neither fire nor sword, nor intrigue, nor ridicule, nor banishment, nor its journey through the wilderness, nor any other thing had prevailed against the Church of Christ. It was fitting, then, at the close of the first half century of its existence that the Saints should rejoice mightily before the Lord.

To ancient Israel every fiftieth year was a jubilee. In it the inheritance which had been sold in the days of misfortune or poverty was restored to the original possessor, and his family returned to the old homestead. The poor debtor was released; the man who had sold himself to his brother, to be his hired servant, was set free, together with all that was his, his wives and his children and they returned to their inheritance.

"Ye shall hallow the fiftieth year," was the word of the Lord to them, "and proclaim liberty throughout all the land unto all the inhabitants thereof." President Taylor resolved that something of this spirit should enter into the teachings and proceedings of the Jubilee Conference. "It occurred to me," said he to the Saints assembled on that occasion, "that we ought to do something, as they did in former times, to relieve those that are oppressed with debt, to assist those that are needy, to break off the yoke of those that may feel themselves crowded upon, and to make it a time of general rejoicing."

Many of the Saints had been gathered from the Eastern States and the countries of the old world through means furnished by the Perpetual Emigration Fund Company. A company organized for the gathering of the poor. The manner in which the poor were assisted to emigrate by this company was as follows:

The company forwarded the means necessary for their emigration and took their notes at the legal rate of interest. When the notes were paid, the money was thrown back into the fund to be used again in assisting others. But many of those thus assisted were old and decrepit; and after their arrival in Utah, poverty refused to release his clutch upon them, and they found it difficult and in some instances impossible to meet their obligations. Then others, the fund company not being importunate in its demands upon them, became careless and neglected to take up their notes. Others lost the faith, and with it, in most cases, all sense of honor, and ignored their obligations. Through these causes a large indebtedness to the fund had accumulated by the year 1880. The principal of the indebtedness amounted to $704,000. The interest, extending along for many years, at 10 per cent. per annum, amounted to $900,000, making in all $1,604,000.

President Taylor proposed that one-half of this amount of the people's indebtedness to the Fund, $802,000, be released; that is, that the worthy poor throughout Zion who were unable to meet their engagements with the Fund be forgiven their indebtedness, not half of it, but the whole. The amount released was to be applied to their benefit in this way. The debtors able to pay were to be held accountable for the amounts they owed. "In former times," said President Taylor, in explaining this matter, "they did not release the rich, it was the poor. The rich can always take care of themselves—that is, so far as this world is concerned."

Then there was a tithing indebtedness on the books of the bishop of the Church against the Saints, amounting to $151,798. President Taylor proposed that one half of that, $75,899, be released to the poor on the same principle that one-half of the Fund indebtedness was released. Both of these propositions were carried by the unanimous vote of the conference.

The year 1879 was a very trying one in Utah. The drought was excessive, and crops consequently light. The winter was one of the severest ever experienced, and thousands of cattle and sheep perished. Some people had lost their last cow, and others all the sheep they had. "Now," said President Taylor, "we propose to raise 1000 head of cows—not old cows which do not give any milk, nor any one teated cows, but good milk cows—and have them distributed among those that may be destitute in the different stakes, under the direction of the authorities thereof." The Church was to put in 300 head of the 1,000, the other 700 head to be furnished by the stakes.

He also proposed that 5,000 head of sheep be appropriated to the poor, to be distributed by the same authorities, 2,000 of which the Church was to furnish, and the stakes the remainder.

For years the servants of the Lord had urged the Saints to store up grain, but only a few had acted upon their advice. The result was that many were without grain even for seed. The Female Relief

Society, however, had been wiser than individuals, and had stored up wheat in nearly all the settlements of the Saints. President Taylor now saw an opportunity to use it, and give a practical illustration of the wisdom that had counseled storing up grain. "Inasmuch as the brethren," he remarked, "had been careless and slow to heed the counsel of President Young in relation to storing away wheat, he [President Young] requested the sisters to do it, and some of us 'lords of creation' thought it a very little thing for our sisters to be engaged in. But we find now they are of some use, and that the 'ladies of creation' can do something as well as we 'lords.' They have 34,761 bushels of wheat? Who of you men can raise that much? Where's your wheat?" (Laughter.)

"Now," he continued, "those 34,761 bushels of wheat will be of considerable importance judiciously managed, and loaned out to some of our poor brethren. It will furnish seed wheat and after harvest they can return it again. We do not want any more harsh talk about the woman question after this."

A voice. "May they [the sisters] vote now?"

President Taylor. "Oh, yes, they may vote now if they choose to, everybody is willing they should vote now. [Laughter.] That is, they are willing the sisters shall vote on the wheat question. [Renewed laughter.] We may as well call a vote on this question now. All you sisters who are in favor of carrying out this request, hold up your right hand. [A forest of hands went up.] There they go, you see! [Laughter.] I think that is the most hearty vote yet. I knew they would do it."

A voice. "Is it to be loaned without interest?"

President Taylor. "Somebody asks if it is to be loaned without interest. Why, of course it is; we do not want any nonsense of that kind." Then raising his splendid voice to its grandest notes, so that it sent a thrill through the entire audience, he exclaimed, "IT IS THE TIME OF JUBILEE!"

Having finished with these public matters, President Taylor reminded the brethren that it was just as praiseworthy for private people to forgive one another their debts as it was for corporations to do it.

"If you find people owing you who are distressed, if you will go to work and try to relieve them as much as you can, under the circumstances, God will relieve you when you get into difficulties. I will tell you that in the name of the Lord."

Then in a circular issued to the officers of the Church a few days after the close of the conference, he added: "The rich have a fitting opportunity for remembering the Lord's poor. If you are holding their notes and they are unable to pay, forgive the interest and the principal, or as much thereof as you might desire them to forgive were their and your circumstances reversed, thus doing unto others as you would that others should do unto you. For upon this hang the law and the prophets. If you have mortgages upon the homes of your brethren and sisters who are poor, worthy and honest, and who desire to pay you but cannot, free them in whole or in part. Extend to them a jubilee, if you can consistently. You will have their faith and prayers and confidence, which may be worth more than money. We invite Zion's Co-operative Mercantile Institution as the parent, all other co-operative institutions as the children, and our brethren who are engaged in profitable railroad, banking, mercantile, manufacturing or other remunerative enterprises, to extend a helping hand. Free the worthy, debt-bound brother if you can. Let there be no rich among us from whose tables fall only crumbs to feed a wounded Lazarus. The Church of Christ has set us a worthy example, let us follow it, so that God may forgive our debts as we forgive our debtors."

I have given a detailed account of these philanthropic transactions connected with the Jubilee Conference, hoping that the transactions themselves may not prove uninteresting, but more especially because they throw out in bold relief the noble generosity of President Taylor's character.

Apart from these acts of generosity, looking to the relief and blessing of the poor, the Jubilee Conference was noted for the out-pouring of spiritual power upon the Apostles and other Elders in their teachings, admonitions and testimonies. The regular conference was preceded by a two days' meeting in the Salt Lake Assembly Hall, and the last meeting of the conference was made memorable by ten of the Apostles bearing testimony to the truth of the great work of the last days, President Taylor closing that grand testimony meeting with these words:

"I testify as my brethren have done, that this is the work of God that has been revealed by the Almighty, and I know it. God will sustain Israel; no power can injure us if we will do what is right. This kingdom will roll on, the purposes of God will progress, Zion will arise and shine, and the glory of God will rest upon her. We will continue to grow and increase, until the kingdoms of this world shall become the kingdoms of our God and His Christ, and He will reign forever and forever."

CHAPTER 38 - THE FIRST PRESIDENCY

While it is a well-established rule that the quorum of Twelve Apostles become the presiding quorum at the death or removal of the President of the Church, it is not in accordance with the order of the Priesthood that the Twelve should become the permanent presidency of the Church. The Lord has said that three Presiding High Priests, chosen by the body, appointed and ordained to that office, and upheld by the confidence, faith and prayer of the Church, form a quorum of the presidency of the Church. Therefore it must follow that the presidency of the Twelve Apostles over the Church can only be temporary. But as they stand next, and form a quorum equal in authority to the First Presidency, they have the power and of right preside when for any cause the First Presidency becomes disorganized.

For more than three years the quorum of Twelve Apostles had presided over the Church, from the death of President Young in August, 1877, to October, 1880. The Lord then inspired His servants to organize the First Presidency. For President there was but one choice—John Taylor. The spirit of revelation indicated that he was the man; and he received the unanimous vote of his fellow Apostles for that high office. He named George Q. Cannon as his first counselor, and Joseph F. Smith, the son of Hyrum Smith, for his second. These brethren were also unanimously sustained by their fellow Apostles. But it is not enough that they be sustained by that quorum alone. All the other quorums of the Priesthood have a voice in these important transactions, as also have all the members of the Church.

It was presenting this action of the Apostles for the approval of the various quorums of the Priesthood and the members of the Church, which constituted the leading feature of the Semi-Annual Conference of October, 1880.

Nothing can be more solemn and impressive than the voting of the quorums of the Priesthood, when they meet to act as a general assembly of quorums. The *States-General* of France, assembled in the *Salle des Menus* just before the French Revolution, in all the glory of raised platforms for Throne, Court and Blood-royal; with space for six hundred Commons Deputies in front; with three hundred clergy on the right of the throne and as many *noblesse* on the left; with lofty galleries filled with two thousand spectators, dames of honor, foreign diplomacies, "and other gilt-edge and white-frilled individuals," though constituting the most remarkable assembly the world ever saw, is not equal in imposing grandeur to the assembly and action of the quorums of the Priesthood.

On the present occasion the Apostles occupied the stand set apart for their use in the great Tabernacle, the second one in the tier of three. The space south of the stand was occupied by the Patriarchs, Presidents of Stakes and their Counselors, and the High Councils of the various Stakes. North of the stands the Bishops and their Counselors were seated, with Presiding Bishop Hunter and his Counselors in front. The High Priests occupied the north center of the body of the great hall, with their Presidents in front. The Seventies were seated in the south half of the body of the hall, with the First Seven Presidents in front. The space immediately back of the High Priests was reserved for the Elders, while the north side of the house, under the gallery was set apart for the quorums of the Lesser Priesthood, the Priests, Teachers and Deacons. The gallery, capable of seating three thousand people, was reserved for the use of the members of the Church.

Apostle Orson Pratt, with hair and full beard, made gloriously white by the frosts of sixty-nine winters, presented the several motions to be acted upon. The manner of voting was for the proposition to be presented to each quorum severally, except in the case of the Priests, Teachers and Deacons, who voted all together as the Lesser Priesthood; the members of each quorum rose to their feet as the question was presented and raised the right hand in token of assent, or, if any were opposed to the proposition, they could make it manifest in the same way after the affirmative vote had been taken.

The order in which the quorums voted was as follows:

First, the Twelve Apostles;

Second, the Patriarchs, Presidents of Stakes, their Counselors, and the High Councils;

Third, the High Priests;

Fourth, the Seventies;

Fifth, the Elders;

Sixth, the Bishops and their Counselors;

Seventh, the Lesser Priesthood.

After this the Presidents of the quorums voted on the question and it was then put to the entire assembly which arose *en masse* and voted in the same manner.

It was a remarkable scene. There was not a dissenting vote in all that vast assembly; and there were probably thirteen thousand people crowded into the great Tabernacle. Perfect unanimity prevailed; and as the several quorums registered their votes and the entire assembly arose and with uplifted hands sanctioned what they had done, the scene was indescribably grand and impressive, carrying with it a power and influence that can only come from a righteous people giving their unrestrained assent to that which God has appointed. It was an influence born of a union of *vox dei et vox populi*. It was a Spirit identical with that which in a larger degree pervades the councils of the Gods.

John Taylor was now invested with the highest office and honors which God gives to man on the earth. He was placed on a par with Melchizedek, Moses, Peter, Joseph and Brigham: for by the action of this conference he was made President of the High Priesthood, whose duty it is to preside over the whole Church, to be like Moses, a seer, a revelator, a translator, a prophet, having all the gifts of God which He bestows upon the head of the Church.

The Lord in describing the power and authority of the Higher or Melchizedek Priesthood, says: It holds the keys of all the spiritual blessings of the Church. It has the privilege of receiving the mysteries of the kingdom of heaven; of having the heavens opened to it; the right to commune with the general assembly and church of the first born; and to enjoy the communion and presence of God the Father, and Jesus the Mediator of the New Covenant.

These are the privileges of the High Priesthood, and John Taylor was called to preside over it, with a right to all the gifts and powers associated therewith. What higher authority can man possess? What honor greater can be given him? True, in the ceremonies which invested him with these high dignities, there was no long drawn out pomp, no tapers, processions, chantings, or clouds of incense; no vestures red or white, gold-laced or furred; no scepter or tiara; no peal of bells, no cannon's roar, no formal, solemn *Te deum*! Yet what office created by man—pontifical, princely, kingly—how graced so ever with the formal pomp and show in the bestowal of it, can equal that conferred on John Taylor, by the voice of God and the common consent of his brethren?

There is no man-created office but what is insignificant in comparison with it. Monarchs with powers usurped, the fruits of conquest, or inherited from a long line of princely ancestors, at the best held by the sufferance of those they rule—monarchs who fret and strut out their brief hour upon this world's troubled stage, who come, and see, and conquer and then vanish, are but fools in power compared with him who attains to the God-created office of President of the High Priesthood.

The power of earthly potentates is limited to the earth, often to an insignificant portion of it; and in duration to a few brief years, then they perish, together with their power and glory; while the power of him who attains to the office of President of the High Priesthood, enters within the veil and has effect both in time and in eternity. He binds on earth and it is bound in heaven; he looses on earth and it is loosed in heaven. He hath become a prince to that government to the increase and dominion of which there is no end, and whose scepter is an unchanging scepter of righteousness.

The princes of this world win and sustain their dominion by the sword; he by the preaching of peace on earth, good will to man; they trust to force—to armies and navies—for the perpetuation of their power; he to love unfeigned, persuasion, long suffering, gentleness, meekness, kindness and pure knowledge—reproving with sharpness at times, it is true, but afterwards showing forth a double portion of love towards those reproved, lest reproof be taken for enmity. Moreover, the princes of this world exercise dominion over their subjects, and they that are great, exercise authority upon them—arbitrary, often cruel, authority—and, as one of their own poets hath said, "Play such fantastic tricks before high heaven, as make the angels weep." The Lord hath decreed that it shall not be so in His government; but he that would be chief in it, let him be the servant of all, even as the Son of Man came not to be ministered unto, but to minister. Jesus spake truly when he said: "My kingdom is not of this world."

Such was the office, then, to which President Taylor succeeded; and such the spirit in which its powers are to be exercised. Both his native disposition and experience qualified him for the place. From his earliest youth arrayed on the side of liberty as against arbitrary authority, so pronounced in sentiment in that controversy, so fearless in maintaining it, that he won the proud title of "Champion of Liberty"—it was natural for him in his administration to pay due regard to the principle of common consent, by which all things are to be done in the Church.

With him as President there could be no arbitrary government among the Saints. Teach men correct principles and let them govern themselves, was a doctrine he learned in his early manhood from the Prophet Joseph. He made it a leading principle in his career. He adopted it in his family government, in his presidency of churches, conferences and missions in the eastern states and in foreign lands. It was a prominent characteristic of his administration while President of the Twelve Apostles; it continued to be his motto during his more direct Presidency of the Church. Yet while he respected the principle of common consent, he blended with that respect a native dignity of character and bearing which prevented in his administration that severely democratic principle of government descending into factious opposition: and on occasion could make those with whom he came in contact feel that *vox Dei* as he felt it within his own inspired soul had a right to be heard in the administration of Church affairs, as well as *vox populi*.

President Taylor's accession to the Presidency of the Church reveals another thing in connection with his history which must not be overlooked. It raises the corner of the veil which separates the natural and spiritual worlds, and permits us to form an idea of his career and character in his first estate, when as a spirit he associated with the Gods in the eternal worlds. It is recorded of Abraham that the Lord showed unto him the intelligences that were organized before the world was; "and among all these there were many of the noble and great ones; and God saw these souls that they were good and he stood in the midst of them, and he said: These I will make my rulers; for he stood among those that were spirits, and he saw that they were good; and he said, Abraham, thou art one of them, thou wast chosen before thou wast born."

So with John Taylor. The high place as one of God's rulers which he had now attained proclaimed that he, too, was one of the "noble and great ones;" and like Jesus, [Abraham], Jeremiah, and other prophets, he was chosen before he was born.

CHAPTER 39 - LESS OF THE POET

Although President Taylor, at the time he became President of the Church, was two years past the three score years and ten allotted by the Psalmist as the life of man, he was not bowed down by their weight. His form was erect and his step elastic; and he entered upon the performance of his high duties with a zeal and vigor only to be expected of a younger man. He visited the Stakes of Zion in Utah and the surrounding territories, setting them in order, teaching, counseling and encouraging the Saints with all the energy and kindness of his great soul.

As a sample of his travels and labors among the people I give the following summary of two of his trips during the year 1881: In the latter part of July, in company with several of the Apostles and other brethren, he started on a tour to visit some of the northern Stakes and settlements. He was absent from Salt Lake City seventeen days, during which time he visited five Stakes of Zion, viz., Cache, Rich, Summit, Wasatch and Utah, traveling much of the distance in carriages. Twenty-three meetings were held by the party. President Taylor attended all but three, and spoke at the most of them.

In the latter part of November of the same year, he visited the southern Stakes and settlements, accompanied by his Counselor Joseph F. Smith and several of the Twelve Apostles. This tour occupied five weeks and four days. The party held sixty-eight meetings; besides many council meetings where advice and instructions to Presidents of Stakes, Bishops and other officers of the Church were freely given. Thus he labored incessantly among the people from his accession to the Presidency until he was driven into retirement by the judicial crusade waged against the Saints some years later.

The subject matter in the discourses of President Taylor in these years dealt very largely with the duties of the Saints in all the relations of life; as husbands and wives, parents and children, neighbors and citizens; unity, honor, integrity, honesty, purity in thought and act were his themes—in one word he preached righteousness as essential to the favor of God, and with the favor of God he assured the Saints they need not fear what man or nations could do. "God will be on the side of Israel, if Israel will be on the side of right," was his oft-repeated, confident assertion.

He was particularly careful to set in order the quorums of the priesthood, and charged them to walk in holiness before the Lord. Who does not remember with what earnestness and power in conferences and other public meetings, he was wont to admonish Presidents of Stakes and bishops of wards to set in order the priesthood and institutions under their supervision? And how he urged them to labor with all diligence, long-suffering and kindness for the reformation of the wayward! But if they would not reform, how he then strictly charged the authorities having jurisdiction in the case to sever them from the Church, that God, angels and the world might know that Israel had no fellowship with drunkards, debauchees, thieves, liars or the dishonest.

Alluding to the Priesthood and its organization he would say: "These things are given to us for what? To gratify our ambition? To enable us to ride over and trample under foot our fellow-creatures? To place power and authority upon us? No; not for any man's emolument or aggrandizement. Although there is nothing more honorable, nothing more dignified, nothing to which a man ought so much to aspire to as to be a servant of the living God, and to be commissioned by Him to do His work upon the earth. And what for? To spread correct principles among men; to combat priestcraft, statecraft, oppression, fraud and iniquity of all kinds; and to introduce among men those pure and holy principles by which the Gods are governed in the eternal worlds."

In addition to these things he taught implicit trust in God, showed the Saints their dependence upon Him, and frequently alluded to the source from whence they derived their knowledge of truth. "Any intelligence which we may possess," he would say, "and which we may be able to impart, is not of ourselves, but of God. It did not originate with Joseph Smith, with Brigham Young, with the Twelve Apostles, nor was it received from any institution of learning, or of science, either religious, political or social. Our philosophy is not the philosophy of the world; but of the earth and the heavens, of time and eternity, and proceeds from God."

How like in spirit is this to that famous reply of the Son of God to the Jews, who marveled at his doctrine, saying, "How knoweth this man letters, having never learned?" What humility, what deep reverence for God there is in the reply of Messiah—"My doctrine is not mine, but His that sent me!"

If in these discourses preached in the latter years of his ministry there were fewer of those poetic flights of eloquence so characteristic of his earlier discourses and writings, there was a deeper solemnity, a calmer but more intense, earnestness. If there was less of the poet, there was more of the philosopher. The flower and bloom had fallen, perhaps, but it was only that the ripening fruit and golden grain might appear.

Finally, his counsels, his warnings, his doctrines and promises received the most direct approval by the voice of God Himself, demonstrating that his teachings had all along been inspired. The approval above referred to is contained in the following revelation:

REVELATION GIVEN THROUGH PRESIDENT JOHN TAYLOR AT SALT LAKE CITY, UTAH TERRITORY

October 13TH, 1882

Thus saith the Lord to the Twelve, and to the priesthood and people of my Church: Let my servants George Teasdale and Heber J. Grant be appointed to fill the vacancies in the Twelve, that you may be fully organized and prepared for the labors devolving upon you, for you have a great work to perform; and then proceed to fill up the presiding quorum of Seventies, and assist in organizing that body of my priesthood who are your co-laborers in the ministry. You may appoint Seymour B. Young to fill up the vacancy in the presiding quorum of Seventies, if he will conform to my law; for it is not meet that men who will not abide my law shall preside over my priesthood; and then proceed forthwith and call to your aid any assistance that you may require from among the Seventies to assist you in your labors in introducing and maintaining the gospel among the Lamanites throughout the land. And then let High Priests be selected, under the direction of the First Presidency, to preside over the various organizations that shall exist among this people; that those who receive the gospel may be taught in the doctrines of my church and in the ordinances and laws thereof, and also in the things pertaining to my Zion and my kingdom, saith the Lord, that they may be one with you in my Church and my kingdom.

Let the Presidency of my Church be one in all things; and let the Twelve also be one in all things; and let them all be one with me as I am one with the Father.

And let the High Priests organize themselves, and purify themselves, and prepare themselves for this labor, and for all other labors that they may be called upon to fulfill.

And let the Presidents of Stakes also purify themselves, and the priesthood and people of the Stakes over which they preside, and organize the priesthood in their various Stakes according to my law, in all the various departments thereof, in the High Councils, in the Elders' quorums, and in the Bishops and their councils, and in the quorums of Priests, Teachers and Deacons, that every quorum may be fully organized according to the order of my Church; and, then, let them inquire into the standing and fellowship of all that hold my holy priesthood in their several Stakes; and if they find those that are unworthy let them remove them, except they repent; for my priesthood, whom I have called and whom I have sustained and honored, shall honor me and obey my laws, and the laws of my holy priesthood, or they shall not be considered worthy to hold my priesthood, saith the Lord. And let my priesthood humble themselves before me, and seek not their own will but my will; for if my priesthood, whom I have chosen, and called, and endowed with the spirit and gifts of their several callings, and with the powers thereof, do not acknowledge me I will not acknowledge them, saith the Lord; for I will be honored and obeyed by my priesthood.

And, then, I call upon my priesthood, and upon all of my people, to repent of all their sins and short-comings, of their covetousness and pride and self-will, and of all their iniquities wherein they sin against me; and to seek with all humility to fulfill my law, as my priesthood, my saints and my people; and I call upon the heads of families to put their houses in order according to the law of God, and attend to the various duties and responsibilities associated therewith, and to purify themselves before me, and to purge out iniquity from their households. And I will bless and be with you, saith the Lord, and ye shall gather together in your holy places wherein ye assemble to call upon me, and ye shall ask for such things as are right, and I will hear your prayers, and my Spirit and power shall be with you, and my blessing shall rest upon you, upon your families, your dwellings and your households, upon your flocks and herds and fields, your orchards and vineyards, and upon all that pertains to you; and you shall be my people and I will be your God; and your enemies shall not have dominion over you, for I will preserve you and confound them, saith the Lord, and they shall not have power nor dominion over you; for my word shall go forth, and my work shall be accomplished, and my Zion shall be established, and my rule and my power and my dominion shall prevail among my people, and all nations shall yet acknowledge me. Even so, Amen.

CHAPTER 40 - THE INDICTMENT

In the latter part of December, 1881, the committee appointed to furnish and arrange the affairs of the Gardo House as the family residence of President Taylor, announced that it was ready; and if agreeable to him, suggested that he immediately move into it. They also intimated that they would be pleased to announce to his friends when they could call upon him. He acted upon their suggestion and appointed the 2nd of January as the day that a public reception would be given, between the hours of 11 a. m. and 3 p. m.

At eleven o'clock that day Croxall's Band entered the enclosure and serenaded the President in his new home, after which the doors were thrown open and the stream of callers began filing into the house. President Taylor, surrounded by his family, his counselors and a few personal friends, received them cordially, and exchanged kindly greetings. During the hours of reception Professor C. J. Thomas' orchestral Band serenaded him. The Tabernacle choir came also, and sang several pieces, among which was the grand anthem "And it shall come to pass in the last days," etc., concluding with "Auld Lang Syne." Two large tables in the dining hall were kept replenished with refreshments, of which nearly all who called partook. It was estimated that more than two thousand friends called upon the President that day. All were pleased to greet him, and were full of kindness and the best wishes for the man of God.

GARDO HOUSE

It was a grand day in the life of President Taylor. His youth and manhood had been spent in the service of God. He had never manifested a disposition to desert the ministry, no matter how strained his own circumstances might be. He was never called to do service in the cause of God, but that he answered, "ready!" and now that the frosts of seventy-four winters had made silvery white his hair, he was comfortably established in a magnificent home, surrounded by his family, his friends and brethren and honored by all Israel. No man had fairer prospects for enjoying the one boon ever coveted by age—the privilege—

"To husband out life's taper at the close,

And keep the flame from wasting by repose."

The fair prospect of ease and comfort, however, was soon to be marred by the ruthless machinations of unreasoning hate.

During the year 1881, a bitter agitation of the Mormon question, was inaugurated in Utah and spread throughout the United States. It was the work of sectarian religious bigots and political adventurers.

The efforts of sectarian ministers who have come to Utah as missionaries to convert the Mormons to their creeds, have always ended in dismal failure. Even those Saints who through neglect of religious duty, or for other causes have become indifferent as to their connection with the Church, could not be persuaded to feed upon the dry husks of the dead theology preached by sectarian ministers. While those who were feeding to the full in the rich pastures of the gospel of Christ, would not so much as look in the direction of the barren moors to which these missionaries invited them. The result was rage and disappointment in the vexed souls of these ministers; and they concluded that Mormonism was a thing not to be reasoned with, but to be stamped out by force.

Hunger for the spoils and emoluments of office, explains the motives of the political adventurers who joined in this agitation. In all the recommendations made to Congress by priests and demagogues, it may be seen that the one object to be attained is the complete control of the Territory by them.

Measures ostensibly for the suppression of plural marriage were introduced into Congress; and a call was made upon the churches throughout the country to hold mass meetings and adopt resolutions urging Congress to enact the Edmunds' Bill. These mass meetings were held early in 1882.

The one at Chicago was held at Farwell Hall, and among those present was ex-Vice-President Colfax, the former opponent, it will be remembered, of President Taylor in a discussion of the "Mormon question." His presence at that meeting was a tacit, but none the less emphatic acknowledgment, that he had failed to effect anything by his argument. He had the best of reasons for knowing that argument could not destroy Mormonism; he had tried it, and failed. Hence we see him associated with those who had determined that it must be "stamped out." He was at Farwell Hall that night to give the weight of his character to a meeting, the purpose of which was to urge Congress to enact proscriptive laws, to crush a people against whom he had hurled the thunderbolt of his logic in vain. It was bad taste, to say the least, for him to be present at that meeting. A decent respect for himself and the opinion of mankind, would have suggested that he leave such work to be done by other hands.

Meetings of this character were held in nearly all the large cities in the Union. They were much alike in spirit. Hatred for the Mormon people characterized them all. Bishop Fallows, at the meeting in Chicago, declared that if the measures then pending in Congress were not sufficient to heal the "political cancer," there were three hundred thousand swords ready to cut it out.

I leave it to the reader to judge how much sweet Christian charity there was in a meeting where such a remark was applauded.

As a sample of the charges made against the Saints and the Church in this agitation, I take those presented at the meeting held in St. Louis.

It was alleged that the Mormon Church interfered in political affairs; and that a recent vote for Delegate to Congress in Idaho had been carried by a brief order from George Q. Cannon, directing the Mormons to vote for a certain man:

That its numbers are daily recruited by cunning appeals to the ignorance and base passions of men;

That the number of polygamous felons in Utah is strongly increased by the importation from abroad of thousands who are ignorantly seduced or licentiously attracted to this shameful institution;

That a large proportion of the whole number of polygamists are unnaturalized foreigners who own no allegiance to the United States or its laws;

That it openly derides the authority of the national government, preaches treason publicly, and makes polygamous rebellion a religious duty;

That it degrades women, blotting out of their speech the very notion of home and all the sacred associations which it calls up, making a parody of religion;

And, lastly, that it foolishly assumes to be defiant to and stronger than the government.

As in these meetings it was assumed that these false statements were true, it was not difficult to work up a spirit of indignation throughout the country and to flood Congress with resolutions and petitions to pass the Edmunds Bill.

Meantime the Saints in Utah were not inactive. They did not permit this storm-cloud to gather without remonstrance. In February the Territorial legislature passed resolutions denying the charges made against the great majority of their constituents, and praying Congress to appoint a commission of honorable men to investigate the condition of affairs in Utah.

In addition to this, meetings in all parts of the Territory were held and remonstrances drawn up against the enactment of the measures pending before the national legislature. Memorials were formulated by the men, women and the youth of both sexes respectively. In all these memorials the false charges and base misrepresentations of their detractors were emphatically denied. In the memorial signed by the men, referring to plural marriage, it was said:

"Whatever of polygamy exists among the Mormons, rests solely upon their religious convictions. It is unsupported by any Territorial legislative enactments, and its practice already exposes them to the penalties of Congressional law. And it is better to leave it to the legitimate operations of that law, and the moral influences at work, than to attempt to extirpate it by radically oppressive or revolutionary measures."

On the same subject the women said: "And moreover, we your petitioners hereby testify that we are happy in our homes, and satisfied with our marriage relations and desire no change. And we most solemnly aver before God and man that our marital relations are most sacred, that they are divine, enjoining obligations and ties that pertain to time and reach into eternity. Were it not for the sacred and religious character of plural marriage, we should never have entered upon the practice of a principle which is contrary to our early teachings, and in consequence of which our names are cast out as evil by the Christian world."

The following paragraph occurred in the memorial of the young men: "We deny that the religious institution of plural marriage, as practiced by our parents, and to which many of us owe our existence, debases, pollutes, or in any way degrades those who enter into it. On the contrary, we solemnly affirm, and challenge successful contradiction, that plural marriage is a sacred religious ordinance, and that its practice has given to thousands, honorable names and peaceful homes where Christian precepts and virtuous practices have been uniformly inculcated, and the spirit of human liberty and religious freedom, fostered from the cradle to maturity."

This in the young ladies': "We have been taught and conscientiously believe that plural marriage is as much a part of our religion as faith, repentance and baptism. We solemnly and truthfully declare that neither we nor our mothers are held in bondage, but that we enjoy the greatest possible freedom, socially and religiously; that our homes are happy ones and we are neither low nor degraded; for the principles of purity, virtue, integrity and loyalty to the government of the United States, have been instilled into our minds and hearts since our earliest childhood."

In each memorial the petitioners prayed that Congress would suspend further action on all bills relating to Utah, and send a commission of honorable, intelligent and unprejudiced men and women to enquire into and learn the true state of affairs in said Territory. The signers to the men's petition numbered 16,256; those to the women's, 19,108; young men's, 15,636; young ladies', 14,152; a total of 65,152.

Surely petitions so respectfully worded, solemnly denying such grave charges, asking for so reasonable a thing as an inquiry into the true condition of affairs in Utah, and so numerously signed as these were, had some claim upon the attention of Congress. They were laid aside, after being read, however, and the Edmunds Bill passed with indecent haste. The bill was ably discussed in the Senate, and many constitutional objections urged against it; but when it came to the House, it was "railroaded through," and that with a rush; debate upon it being limited to five minute speeches, the whole discussion not lasting more than two hours. It was approved by the President on the 22nd of March, and then became law.

In addition to defining polygamy and fixing the punishment for it, the new law also made cohabitation with more than one woman, a misdemeanor, to be punished by a fine of not more than three hundred dollars and six months' imprisonment; it provided that counts for polygamy and unlawful cohabitation might be joined in the same indictment; it made actual polygamists and those who believed in the rightfulness of it, incompetent as jurors in any prosecution for polygamy or unlawful cohabitation; it also made polygamists, or those cohabiting with more than one woman, incompetent to vote or hold office. It vacated all registration and election offices of every description, and placed the registration of voters and the management of elections under a federal returning board, known as the Utah Commission.

When the news of the full enactment of this law reached Utah, President Taylor, knowing the vindictive hatred of the conspirators in Salt Lake City who had concocted that law and aroused the popular clamor which induced Congress to enact it; and knowing that they would seek first to entangle him within its meshes because he was President of the Church; and further knowing that such were the nature of his duties to the Church that it was imperative that he have his liberty, that he might watch over the interests of the great people committed to his care—he resolved to make a great personal sacrifice by submitting to this law, unjust, cruel and infamous as it was. He therefore took counsel with his family and it was arranged that his wives return to their former homes, while he continued to reside at the Gardo House.

CHAPTER 41 - A STORM IS COMING

The morning of the second day's conference in April, 1882, was stormy and cold. The wind blew in fitful gusts, pelting the Saints with sleet as with bowed heads and turned up collars they hurried along to attend the conference. President Taylor made an impressive allusion to this storm in the course of his remarks that day.

Referring to the late enactment of Congress—the Edmunds Bill—and the bitter prejudice aroused against the Saints, he warned them that a storm was coming; and that it would break in its fury upon them. "Let us treat it," said he, half humorously "the same as we did this morning in coming through the snow-storm—put up our coat collars (suiting the action to the word) and wait till the storm subsides. After the storm comes sunshine. While the storm lasts it is useless to reason with the world; when it subsides we can talk to them."

In the afternoon he again referred to this matter: "I stated this morning that there was a storm coming—in fact it is raging at present and has been for some little time, and that it would be well for us to keep up our coat collars and protect ourselves as best we could until the storm passed over. There will be a storm in the United States after a while; and I want our brethren to prepare themselves for it. At the last conference, I think, I advised all who were in debt to take advantage of the prosperous times and pay their debts; so that they might not be in bondage to anyone, and when the storm came they might be prepared to meet it. There will be one of that kind very soon; and I thought I would give you this warning again, and repeat this piece of advice—the wise will understand."

On the last day of the conference—the 9th of April—President Taylor preached one of the most remarkable and powerful sermons of his life. He occupied more than two hours in delivering it; and throughout, the immense congregation which filled the great Tabernacle to its utmost capacity listened with rapt attention.

In addition to sketching the rise and progress of the work of the Lord in these last days, he refuted by the most positive testimony the base slanders on which the late agitation against the work was founded. Referring to the assault made upon the Saints under the pretext of suppressing polygamy, he thus defined the position and policy of the Church:

"We covet no man's possessions. But we expect to maintain our own rights. If we are crowded upon by unprincipled men or inimical legislation, we shall not take the course pursued by the lawless, the dissolute and unprincipled. We shall not have recourse to the dynamite of the Russian Nihilists, the secret plans and machinations of the communists, the boycotting and threats of the Fenians, the force and disorder of the Jayhawkers, the regulators or the Molly Maguires, nor any other secret or illegal combination; but we still expect to possess and maintain our rights; but to obtain them in a legal, peaceful and constitutional manner. As American citizens, we shall contend for all our liberties, rights and immunities, guaranteed to us by the Constitution; and no matter what action may be taken by mobocratic influence, by excited and unreasonable men, or by inimical legislation, we shall contend inch by inch for our freedom and rights, as well as the freedom and rights of all American citizens and of all mankind.

"As a people or community, we can bide our time; but I will say to you Latter-day Saints, that there is nothing of which you have been despoiled by oppressive acts or mobocratic rule, but that you will again possess, or your children after you. Your possessions, of which you have been fraudulently despoiled in Missouri and Illinois, you will again possess, and that without force, or fraud or violence. The Lord has a way of His own in regulating such matters. We are told the wicked shall slay the wicked. He has a way of His own of 'emptying the earth of the inhabitants thereof.' A terrible day of reckoning is approaching the nations of the earth; the Lord is coming out of His hiding place to vex the inhabitants thereof; and the destroyer of the Gentiles, as prophesied of, is already on his way. Already combinations are being entered into which are very ominous for the future prosperity, welfare and happiness of this great republic. The volcanic fires of disordered and anarchial elements are beginning to manifest themselves and exhibit the internal forces that are at work among the turbulent and unthinking masses of the people.

"Congress will soon have something else to do than to prescribe and persecute an innocent, law-abiding and patriotic people. Of all bodies in the world, they can least afford to remove the bulwarks that bind society together in this nation, to recklessly trample upon human freedom and rights, and to rend and destroy that great palladium of human rights—the Constitution of the United States. Ere long they will need all its protecting influence to save this nation from misrule, anarchy and mobocratic influence. They can ill afford to be the foremost in tampering with human rights and human freedom, or in tearing down the bulwarks of safety and protection which that sacred instrument has guaranteed.

"The internal fires of revolution are already smoldering in this nation, and they need but a spark to set them in a flame. Already are agencies at work in the land calculated to subvert and overthrow every principle of rule and government; already is corruption of every kind prevailing in high places and permeating all society; already as a nation, we are departing from our God, and corrupting ourselves with malfeasance, dishonor and a lack of public integrity and good faith; already are licentiousness and debauchery corrupting, undermining and destroying society; already are we interfering with the laws of nature and stopping the functions of life, and have become the slayers of our own offspring, and employ human butchers in the shape of physicians to assist in this diabolical and murderous work.

"The sins of this nation, the licentiousness, the debauchery, the murders are entering into the ears of the Lord of Sabaoth, and I tell you now [addressing himself to the nation], from the tops of these mountains, as a humble servant of the living God, that unless these crimes are stopped, this nation will be overthrown, and its glory, power, dominion and wealth will fade away like the dews of a summer morning. I also say to other nations of the earth, that unless they repent of their crimes, their iniquities and abominations, their thrones will be overturned, their kingdoms and governments overthrown, and their lands made desolate.

"This is not only my saying, but it is the saying of those ancient prophets which they themselves profess to believe; for God will speedily have a controversy with the nations of the earth, and, as I stated before, the destroyer of the Gentiles is on his way to overthrow governments, to destroy dynasties, to lay waste thrones, kingdoms and empires, to spread abroad anarchy and desolation, and to cause war, famine and bloodshed to overspread the earth."

Reverting again to the position to be assumed by the Church in relation to the Edmund's law, he expressed himself thus:

"We do not wish to place ourselves in a state of antagonism, nor act defiantly towards this government. We will fulfill the letter, so far as practicable, of that unjust, inhuman, oppressive and unconstitutional law, so far as we can without violating principle; but we cannot sacrifice every principle of human right at the behest of corrupt, unreasoning and unprincipled men; we cannot violate the highest and noblest principles of human nature and make pariahs and outcasts of high-minded, virtuous and honorable women, nor sacrifice at the shrine of popular clamor the highest and noblest principles of humanity!

"We shall abide all constitutional law, as we always have done; but while we are God-fearing and law-abiding, and respect all honorable men and officers, we are no craven serfs, and have not learned to lick the feet of oppressors, nor to bow in base submission to unreasoning clamor. We will contend inch by inch, legally and constitutionally, for our rights as American citizens. We stand proudly erect in the consciousness of our rights as American citizens, and plant ourselves firmly on the sacred guarantees of the Constitution. We need have no fears, no trembling in our knees about these attempts to deprive us of our God-given and constitutional liberties. God will take care of His people, if we will only do right."

The speaker concluded as follows:

"Our trust is in God. You have heard me say before, Hosanna, the Lord God Omnipotent reigneth; and if this congregation feels as I do, we will join together in the same acclaim. Follow me. HOSANNA! HOSANNA! HOSANNA TO GOD AND THE LAMB, FOREVER, AND EVER, WORLDS WITHOUT END. AMEN, AMEN, AND AMEN!"

Thrice was the shout repeated, the vast congregation of from eleven to thirteen thousand followed President Taylor as with one voice. The grand words of praise and triumph were not new to Israel. They had shaken the walls of the Temple at Nauvoo during the one day that it stood resplendent in all the glory of the House of God—though the Saints knew they would be compelled to abandon it the next day to their enemies. The same glorious shout in the midst of toil and hardships had rolled through the woods bordering the streams of Iowa, and had broken the silence that for ages brooded over the vast prairies of the west. Indeed the shout was older than that, older than the everlasting hills which now listened to it—aye, older than the earth itself! For was not this the shout which shook the heavens before the foundations of the earth were laid, when "the morning stars sang together and all the sons of God shouted for joy?"

A celebrated press correspondent, who was present in the interest of the New York *World*, thus describes the closing scenes of that conference:

"Acquainted though I am with displays of oriental fanaticism and western revivalism, I set this Mormon enthusiasm on one side, as being altogether of a different character; for it not only astonishes by its fervor, but commands respect by its sincere sobriety. The congregation of the Saints assembled in the Tabernacle, numbering, by my own careful computation, eleven thousand odd, and composed in almost exactly equal parts of the two sexes, reminded me of the Puritan gatherings of the past as I had imagined them, and of my personal experiences of the Transvaal Boers as I knew them. There was no rant, no affectation, no straining after theatrical effect. The very simplicity of this great gathering of country-folk was striking in the extreme, and significant from first to last of a power that should hardly be trifled with by sentimental legislation. Nor could anything exceed the impressiveness of the response which the people gave instantaneously to the appeal of their President for the support of their voices. The great Tabernacle was filled with waves of sound as the 'Amens' of the congregation burst out. The shout of men going into battle was not more stirring than the closing words of this memorable conference, spoken as if by one vast voice."

CHAPTER 42 - TEST OATH

Notwithstanding the cares, labors and anxiety which his position as President of the Church thrust upon him, in these eventful years of which we are now writing, President Taylor still found time to write works on the gospel. In the year 1882 he issued his work on the Mediation and Atonement of our Lord and Savior Jesus Christ. It is a book of some two hundred royal octavo pages.

In the main, it is a collection of scriptural passages bearing upon the subject, brought together from both ancient and modern revelations, and arranged in such manner as to develop the necessity, sufficiency, efficacy, glory, power and completeness of the atonement made by Messiah, for the sins of the world. It is not a work ambitious of displaying literary skill, or written with a view to meet the shallow and trifling objections urged against this great, central fact of the gospel by glib-tongued infidels and repeated without thought by their apish followers. It was the object of the author to bring together all the testimonies to be found in holy writ on this subject, as well in modern as in ancient scripture; and most admirably did he succeed, linking the testimonies together with such remarks as make their meanings and bearings clear, and increase the value of the original passages. The student of the great subject of the atonement, will find in President Taylor's work a most valuable collection of material for his consideration.

In chapter XXIII he will also find a most valuable reference to the doctrine of evolution as believed in by the Darwinian school of philosophers—a school of philosophy which professes to trace living phenomena to their origin, and which, if it were true, would at once destroy the doctrine of the Atonement.

In the appendix to the work, also will be found some interesting information in relation to the ideas of a general atonement and redemption entertained by the ancient heathen nations, traces of which may still be found in the traditions of their descendants. From these facts some noted infidel writers have sought to make it appear that the Christian doctrine of the atonement was derived from the heathens; but President Taylor clearly proves that the heathens originally derived their knowledge of these things from the earlier servants of God, and have preserved those truths, though in a mutilated form, in their traditions. "Exhibiting," as President Taylor writes, "that the atonement was a great plan of the Almighty for the salvation, redemption and exaltation of the human family; and that the pretenders in the various ages, had drawn whatever of truth they possessed, from the knowledge of those principles taught by the priesthood from the earliest periods of recorded time; instead of Christianity being indebted, as some late writers would allege, to the turbid system of heathen mythology, and to pagan ceremonies."

About this time he also wrote a pamphlet of some forty-five pages on the Aaronic Priesthood, chiefly relating to the authority and duties of Bishops.

The Mormon question having come once more prominently before the country through the enactments of Congress against it, the editor of the *North American Review* visited Utah for the express purpose of soliciting President Taylor to write an article on the then present state of the Mormon question, which he did, reviewing the operations of the recently passed Edmunds law; and in addition to that, refuted many of the false, slanderous misrepresentations, both new and old, respecting the Saints.

Meantime the storm which President Taylor had predicted at the April conference in 1882, burst upon the Saints in all its fury. The conspirators against the Church of Christ, in the Edmunds enactment, had a law under which they hoped to be able to destroy its power.

The first act of the Commission appointed by that law, was to frame a test oath which they required every person to take before he was permitted to register or vote. This practically disfranchised a whole Territory at one fell swoop; and in order to be reinstated as a voter, every man had to take the oath, which required him to swear that he had never simultaneously lived with more than one woman "*in the marriage relation*;" or if a woman, that she was not the wife of a polygamist, nor had she entered into any relation with any man in violation of the laws of the United States concerning polygamy and bigamy.

By this arrangement it will be seen that those who cohabited with more than one woman in adultery or prostitution, were not affected by its provisions. The *roué*, the libertine, the strumpet, the brothel-keeper, the adulterer and adulteress could vote. No matter how licentious a man or a woman might be, all but the Mormons were screened and protected in the exercise of the franchise by the ingenious insertion of the clause, "in the marriage relation," a clause which nowhere appears in the Edmunds law. Such broad constructionists were the Commission that they declared no man or woman who had ever been a member of a family practicing plural marriage, should be permitted to register or vote, no matter what their present status might be. As a case in point, President Taylor himself relates the following incidents connected with the operations of this law. They are from the article above referred to in the *North American Review*:

"A former mayor of Salt Lake City, Mr. Feramorz Little, a very honorable gentleman and highly respected, came to this Territory many years ago, before there was any law of Congress against plural marriage, and espoused two wives. Subsequently, one of these wives died, then the other, and at the time that this incident occurred he had been for years without a wife. He had a son who was appointed registrar for a certain district in this city, and this son had the mortification of being compelled, under the ruling of the Commission, to refuse his father permission to register, and consequently deprived him of the right to vote—a privilege which he had a perfect right to exercise, both because of the provision in the

Constitution that no *ex post facto* law shall be made, and again by reason of the statute of limitations, which bars all action in any such cases after the expiration of three years. Soon after the refusal of the registrar to place his father's name on the registration list, a well-known keeper of a bagnio and her associates presented themselves, and the son had the humiliation of having to permit them to register. These courtesans afterward voted.

"Another case: A man came to the place of registration, and remarked to the officer that he supposed he could not register, as he had a wife and also kept a mistress. This man might be considered a very straight-forward fellow to make so ready an acknowledgment, but I fail to see anything straight-forward in such a crooked transaction as the breaking of the marriage vows and marital infidelity. But the officer knew what was in the oath better than this man, and advised him to read it. He did so. When he came to the words, 'in the marriage relation,' he immediately said, 'Yes, I see. I can go that,' and was at once sworn and registered."

Having begun the application of the law so as to effect the franchise of the party in the majority, the next move of the conspirators was to begin action judicially.

The first case prosecuted under the new regime was that of Rudger Clawson, a young man highly respected in the community. His case marks the inauguration of as cruel and unjustifiable a judicial crusade as was ever perpetrated against a free people in a professedly free government. He was arraigned both for polygamy and unlawful cohabitation, found guilty and sentenced on the 3rd of November, 1884. His sentence on both charges covered a period of four years imprisonment, and eight hundred dollars in fines.

President Taylor was subpoenaed as a witness in his case, but the testimony he gave was not material. Indeed the prosecution seemed more anxious to involve him in a conflict with the court than to elicit any fact he might know in relation to this particular case. His description of the scene in court during this trial, the character of the man being tried, and that of the men trying him, with a review of their methods and the principles involved in the controversy, together with the picture he draws of the present state of society as he described them off hand in a discourse delivered in Ogden, a few days after the trial, is too important to be omitted; and it demonstrates that the fire of President Taylor's eloquence could still burn brightly on occasion, until it scorched and burned an opponent, and vindicated the right. He said:

"While I was in court a few days ago, and gazing upon the assembly of judges, lawyers, marshals, witnesses, spectators, etc., many reflections of a very peculiar character passed through my mind, some of which I will here rehearse:

"I could not help thinking as I looked upon the scene, that there was no necessity for all this; these parties [Rudger Clawson and his plural wife] need not have placed themselves in this peculiar dilemma. Here was a young man blessed with more than ordinary intelligence, bearing amongst all who know him a most enviable reputation for virtue, honesty, sobriety and all other desirable characteristics that we are in the habit of supposing go to make a man respected and beloved, the civilized world over. He had been trained from early childhood in the nurture and admonition of the Lord, had been an attendant at Sabbath school and Young Men's Improvement Societies, where his course was of the most pleasing kind; more than this, some years ago when quite a youth, he had shown his devotion to the faith in which he had been reared, by going forth without purse or scrip to preach in the midst of the unbelieving the doctrines of a most unpopular faith. And as I reached this point in my reflections, my mind instinctively wanders to a monument I gazed at in Salt Lake City cemetery but a few days ago. That monument records in fitting words of respect and admiration the devotion of two young missionaries in a far-off southern state, one of whom had fallen a victim to mob violence, had sealed with his blood the testimony which he bore, the other had stood by him in his hour of sore need, and rescued his mangled body and brought it safely for thousands of miles to the home of his bereaved parents and sorrowing co-religionists.

"This heroic young man is the one now arraigned before the courts of his country, for an alleged offense against the morality of the age! Assuming that the reports pertaining to him should prove to be correct, and he really has a plural wife, what then would be the position? He from his earliest recollection, had been taught to reverence the Bible as the word of God, to revere the lives and examples of the ancient worthies whom Jehovah honored by making them His confidents, and revealing unto them the secrets of his divine purposes; he had read of one who was called 'the friend of God and the father of the faithful;' of another who was said to be a 'man after God's own heart;' of a third who in all things is said to have done the will of heaven, and so on until they could be numbered by the score; yet all these men, the friends, associates and confidents of the great Creator of heaven and earth, were men with more than one wife, some with many wives, yet they still possessed and rejoiced in the love and honor of the great judge of all the world, whose judgments are just, and whose words are all righteousness. This young man is charged with following these worthy examples; it is asserted that he has taken to wife a beautiful and virtuous young lady, belonging, like himself, to one of our most respected families, and who also believes in the Bible, and in the example set her by those holy women of old, such as Rachel, Ruth, Hannah, and others, who honored God's law, and became the mothers of prophets, priests and kings.

"And as my cogitations ran, I thought what need had these two to follow such examples of a by-gone age; why not walk in the way of the world today, unite with our modern Christian civilization, and if passion guide their actions why call each other husband and wife, why hallow their associations by any sacred ceremony—was there any need of such? Why not do as tens of thousands of others do, live in the condition of illicit love? And then if any child should be feared from this unsanctified union, why not still follow our Christian exemplars, remove the foetal encumbrance, call in some copyist of Madame Restell, the abortionist, male or female that pollute our land? That would have been, *sub-rosa*, genteel, fashionable, respectable, Christian-like, as Christianity goes in this generation.

"If this did not succeed, the young man might have turned his victim into the street to perish, or die of pollution as is done in tens of thousands of instances, in the most sanctified manner by the hypocrites of the day. Then in either of these cases, the young gentleman could have been received into good society, be petted and applauded; could hold a position under our government, be even a deputy marshal, registrar or what not, and still further, be able to answer all necessary questions; and be admitted as a grand juror without being brought in as a gutter snipe on an open venire, but as a respectable citizen on the regular panel.

"Or, again, these two, in the event of a child being born, might consign it to the care of some degraded hag, some 'baby farmer,' where gradually and quietly its innocent life would ebb out, and bye and bye the grief-stricken parents would receive the anticipated notice that their dear little offspring, notwithstanding every care, was dead and buried! This is a respectable crime, a crime committed principally by those who go to high-toned churches and fashionable meeting houses in velvets and feathers, in silks and satins, and who with upturned eyes and hypocritical voices, insult the majesty of heaven by drawling out, 'Lord have mercy upon us, miserable sinners!' Yet they are murderers—murderers of the worst kind, the shedders of innocent blood, consumers of their own flesh, whom the vengeance of God awaits!

"This young man and woman could have done all this and no marshals with ready feet would have dogged their steps, no packed grand juries with unanimous alacrity would do the bidding of over-zealous prosecuting attorneys; no federal judge would overturn precedent, ignore law, disregard justice on purpose to convict. No, they might have been the friends, associates, companions of judge and prosecutor, governor and commissioner; but now, as they would neither associate unrighteously, nor take means to destroy the results of their union, but honestly and virtuously live, as is claimed, as husband and wife, he stands in the felon's dock, charged with an offense against the dignity of the United States, and to convict him, oppressive laws, more oppressively administered are brought to bear with all the ingenuity that malice can devise and hatred adopt.

"And there, in this ignominious position, he stands with every person who might possibly be his friend, excluded from the jury, without the possibility of a fair trial by his peers, not one of the panel being in the least sympathy with himself; by such people this unfortunate young gentleman has to be tried, judged, prosecuted, proscribed and condemned because of his firm and unswerving faith in the God of Abraham, Isaac and Jacob; of David, Solomon, and numerous other God-fearing and honorable men, who, like him, have despised the cant and hypocrisy of an ungodly world, and dared to obey the behests of Jehovah.

"Of these things he had learned from the Bible, in the Sunday School; no wonder then that our would-be reformers are so anxious to exclude the Bible from our district schools, as its teachings and examples so emphatically condemn the theories on which the acts and legislation of Congress are based, as well as the course pursued by those who seek to aid in the regeneration of Utah, by adding to or taking from the law as is best suited to shield their own corrupt practices; or, on the other hand, by extra judicial proceedings, under cover of law, they pervert, to prosecute and persecute the Mormons.

"Where was this scene enacted? In the gorgeous palaces of Belshazzar, surrounded by his wives, concubines, and nobles, and where was seen written on the walls '*Mene, Mene, Tekel Upharsin*?' No. Was it at the destruction of Sodom and Gomorrah, when ten righteous persons could not be found to avert the wrath of an offended God, or in Pompeii or Herculaneum, which, in their turn, for their libidinous and unrighteous practices, as Sodom and Gomorrah, suffered the vengeance of eternal fire? No. Was it at the Saturnalia of the Bacchanals of ancient Greece and Rome? No. Those nations have long been overthrown and are now only known to a few readers of ancient history. Was it during the reign of the first French Republic, when they elevated a prostitute as the goddess of reason? No. Was it in the days of the inquisition, when the rack, the gibbet, the faggot and the flames were brought into requisition to force unwilling victims to testify of things which their conscience forbade, and who perished by thousands for daring to think, and act, and believe in and worship God according to their own consciences? No. Was it under the influence of Bacchus, or in the midnight revelings as exhibited in Rome under Nero? No; this scene was enacted in mid-day, in the nineteenth century, in the year of our Lord, 1884, in the Federal court house, in Salt Lake City, at a court presided over by Judge Charles S. Zane, Chief Justice for the United States in the Territory of Utah, assisted by Prosecuting Attorney William H. Dickson, and the other adjuncts of the law, and in the presence of several hundred American citizens!"

CHAPTER 43 - LAST SERMON

The "storm" increased in violence. Special appropriations were made in Washington to aid in the enforcement of the infamous Edmunds law. With those funds deputy marshals were multiplied, some of them being men of notoriously immoral lives. They usually went in squads, pouncing first upon one village and then another, raiding the homes of the most respected and honorable men in the community, who were suspected of living with their plural wives—with women they had honored with the name of wife in some instances for more than a quarter of a century, by whom they had reared large and respectable families: and because they would not abandon them—thrust them away like unclean, nameless things—this pack of human hounds were turned loose upon them, to dog their footsteps, to invade their homes and insult their families.

Spotters and spies were employed to betray their neighbors; children were hailed upon the streets and questioned about the affairs of their parents; wives—lawful wives—were dragged into the courts and compelled to testify against their husbands; shamefully indecent questions were put to modest maidens in jury rooms and in open court; juries were packed to convict; a Mormon accused of violation of the anti-polygamy laws stood before a jury of his avowed political and religious enemies; suspicion was equivalent to accusation; accusation to indictment; indictment to conviction; and conviction met almost invariably with the full penalty of the law, unless the victim was so recreant to every sense of honor as to push from him the women he had taken as wives for time and all eternity!

In the midst of this judicial "storm" which broke upon the Church in Utah and the surrounding territories, President Taylor moved calmly on, discharging his duties, counseling, encouraging and strengthening the people. At the same time he did not fail to rebuke and proclaim the hypocrisy of the men who were the prime movers in this unholy crusade, carried on, professedly, in the interests of morality. For this purpose he published the criminal statistics of Utah for the year 1883, by which he demonstrated that while the Gentile population was greatly in the minority, they furnished the overwhelming majority of criminals. Following are his statements:

"The population of Utah may be estimated at one hundred and sixty thousand in 1883.

"Of these say one hundred and thirty thousand are Mormons, and thirty thousand are Gentiles—a very liberal estimate of the latter.

"In this year there were forty-six persons sent to the penitentiary convicted of crime. Of these thirty-three were non-Mormons, and thirteen reputed Mormons.

"At the above estimate of population the ratio or percentage would be one prisoner for every ten thousand Mormons, or one hundredth of one per cent., and of the Gentiles one convict in every nine hundred and nine, or about one ninth of one per cent. So that the actual proportion of criminals is more than ten times greater among the Gentiles of Utah, with the above very liberal estimate, than among the Mormons.

"It is urged that these non-Mormon prisoners are not a fair representation of the average of crime throughout the country, but are the result of the flow of the desperate classes westward to the borders of civilization; with greater truth we reply that the Mormon prisoners are not representatives of Mormonism, nor the results of Mormonism, but of the consequences of a departure from Mormon principles; and of the thirteen prisoners classed as Mormons, the greater portion were only so by family connection or association.

"ARRESTS IN SALT LAKE CITY IN 1883:

Mormons 150

Non-Mormons 1,559

Or more than ten times the number of Mormon arrests.

"Again it is estimated that there are six thousand non-Mormons and nineteen thousand Mormons in Salt Lake City, which shows of Mormons one arrest in one hundred and twenty-six and two-thirds.

"Non-Mormons, one arrest in a fraction less than four, or rather more than twenty-five per cent.

"If we were not on the defensive in this case," observed President Taylor, when presenting the above facts, "I would say nothing about these things; but it ill-becomes men who have ten criminals to our one, to come here as our reformers, and try to disfranchise men who are ten times as good as they are. These are facts that are not of my own getting up. They come from the public records and can be verified by the prison and other statistics."

In order to still further explode the defense made by those whom these facts placed in so unenviable a position, *viz*: that the scum of society from the eastern states had floated out here to the west, and consequently the Gentile population in Utah was not representative of Gentile communities elsewhere, he collected a number of statements from the sermons and writings of leading ministers and writers from various parts of the Union, on the subject of infanticide, foeticide and kindred crimes, that told a sad tale of sexual immorality, which every year, according to the authors he quoted, was growing worse and worse—something too much of this:

Handle it carefully,
Deal with it gently,
Speak of it tenderly,
Poor justice is blind!

The Stakes of Zion located in Arizona suffered quite as much from this judicial crusade as those living in Utah, and they were further away from the chief pastors of the flock, and hence greater perplexity and excitement. On learning of this, President Taylor determined to visit them, learn the true situation of their affairs and counsel them as the Lord should give him wisdom.

Accordingly a party of brethren was made up including his second counselor, Joseph F. Smith, and also Apostles Moses Thatcher and Francis M. Lyman, Bishop John Sharp and others. They were joined in the south also by Apostle Erastus Snow.

The party left Salt Lake City on the 3rd of January, 1885, by the Union Pacific Railway to Denver, thence to Albuquerque, in New Mexico, thence to the settlements of the Saints in Apache County, Arizona, in the vicinity of Winslow.

President Taylor went to St. David, in the extreme south-east corner of Arizona, near Benson, where he met with the Presidents of the four Stakes in that Territory; Jesse N. Smith, Christopher Layton, Alexander F. McDonald and Lot Smith. He found the Saints in a lamentable condition. They had been set upon in the most ruthless manner by their enemies. Nearly all the forms of law had been abandoned in dealing with them, and outrages had been heaped upon them, under the pretext of executing the law, that were well-nigh unendurable. Those who had been convicted and sentenced had been shipped off to Detroit, a distance of two thousand miles, notwithstanding there was a good available prison at Yuma, within the Territory.

Under these circumstances President Taylor thought it better for the brethren to evade the law; and in order that those who were being hunted might find a temporary place of refuge, he sent two parties down into Mexico to find suitable place for the settlement of those who had to flee from this unhallowed persecution.

During the absence of these parties, he visited with a portion of his party Guaymas, on the Gulf of California, in the state of Sonora, Mexico. On the return trip he stopped off at Hermosillo, the capital of the state of Sonora, where he and his party were received at the residence of Governor Torres, with distinguished consideration.

Returning to Benson he met with the brethren sent in search of a place of refuge, and decided in his capacity as Trustee-in-Trust of the Church to assist in purchasing a place which had been selected by Christopher Layton, just over the line in the state of Sonora.

After giving general directions to guide the Presidents of the Stakes in Arizona as to their future policy and movements, President Taylor and party visited the settlements of the Saints in Maricopa County, on Salt River; and from thence *via* Los Angeles went to San Francisco. Here he spent a day or two visiting points of interest. Among other features of his visit was a call at the famous library of the veteran historian, Hurbert H. Bancroft.

While in San Francisco he received dispatches to the effect that it would not be safe for him to return home, as his arrest had been determined upon. Notwithstanding this information he immediately started for Salt Lake City, where he arrived on Tuesday, January 27th, 1885, having traveled nearly five thousand miles since the 3rd of the same month.

The Sunday following, February 1st, he preached his last public sermon. In it he related the principal incidents of his late mission into Arizona, described the wrongs inflicted upon the people there, and told the council he had given them.

As the vindictiveness of the courts had increased during his absence, he gave the same advice to the people of Utah.

He deplored the condition of things in the Territory, not so much on account of the Latter-day Saints, as on the account of the great government of the United States, which had stooped from the proud position it had hitherto boasted as the asylum for the oppressed of all nations, to that of a persecutor of a righteous people for their religion, until they had to find an asylum in an adjoining republic! Referring to the outrages perpetrated both in Arizona and in Utah, he asks:

"What would you do? Would you resent these outrages and break the heads of the men engaged in them, and spill their blood? No;" said he, "avoid them as much as you possibly can—just as you would wolves, or hyenas, or crocodiles, or snakes, or any of these beasts or reptiles. Get out of their way as much as you can. What! Won't you submit to the dignity of the law? Well, I would if the law would only be a little more dignified. But when we see the dignity of the ermine bedraggled in the mud and mire, and every principle of justice violated, it behooves men to take care of themselves as best they can. But no breaking of heads, no bloodshed, rendering evil for evil. Let us try to cultivate the spirit of the gospel, and adhere to the principles of truth. While other men are seeking to trample the Constitution under foot, we will try to maintain it. I will tell you what you will see by and by. You will see trouble! *Trouble*! TROUBLE enough in these United States. And as I have said before, I say today—*I tell you in the name of God,* WOE! *To them that fight against Zion, for God will fight against them!*"

Such was his last admonition, his last warning, his last prophecy delivered in person in public to the people of God, to the nation in which he had labored as a faithful servant of God, with such untiring zeal, wisdom and skill for half a century.

That night he went into retirement, to escape the ruthless persecution aimed at him by the unrelenting and hate-blinded enemies of the Church of Christ.

CHAPTER 44 – COHABITATION

From his places of retirement among the Saints, President Taylor continued to preside over the Church, and under God to shape its policy and direct its movements. Prevented by the mistaken zeal of the United States officials and the vigilance of their myrmidons—the spotters and spies—from attending the public meetings and conferences of the Church, he, with his counselors, addressed general epistles to the Saints in which they imparted such counsel and instruction as they considered necessary and suited to the conditions by which they were environed.

These papers are remarkable for their conservative tone and wisdom; for the total absence of anger or vindictiveness, as also for the scope and variety of the subjects they treated upon. They compare favorably with the wisest and best state papers ever issued by kings or presidents, ministers of state or cabinet councils. The flock of Christ, therefore, was not left without the counsel of heaven or the care of the shepherds.

Still those were dark days. The seats reserved and usually occupied by the leaders of Israel in the public assemblies were either vacant or filled by comparative strangers. The recent enactments of Congress infamous in themselves, were still more infamously enforced. The courts and United States officials in Utah seemed utterly reckless in their methods of executing the law. Men who at the most were guilty of what the law defined to be a misdemeanor, punishable by six months imprisonment and three hundred dollars fine, were hunted as if they were guilty of the grossest crimes which could endanger the peace and safety of the community.

Frequently, and I may say usually, deputy marshals in the night would surround the houses suspected as being the places where their victims were to be found, and then in the morning, before the inmates were astir, would pounce upon them in the most unceremonious and brutal manner. No place was so sacred in the homes of the people but these minions under the color of law would force their way into it. Even the bed chambers of modest maidenhood were rudely entered before the occupants could dress, and in some instances the covering of their beds stripped from them in the pretended search for violators of the law; and they the while compelled to listen to their low blasphemies.

In proof of these allegations, which may seem too hard for belief as time with its ever-moving wheels carries us away from the years in which these acts of petty tyranny were perpetrated, I insert a few statements of parties who suffered them. These statements are to be found in a memorial addressed to Congress by the women of Utah, presented in the Senate on the 6th of April, 1886, by Senator Blair of New Hampshire, and ordered printed by that body:

"On January 11th, 1886, early in the morning, five deputy marshals appeared at the residence of William Grant, American Fork, forced the front door open, and, while the inmates were still in bed, made their way up stairs to their sleeping apartments. There they were met by one of the daughters of William Grant, who was aroused by the intrusion and, despite her protestations, without giving time for the object of their search to get up and dress himself, made their way into his bedroom, finding him still in bed and his wife *en deshabille* in the act of dressing herself."

Mrs. Easton, of Greenville, near Beaver, relates the following:

"About seven a. m. deputies came to our house and demanded admittance. I asked them to wait until we got dressed, and we would let them in. Deputy Gleason said he would not wait, and raised the window and got partly through by the time we opened the door, when he drew himself back and came in through the door. He then went into the bedroom; one of the young ladies had got under the bed, from which Gleason pulled the bedding and ordered the young lady to come out. This she did, and ran into the other room, where she was met by Thompson. I asked Gleason why he pulled the bedding from the bed, and he answered, 'By God! I found Watson in the same kind of a place.' He then said he thought Easton was concealed in a small compass, and that he expected to find him in a similar place, and was going to get him before he left."

Miss Morris, of the same place, says:

"Deputy Gleason came to my bed and pulled the clothing off me, asking if there was any one in bed with me. He then went to the fireplace and pulled a sack of straw from there and looked up the chimney. One of them next pulled up a piece of carpet, when Gleason asked Thompson if there was anyone under there. Thompson said 'No,' and Gleason exclaimed, 'G—d d—it, we will look, anyway.' They also looked in cupboards, boxes, trunks, etc., and a small tea chest, but threw nothing out."

Deputy Thompson, referred to in the above, is the man who, a few months afterwards, December 16th, 1886, killed Edward M. Dalton at Parowan by shooting him down in the street under the plea that Dalton was trying to escape arrest for unlawful cohabitation. The testimony of eye witnesses to the whole transaction, however, does not bear out the claims of the man upon whose hands will be found innocent blood when he shall stand before that tribunal where there is no shuffling—where the action will be seen in its true light—where the guilty man himself, even in the teeth and forehead of his offending, must give in the evidence.

The following which occurred in Idaho is also from the aforesaid Memorial:

"February 23rd, 1886, at about eleven o'clock at night, two deputy marshals visited the house of Solomon Edwards, about seven miles from Eagle Rock, Idaho, and arrested Mrs. Edwards, his legal wife, after she had retired to bed, and required her to accompany them immediately to Eagle Rock. Knowing something of the character of one of the deputies, from his having visited the house before, when he indulged in a great deal of drinking, profanity, and abuse, she feared to accompany them without some protection, and requested a neighbor to go along on horseback while she rode in the buggy with the two deputies. On the way the buggy broke down and she, with an infant in her arms, was compelled to walk the rest of the distance—between two and three miles. They could have no reason for subpoenaing her in the night, and compelling her to accompany them at such an untimely hour, except a fiendish malice or a determination to heap all the indignities possible upon her, because she was a Mormon woman, for she never attempted to evade the serving of the warrant, and was perfectly willing to report herself at Eagle Rock the next day. She was taken to Salt Lake City to testify against her husband."

After reading such atrocities—such unjustifiable invasions of the homes of the people—one instinctively asks himself if in the great republic the wheels of civil liberty have not been turning backward instead of forward. More than a century before these things transpired, the eloquent Lord Chatham announced the great doctrine for all England and her colonies, including those in America, that a man's house was his castle; that though it might be so poor that the rains of heaven could penetrate it, and the winds whistle through its crevices, yet the king of England could not cross its threshold without its owner's permission.

Not satisfied with the penalties affixed to the laws against unlawful cohabitation, the Utah courts determined to increase them by means little short of legislation itself. The trick resorted to was to decree that the time a man had cohabited with more women than one as wives, could be divided up into years, months or weeks, and separate bills of indictment be found for each fragment of time. So ruled the Chief Justice, Charles S. Zane. Judge Orlando W. Powers of the First Judicial District, carried the infamous doctrine still further, and in charging a grand jury, on the 23rd of September, 1885, said: "An indictment may be found against a man guilty of unlawful cohabitation, for every day, or other distinct interval of time, during which he offends. Each day that a man cohabits with more than one woman, as I have defined the word cohabit, is a distinct and separate violation of the law, and he is liable for punishment for each separate offense."

His definition of cohabitation was as follows:

"The offense of cohabitation is complete when a man, to all outward appearances, is living or associating with more than one woman as his wife. To constitute the offense it is not necessary that it be shown that the parties indulge in sexual intercourse. The intention of the law-making power, in enacting the law, was to protect monogamous marriage by prohibiting all other marriage, whether evidenced by a ceremony, or by conduct and circumstances alone."

So held all the courts, and under that ruling such infamies as the following were possible:

"In the case of Solomon Edwards recently accused of this offense—unlawful cohabitation—it was proved by the evidence for the prosecution that the defendant had lived with one wife only since the passage of the Edmunds act, but after having separated from his former plural wife, he called with his legal wife at the former's residence to obtain a child, an agreement having been made that each party should have one of the two children, and the court ruled that this was unlawful cohabitation in the meaning of the law, and defendant was convicted."

It is but proper to say that the Supreme Court of the United States, on an appeal being taken to it, decided against this infamous doctrine. But it held sway for a time and exhibited the venomous disposition of those entrusted with the execution of the laws in Utah.

In this crusade every effort was made to find President Taylor. His own houses, the Church offices, and the Gardo House, were well-nigh always under the surveillance of spies or deputy marshals, and the latter places were several times searched, but always in vain. That the place of his concealment was not discovered is little short of the miraculous, since the business to which he continued to give his personal attention was considerable, and required frequent communication with agents who were at liberty to act. He owed his safety, however, more to the promptings of the Holy Spirit than to the cunning of man. More than once, in obedience to its whisperings, and when to all outward appearances there was no danger to be feared, he would leave his place of temporary abode. By frequently changing his place of concealment, while running considerable risk of discovery in moving, he kept his enemies mystified as to his whereabouts.

Though driven into retirement by a malicious and perverted administration of the Edmunds law, he never allowed it to embitter his thoughts or disturb the calmness and patience of his disposition. No, not even so much as to lead him to speak evil of those who persecuted him. "God forgive them," he would say, "They know not what they do." "I pity them, with all my heart." The following letter addressed to his family that had convened to celebrate the anniversary of his birth—a custom with them for years—is the very best evidence both as to his sentiments toward his enemies and the grandeur of his soul.

CHAPTER 45 - LETTER TO HIS FAMILY

"To my wives, my children, relatives and friends, who may have assembled at the Gardo House, to celebrate the return of my birthday, November 1st, 1886:—

"As I am prevented from being with you on the present occasion, I desire to send to you my benediction and blessing; and to say unto you: May grace, mercy and peace be extended to you from God our Eternal Father, through our Lord Jesus Christ, who is our Savior, Redeemer and Friend.

"I need not say unto you, that it would have afforded me very great pleasure to have been with you on the present occasion, and to have saluted you personally, as I know it would have been very gratifying unto you. But, through the dispensation of an All-wise Providence, things are not in a position that we would desire to have them; they are in accordance, however, with the design of our Heavenly Father, who ordains all things in harmony with the dispensation of His providence towards the children of men.

"Some people suppose that persecutions and trials are afflictions; but sometimes, and generally, if we are doing the will of the Lord and keeping His commandments, they may be truly said to be blessings in disguise. When our great Redeemer was on earth, He said to His disciples: 'Blessed are ye when men shall revile you, and persecute you, and shall say all manner of evil against you falsely, for my sake. Rejoice and be exceeding glad, for great is your reward in heaven, for so persecuted they the prophets which were before you.'

"Although for the time being, these things may be painful, yet if properly comprehended and realized, we should look at them in another view, and feel as Paul said to the saints in his day: 'For our light affliction, which is but for a moment, worketh for us a far more exceeding and eternal weight of glory; while we look not at the things which are seen, but at the things which are not seen; for the things which are seen are temporal, but the things which are not seen are eternal,' and will lead us to reflect in most instances even as John Wesley sang:

"'Shall I be carried to the skies,
On flowery beds of ease;
While others fought to win the prize,
And sailed through bloody seas!

"'No; I must fight, if I would reign,
Increase my courage, Lord;
I'll bear the toil, endure the pain,
Supported by thy word.'

"The foregoing are my sentiments, which I express from the bottom of my heart; and I would state further, that if we expect to be united with the hundred and forty-four thousand of which John speaks; who are clothed in white raiment, and who were gathered together from every nation, kindred, people and tongue, and who had washed their robes and made them white in the blood of the Lamb (therefore were they next the throne and serve their Maker day and night); we must pass through the same ordeal they did.

"These people who were so honored of God, and of the Redeemer, and the heavenly hosts, were those who had come up through much tribulation; and we are further told in late revelations which God has given us through the Prophet Joseph, that 'After much tribulation cometh the blessing.'

"I was very sorry to learn, in the midst of other things, of the sickness of my wives Jane and Sophia, and my heart has gone out in prayer for them, accompanied by my brethren, that they may be healed, and I am pleased to learn that there is some slight improvement in the health of Aunt Jane, and also that there are some reasonable hopes of the removal of the terrible affliction that has overtaken Aunt Sophia. I would here remark that in speaking of these strokes, I have been making careful inquiry about them since her sad affliction, and learned that it is no uncommon thing for people to be healed of this kind of disease. A lady of about her age that I conversed with quite recently, said she had had two strokes of that kind, and she is now quite well, hale and hearty. I mention these things in hopes that it will afford some consolation to Aunt Sophia and to you, her friends.

"I am pleased to be informed that the health of the family is generally good, and that the disposition and feeling of both wives and children is to fear God, to work righteousness, and to yield obedience to His laws. For if we expect to obtain a celestial glory and exaltations with thrones, principalities and powers in the celestial kingdom of our God, we must abide a celestial law. For it is expressly stated that we can only inherit such a kingdom, such glory, and blessings as we prepare ourselves for, by yielding obedience to the laws thereof; whether it be a celestial, or terrestrial or telestial.

"We are engaged in a great work, and laying the foundation thereof—a work that has been spoken of by all the holy prophets since the world was; namely, the dispensation of the fullness of times, wherein God will gather together all things in one, whether they be things in the earth, or things in the heavens; and for this purpose God revealed Himself, as also the Lord Jesus Christ, unto His servant the Prophet Joseph Smith, when the Father pointed to the Son and said: 'This is my beloved Son, in whom I am well pleased, hear ye Him.' He further restored the everlasting gospel; together with the Aaronic and Melchizedek Priesthoods; both of which are everlasting as God is; and in the interest of humanity sent forth His gospel to the nations of the earth. I am happy to say that I have been a bearer of this gospel to several nations, and have been the means of bringing many to the knowledge of the truth; among which are some of you, my wives. We have been gathered together, according to the word of the Lord, and the order of His Priesthood, to our present homes, our lands and our possessions. We have had the privilege of assisting in building temples to the Lord, and administering therein. The principles which have been developed for the progression, the happiness and exaltation of the faithful in Christ Jesus; and some of you, my sons, have been favored with the Holy Priesthood, which is after the order of Melchizedek, after the order of the Son God and of God the Eternal Father, and after the power of an endless life. We expect and have faith, that this earth will yet be renovated and purified, the wicked will be rooted out of it, and the righteous inherit it; and we further look forward to the time when there will be a new heaven and a new earth, wherein dwelleth righteousness; and a new Jerusalem, wherein the Lord God and the Lamb will be the light thereof, and you, my wives, and also my children who have come to years of maturity, will have the privilege, if faithful to your covenants, of entering into and partaking of the most exalted, glorious, and eternal blessings, which any men or women on earth have enjoyed in this world, or in the world to come; and will eventually be associated with the Gods in the eternal worlds.

"We are here gathered together in this land of Zion for the purpose of purifying, instructing and building up the Church of God; and also building up a Zion of God, and establishing the rule and government of God on the earth, and fulfilling that which is spoken of by the Prophet: 'The Lord is our Judge, the Lord is our Lawgiver, the Lord is our King; He will save us.'

"In view of the many great and precious promises which are made to us, and which fall to our lot through obedience to the laws of God; we should at all times place ourselves in conformity with the laws, usages and requirements of the Church and kingdom of God upon the earth. Our lives should not be a blank. We are heirs of eternal lives. We ought to use all our energies in the interest of humanity, in the establishment of the Zion of God, and the building up of the kingdom of God on the earth.

"It would be very proper for you, my wives, and daughters who are of sufficient age, if you have not already done so, to associate yourselves with the Relief Societies; and of my sons and daughters to unite themselves with the Young Men's and Young

Women's Mutual Improvement Associations; and thus, while you are receiving information and benefit, you, at the same time may make yourselves useful and a blessing unto others. Let me here say, that the Prophet Joseph Smith instituted the Ladies' Relief Society for that purpose. It is proper that you should all reverence the Lord your God in all things, and cultivate His love and fear in your hearts. All ought to dedicate themselves daily, morning and evening to the Lord, and seek for His mercy, blessing and oversight, both day and night. You who have families ought to gather them together every morning and every evening, and dedicate yourselves to the Lord. And this dedication ought to be in private, between yourselves only and the Lord, as well as in public or family prayer. The Prophet Joseph gave a special charge to me while living, as near as I can remember as follows: 'Brother Taylor, never arise in the morning or retire at night, without dedicating yourself unto God and asking His blessings upon you through the day or night, as the case may be, and the Lord God will hear and answer your prayers; and don't let any circumstances prevent it.' I had been in the habit of doing so, for years before this; but since that time I have not omitted, to my knowledge, the observance of this duty, morning or evening.

"Never do an act that you would be ashamed of man knowing, for God sees us always, both day and night, and if we expect to live and reign with Him in eternity, we ought to do nothing that will disgrace us in time.

"We should be strictly honest, one with another, and with all men; let our word always be as good as our bond; avoid all ostentation of pride and vanity; and be meek, lowly, and humble; be full of integrity and honor; and deal justly and righteously with all men; and have the fear and love of God continually before us, and seek for the comforting influence of the Holy Ghost to dwell with us. Let mothers be loving, kind and considerate with their children, and the children kind and obedient to their mothers, and to their Fathers; and seek always to be governed by good and wise counsel, and so to live every day, and in all our acts, as to keep a conscience void of offense towards God and man. Be kind and courteous to all, seek to promote the welfare of all, be gentlemen and ladies, and treat one another, and all men with proper courtesy, respect and kindness. So shall you be honored by the good and virtuous, enjoy the blessings of a good conscience, and secure the approbation of God, and of the holy angels, in time and throughout all eternity.

"The protecting care of the Lord over me and my brethren has been very manifest since my absence from home, for which I feel to bless and praise His holy name. I always am very desirous to acknowledge His hand in all things, and I am very anxious that you should do the same. For to the Lord we are indebted for every blessing which we enjoy, pertaining to this life, and the life which is to come.

"While we seek to God our Heavenly Father for His blessings, let us be careful to so live that we can secure and claim them, by our obedience to His laws. Be merciful, and kind, and just, and generous to all. Preserve your bodies and your spirits pure, and free from contamination. Avoid lasciviousness, and every corrupting influence; that you may be indeed the sons of God without rebuke, in the midst of a crooked and perverse generation.

"I pray God the Eternal Father that when we have all finished our probation here, we may be presented to the Lord without spot or blemish, as pure and honorable representatives of the Church and kingdom of God on the earth, and then inherit a celestial glory in the kingdom of our God, and enjoy everlasting felicity with the pure and just in the realms of eternal day, through the merits and atonement of the Lord Jesus Christ, our Savior and Redeemer, in worlds without end. Amen.

"To those present of my friends and not of my immediate family, I present a most hearty welcome, and an affectionate regard.

"I thank you all for your sympathetic, kind and generous feelings manifested through the letters I have received. I must also beg you to exercise to me a spirit of benevolence and charity, over my apparent negligence, at times, in not being as prompt as desirable in answering your communications. For while I profoundly respect and appreciate your kindness, it is not always convenient for me to send an immediate reply, as I have daily to attend to all my official duties as when in my office at home.

"In regard to my position and that of my brethren who are with me, I am happy to inform you that we now are, and always have been, during our exile, supplied with everything that is necessary to our comfort and convenience. Go where we will, we have good accommodations, plenty of food and the necessaries of life, kind and sympathetic friends, and the best of treatment. I am also happy in the belief that you are comfortably situated. If there is anything that any of you require and you will inform me, I shall be happy to supply it, if within my power. Some of you have written that you 'would like to have a peep at me.' I heartily reciprocate that feeling, and would like to have a 'peep' at you on this occasion; but in my bodily absence my spirit and peace shall be with you.

"God bless you all, in time and throughout the eternities to come, is the prayer of your affectionate husband, father and friend in the new and everlasting covenant—

"JOHN TAYLOR"

CHAPTER 46 - HALF MAST

Such was the man whom the United States officials in Utah thought it necessary to hunt down like an atrocious felon, and even put a price upon his head for his apprehension! This is the man adjudged unworthy by the Edmunds law to vote or hold office in the United States! This is the man who must be driven from his family and the comforts of home to satisfy the clamor of an unthinking, prejudiced populace, aroused to a frenzy of excited intolerance by misrepresentation and an appeal to passion! It is a sad comment on the subserviency of our national legislators to have it to say that they yielded a ready submission to the clamors of the multitude, and steadily refused to investigate the charges against the Latter-day Saints before enacting the proscriptive legislation under which President Taylor and men of like character suffered.

His wife Sophia mentioned in the foregoing letter, who was suffering from the effects of a paralytic stroke at the time it was written, died on the 27th of February following. During her distressing illness he could not visit her; nor yet when the last sad rites that men performed for the dead were held over her remains could he be present to look upon the face of this loving and faithful wife. During her illness her house was closely watched by spies, and even while she was dying it was searched in hopes of finding him. Though his heart was torn with anguish under these trying circumstances, he bowed to the hard conditions with that Christian fortitude which had been characteristic of him all his life.

When President Taylor retired from public view on the evening of the 1st of February, 1885, it was not out of any consideration for his personal safety, or ease or comfort, but for the public good and in the interests of peace. There can be no question but that there was a cunningly devised plan on the part of the assailants of the Church to involve the Saints in difficulty with the government, to provoke them to acts of violence against the alleged execution of the law, that a pretext might be found for their destruction or expulsion from the land they had redeemed from the desert. What meant, else, that unwarranted invasion of the homes of the people? What meant this inhuman hounding of men so highly honored in the community? What meant this reign of terror in which laws were perverted, time-honored precedents overturned, and nearly all the rules of jurisprudence ignored? What meant the repeated efforts to engage the military power in the settlement of Utah affairs if violence was not contemplated? That a pre-text for violence was eagerly sought is clearly seen in the following:

On the 4th of July, 1885, the United States flag was raised at half-mast at the City Hall, in Salt Lake City, and over some other buildings, among them, Z. C. M. I., *Deseret News* Office and Tabernacle. This action was designed to express sorrow at the subversion of those principles of religious and civil liberty in our Territory for which the founders of our government had fought and died. This act was construed to be an insult to the flag, and to portend treason and rebellion. The wildest excitement prevailed; and threats of violence were indulged in by the enemies of the Saints.

"Pioneer Day," the 24th of July, was not far off, and it was alleged by the enemies of the Saints that it was the intention of the "Mormons" to again "insult" the flag by putting it at half-mast, and draping it in mourning. By industriously circulating such a rumor the country expected a conflict on that date, and General O. O. Howard, deceived by the misrepresentations of the anti-Mormon clique, in Salt Lake City, made such representations to President Cleveland that he was directed to keep all posts of the Western Platte department of the army in full strength and be prepared for any emergency that might arise in Utah in the near future. General Hatch with the Fifth Cavalry was ordered to remain in readiness at Ogallala, Nebraska, to proceed by express train to Salt Lake City if necessary.

On the 18th of the month there was a meeting of Lincoln Post No. 2, Grand Army of the Republic, in Butte, Montana. After some minor business, the subject of the approaching Pioneer Day and Mormon celebration at Salt Lake, July 24th, and General Howard's dispatches in relation thereto was taken up and fully discussed. The result was the appointment of a committee on resolutions. That committee reported the following, which was unanimously adopted.

"LINCOLN POST, G. A. R.,

"BUTTE CITY, M. T., July 18, 1885.

"WHEREAS, from the report of General Howard and information received from comrades of the G. A. R., residents of Utah, we are advised that the representatives of the twin relic of barbarism design on the 24th inst., to repeat their treasonable actions of July 4th and threaten to trample the flag of our country in the dust, therefore, be it

"*Resolved*, that the comrades of Lincoln Post, No. 2, G. A. R., tender to Governor Murray, of Utah, and to H. C. Wardleigh, Commander of the Department of Utah, G. A. R., the services of this Post at Salt Lake City on July 24, and 'continue during the war.'

"*Resolved*, that the members of this Post hold themselves in readiness to 'move together' upon the request of our comrades in Utah; that the Quartermaster be instructed to at once issue members of the Post arms and ammunition, and the Adjutant be instructed to notify every member of this Post to report for duty at once.

"(Signed) E. L. HOLMES,

"J. D. JENKS,

"F. R. VINCENT."

"SPECIAL ORDER."

"HEADQUARTERS LINCOLN POST, no. 2,

"DEPARTMENT OF MONTANA, G. A. R.,

"BUTTE, Montana, July 18, 1885.

"Special Order No. 4."

"I. COMRADES: In obedience to resolutions this day passed by Lincoln Post, each comrade will hold himself in readiness to report for duty, armed, uniformed and equipped.

"II. This Post is divided into two companies, A and B. Comrade C. S. Shoemaker is assigned to the command of A. company, and Comrade John Bechtel is assigned to the command of B. Company.

"III. Harry C. Kessler, Quartermaster will at once issue arms and ammunition to each comrade, and make the proper arrangement for such transportation, subsistence and supplies as the occasion may require.

"[By order of the Post Commander.]

"J. J. YORK, Adjutant."

The cause of such a movement as this doubtless occurred at the instance of the bitter anti-Mormons in Salt Lake. Eight days before, their organ, the Salt Lake *Tribune*, said:

"The ex-Confederate soldiers are talking of holding an indignation meeting here on the 24th inst., to express their views on the insult offered to the flag on July 4, by the Mormon Church in this city. The federal court room has been obtained, the railroads have agreed to give half-fare rates from the Park, Ogden and the mining camps, and the hotels such reasonable rates as to make it an object. The sentiments of the ex-Confederates are to be embodied in the form of resolutions to be sent to the Southern States and Congressmen, politicians and newspapers in that section. It is believed that the southern people should be made aware of the true condition of affairs in Utah, and that they will listen to and believe what the ex-Confederate soldiers living here may say on the subject, with more readiness than they would were the information to come to them from all loyal citizens of Utah without distinction. It is a good move, and for another reason. There is talk on the streets to the effect that on the 24th—Pioneer's Day—the Mormons intend to drape the flag in mourning and float it at half-mast. That would be a good day for the presence in this city of two or three thousand old soldiers, Federal and Confederate. It would probably result in a speedy and effectual settlement of the whole Mormon business, for with such men here in force the nation's flag would not be insulted with impunity."

In all this one may see the wolf accusing the lamb with fouling the water, though the latter stood below him in the stream: or the big bully of a boy, though a coward at heart, strutting about with a chip on his shoulder daring little urchins to knock it off. There can be no question but what it was the design of the anti-Mormon agitators to have present on that day if not "two or three thousand old soldiers," at least that many desperate men to precipitate a crisis by provoking the people to resistance, that there might be a "speedy and effectual settlement of the whole Mormon business." With such a gathering not even the aid of conjecture is necessary to determine how "the settlement" would have been attempted.

It is needless to say there had been no intention to insult the flag, by putting it at half-mast on the 4th of July. The people had cause to mourn, and they did it quietly and respectfully with the flag which they revered at half-mast; and no one but blustering demagogues, seeking cause of quarrel could see in that treasonable designs on the government, or disrespect to the flag. Neither had there been any determination to drape the flag in mourning and fly it at half-must on the 24th of July. All that originated in the depraved minds of men who were only too anxious to have the Saints do something that would furnish an excuse for making war upon them. The most formidable thing contemplated on that day, on the part of the Saints, was a gathering of Sunday school children at the Tabernacle.

All these war-like demonstrations on the part of the enemies of the Saints, however, were very singularly quieted. General U. S. Grant, who for some time had been having a stubborn fight with death, surrendered quietly to the dread monarch on the morning of July 23rd. The same day the Governor of Utah, Eli H. Murry, issued a proclamation recommending that "flags draped in mourning be placed on all public buildings, and, as far as practicable, on business houses and on the houses of the people, and that they so remain until the burial."

Thus the crisis passed.

This incident reveals the need there was of taking every precaution to avoid excitement, and vindicates the wisdom of President Taylor's course in going into exile. He had observed the determination of men in official positions to involve the Saints in serious trouble, and was determined that so far as he was concerned, they should have no pretext on which to base their actions.

The Latter-day Saints appreciated his motives, and sent to him in his exile cheering words of blessing, confidence and support. As the conference held at Provo, in April, 1887, was drawing to a close, Apostle F. D. Richards arose and said:

"In view of recent occurrences, and the assaults which have been made upon the First Presidency of the Church of Jesus Christ of Latter-day Saints,

"I move that we, the officers and members of the Church, in general conference assembled, express to our faithful brethren who preside over us, and to the world at large, by our vote, our undiminished confidence in and love for them.

"That, inasmuch as President John Taylor is our Prophet, Seer and Revelator, chosen by the Lord, we do express to him in this manner, our love and respect for him, and unite in saying that we have viewed with admiration the steadfastness, integrity and valor which he has displayed in the cause of God.

"That, as Trustee-in-Trust, we approve of his course, and endorse and ratify his official acts, and have entire confidence in his integrity in this capacity.

"And that we also entertain the same feelings for his two Counselors, Presidents George Q. Cannon and Joseph F. Smith, in their places; and desire to assure these, our beloved brethren, that we do uphold them by our faith, prayers, and works; and that we look forward with delight to the time when we shall have the privilege of again beholding the faces of these, our brethren, the First

Presidency of the Church, and hearing their voices in our public assemblies."

This was carried by a hearty, unanimous vote.

But the Saints were no more to have the privilege in this life of seeing the face and hearing the voice of President Taylor. Though his age had been as a lusty winter, frosty but kindly; though in his youth never had he partaken of hot and rebellious liquors to inflame or contaminate his blood, nor with unbashful forehead wooed the means of weakness and debility, yet his long exile and the confinement incidental thereto, at last broke down his health. Notwithstanding the kind attentions of his associates in exile, and trusted friends who gladly received him into their houses, their friendly administrations could not fill the place of home and its joys, its happy reunions and associations. Nor could he have that regular exercise in exile that he would have had in freedom. Add to these things the cares and anxieties forced upon him by reason of the unwarranted and inhuman assaults made upon himself and the people over whom he presided, and you have at once the causes of his last illness and death. Had it not been for these things President Taylor undoubtedly would have lived many years longer to direct the affairs of the Church of Christ.

His health commenced failing about a year before his death, but his last illness began about five months before that sad event. Sustained by his marvelous will-power, he resisted the approach of death with all his characteristic determination. He would neither permit himself nor others to believe that he was seriously ill. But his decreasing inclination to take what little exercise he could under the circumstances; and periods of prostration occurring with increasing frequency, told its own story as to how the battle was going.

The tenth of July marked a crisis in the struggle for life which alarmed his friends and attendants. The tenth occurred on Sunday. It had been his custom in these years of exile to hold religious service on the Sabbath and fast days, the first Thursday of every month. The brethren who were with him usually took turns in presiding in these meetings. The service consisted of singing, prayer, administering the sacrament and such remarks as the brethren felt inclined to make.

On the tenth of July before named, the meeting was called as usual and opened, but no one could speak. President Taylor's illness had taken a turn for the worse and the unpleasant conviction forced itself on those about him least willing to believe it, that he was gradually sinking. The day after the memorable tenth of July, his first Counselor, George Q. Cannon, wrote the following to Daniel H. Wells:

"It gives me great pain to be obliged to communicate to you the intelligence that, I think, President Taylor is gradually passing away, and according to present appearances, may not live many days or a week at the farthest. For four months past he has been ailing, and his health and strength gradually failing him; but he has been so full of hope and pluck that he has impressed us all who have been with him with a feeling that he would recover. Through all his sickness up to the present he has steadily maintained that he would get better, and knowing how much the faith of the people has been exercised in his behalf, it has been difficult to resist the conviction that he would get well. I addressed letters to the Twelve who are absent from the city on the 1st inst. advising them of his condition. On the 5th, being in the city, I addressed letters to them again, advising them that I had heard such good reports from President Taylor, that I felt it my duty to communicate it to them. He appeared to have taken a very favorable turn, and asserted that now he would get better; but this lasted only a few days. An unfavorable change took place yesterday and I think he is sinking.

"It is with a great reluctance that I admit this to myself; but I feel it my duty to try and communicate it to you and to all the brethren of the Council."

Letters similar in import were written to the Apostles; but after this he rallied again and inspired those around him for several days with new hopes. On the 18th his second Counselor, Joseph F. Smith, arrived from the Sandwich Islands. President Taylor was very weak and low but still conscious; and as he looked up and recognized Brother Joseph, and his attention was called to the fact that the First Presidency were together once more—the first time since December, 1884—he said:

"I feel to thank the Lord!"

After this he continued to grow weaker, with only intervals of consciousness, until the evening of the 25th.

It was at the house of Thomas F. Rouche, of Kaysville, that President Taylor was fighting out this last battle, with such remarkable determination. On the above named evening, the few friends who were permitted to be with him, among whom were his two Counselors, two of his wives, Mary Oakey Taylor and Maggie Young Taylor, and the Rouche family, were gathered about his bed as he slowly sank under the hand of Death. He was passing away without a struggle, quietly as a child falls asleep. At five minutes to eight o'clock, "the weary wheels of life stood still"—the great spirit had left its earthly tabernacle.

CHAPTER 47 - RESOLUTIONS OF RESPECT

The next day the sad event of President Taylor's death was announced to the Church and the world in the following communication from his counselors to the *Deseret News*:

"Once more the Latter-day Saints are called upon to mourn the death of their leader—the man who has held the keys of the kingdom of God upon earth. President John Taylor departed this life at five minutes to eight o'clock on the evening of Monday, July 25th, 1887, aged 78 years, 8 months and 25 days.

"In communicating this sad intelligence to the Church, over which he has so worthily presided for nearly ten years past, we are filled with emotion too deep for utterance. A faithful, devoted and fearless servant of God, the Church in his death has lost its most conspicuous and experienced leader. Steadfast to and immovable in the truth, few men have ever lived who have manifested such integrity and such unflinching moral and physical courage as our beloved President who has just gone from us. He never knew the feeling of fear connected with the work of God. But in the face of angry mobs, and at other times when in imminent danger of personal violence from those who threatened his life, and upon occasions when the people were menaced with public peril, he never blenched—his knees never trembled, his hand never shook.

Every Latter-day Saint always knew beforehand, on occasions when firmness and courage were needed, where President John Taylor would be found and what his tone would be. He met every issue squarely, boldly and in a way to call forth the admiration of all who saw and heard him. Undaunted courage, unyielding firmness were among his most prominent characteristics, giving him distinction among men who were distinguished for the same qualities. With these were combined an intense love of freedom and hatred of oppression. He was a man whom all could trust, and throughout his life he enjoyed, to an extent surpassed by none, the implicit confidence of the Prophets Joseph, Hyrum and Brigham and all the leading men and members of the Church. The title of "Champion of Liberty," which he received at Nauvoo, was always felt to be most appropriate for him to bear. But it was not only in the possession of these qualities that President Taylor was great. His judgment was remarkably sound and clear, and through life he has been noted for the wisdom of his counsels and teachings. His great experience made his suggestions exceedingly valuable; for there has scarcely been a public movement of any kind commenced, carried on, or completed, since he joined the Church in which he has not taken part.

"But it is not necessary that we should, even if time permitted, rehearse the events of his long and busy life. To do so would only be to give the greater part of the history of the Church; for with it his biography is inseparably interwoven.

"The last time President Taylor appeared in public was on Sunday, February 1st, 1885. On that occasion he delivered a lengthy discourse in the Tabernacle, in Salt Lake City. Rumor had been floating around for some time that his arrest was contemplated. In fact, while returning from a trip to the settlements in Arizona, he was advised in California that he was in great danger, and it was suggested that perhaps it would be better for him not to return to Salt Lake City. He listened to these cautions but still resolved to take the risk, and came back and fearlessly went about his business for some time. But on the evening of Saturday, February 1st, he concluded to withdraw himself from the public performance of his numerous and important duties.

In taking this step he did so more to preserve peace and to remove all possible cause of excitement, than from any desire of personal safety. He perceived that there was a determination on the part of men holding official position here to raise an issue, and, if possible, involve the Latter-day Saints in serious trouble. He had not broken any law. He knew he was innocent and that if he were arrested and could have a fair trial, nothing could be brought against him. He had taken every precaution that a man could take under his circumstances to make himself invulnerable to attack. He was determined that, so far as he was concerned, he would furnish no pretext for trouble, but would do everything in his power to prevent the people over whom he presided from being involved in difficulty.

"From that date, upwards of two years and a half ago, when he left his home in Salt Lake City, he had not the opportunity of crossing its threshold again. To home and its joys, its delightful associations and its happy reunions he has been a stranger. He has lived as an exile—a wanderer in the land, to the development and good government of which he has contributed so much! While living in this condition, one of his wives was stricken with disease, and though his heart was torn with anguish at the thought of her condition, and with anxiety to see her and minister to her in her deep distress, her residence was closely watched by spies, and when she was in a dying condition, was even searched with the hope of entrapping him! Thus she was deprived of the privilege of looking upon his beloved face, and he had not even the sad consolation of witnessing or taking any part in her funeral ceremonies.

"During the two years and a half that President Taylor has been living in this condition, he has been cut off from all the society and loving ministrations of his family. But though this was so hard to bear at his time of life, he never murmured. He was always full of courage and hope, cheering everyone with whom he was brought in contact, and lifting his companions by his noble example out of despondency and discouragement.

With the same courage with which he stood by the Prophet of God and with a walking cane parried the guns of the mob when they vomited their sheets of flame and messengers of death in Carthage jail, he confronted the difficulties and the trials which he had to meet when compelled to leave his home and the society of those whom he loved. His demeanor throughout this long ordeal has been most admirable. Everyone who has seen him has been impressed by his equanimity and stately bearing. Always distinguished for his courtesy and dignity of character, at no period of his life did he ever exhibit those traits to greater advantage than he has during his exile. He has never condescended even to speak evil of those who so cruelly persecuted him.

"By the miraculous power of God, President John Taylor escaped the death which the assassins of Carthage jail assigned for him. His blood was then mingled with the blood of the martyred Prophet and Patriarch. He has stood since then as a living martyr for the truth. But today he occupies the place of a double martyr. President John Taylor has been killed by the cruelty of officials who have, in this Territory, misrepresented the Government of the United States. There is no room to doubt that if he had been permitted to enjoy the comforts of home, the ministrations of his family, the exercise to which he had been accustomed, but of which he was deprived, he might have lived for many years yet. His blood stains the clothes of the men, who with insensate hate have offered rewards for his arrest and have hounded him to the grave. History will yet call their deeds by their right names; but one greater than the combined voices of all historians will yet pronounce their dreadful sentence.

"It is now some time since President Taylor was attacked by disease. It came upon him by degrees, manifesting itself in the beginning by a swelling of the limbs for the want of proper exercise. He fought disease with his characteristic pluck and determination. He would not yield. He would neither allow himself nor anyone else to think that his sickness was serious. He would not permit his family to know his real condition, as he did not wish them to have any anxiety on his account, and it was almost against his express wishes they were told how sick he was. When messages were sent by him to them, they were always of a re-assuring character. Up to the last day or two he was able to sit in his chair, and until quite recently he was able to assist himself in getting in and out of bed. The strength he has exhibited and his tenacity of life have been very wonderful; for though so strong, he had partaken of scarcely and nourishment for the past six weeks. So peacefully did he pass away, and so like a babe falling asleep that a brief period elapsed before those who stood around his bed were sure that his spirit had taken its flight.

"As the sad intelligence which we now communicate will spread through these valleys and mountains, sorrow will fill the hearts of all at hearing of the last days of their beloved and venerable President. We know how deep has been the sympathy that has filled the hearts of the Saints for him in his advanced years, in thinking of his condition and of his being compelled to live as an exile from his family the people. The expressions of esteem love which have come to him from all parts of the land have deeply touched him and caused him great pleasure in thinking how much he was beloved and how much his welfare was desired by all the Saints throughout the earth.

"His constant desire was to do everything in his power to relieve the Latter-day Saints from the oppressions under which they suffer. Every pulsation of his heart beat with a love of Zion and a desire for her redemption. We desired, and the desire was general, we believe, throughout the Church—that he might live to emerge from his exile and be once more a free man among the people whom he loved. But this has been denied us. He has gone to mingle with the holy and the pure, and to quote his own eloquent words, written concerning his dear friend, Joseph the Seer:

"Beyond the reach of mobs and strife,
He rests unharmed in endless life;
His home's in the sky, he dwells with the Gods,
Far from the furious rage of mobs."

And though we have lost his presence here, his influence will still be felt. Such men may pass from this life to another, but the love which beats in their hearts for righteousness and for truth cannot die. They go to an enlarged sphere of usefulness. Their influence is extended and more widely felt, and Zion will feel the benefit of his labors, as it has the labors of others who have gone before him. The work of God will roll forth. One after another of the mighty men—the men who have spent their lives in the cause of God—may pass away, but this will not affect the purposes of our Great Creator concerning His latter-day work. He will raise up others, and the work will go on increasing in power, in influence, and in all true greatness, until it will accomplish all that God has predicted concerning it.

"We feel to say to the Latter-day Saints: Be comforted! The same God who took care of the work when Joseph was martyred, who has watched over and guarded and upheld it through the long years that have since elapsed, and who has guided its destinies since the departure of Brigham, still watches over it and makes it the object of His care. John has gone; but God lives. He has founded Zion. He has given His people a testimony of this. Cherish it in your heart of hearts, and live so each day that when the end of your mortal lives shall come, you may be counted worthy to go where Joseph, Brigham and John have gone, and mingle with that glorious throng whose robes have been washed white in the blood of the Lamb.

"This is the earnest prayer for all Saints, and for all the honest in heart, of your unworthy servants in Christ,

"GEORGE Q. CANNON,

"JOSEPH F. SMITH"

This announcement cast an inexpressible gloom over the entire community. Everywhere could be heard expressions of esteem for the departed: "We did not think when he was driven into exile that we would never see him in life again," said some. "Well, he is beyond the reach of the minions of the law now," said others. "How we would like to have seen his face and heard his kindly voice once more before he left us!" "This makes twice he has suffered martyrdom!"

The *Deseret News*, in concluding a lengthy biographical sketch of him said:

"The soul of honor, of indomitable energy and unflinching firmness when convinced of the right, President Taylor was the embodiment of dignity and urbane authority. His record is without a stain, and his name will be inscribed in the archives of heaven, among those of the mighty spirits who have helped to sway the destinies of this world. He has gone to mingle with his brethren of the last dispensation who laid the foundation of this great work, and with them he will shine in eternal splendor as a son of God, an heir to the royal Priesthood, a ruler in the Father's kingdom. May peace and comfort rest upon the bereaved!"

Following are the resolutions of respect adopted by the Board of Directors of Z. C. M. I.—of which he was President,—at their first meeting after his death:

"*Whereas,* On the 25th day of July, 1887, it pleased an All-wise Creator to remove from our midst, by the hand of death, President John Taylor; and,

"*Whereas,* He was elected a director of the Z. C. M. I., October 7th, 1877, and served in that capacity until October 5th, 1883, when he was elected president of this institution, and acted in that office continuously from that date until his demise; and,

"*Whereas,* His whole life has been prominent for unblemished rectitude and distinguished ability, the last fifty years of it having been devoted almost exclusively to the benefits of his fellow men—as an able companion of human liberty—and advocate of correct religious principles, as a journalist, legislator and a leader of a great people. Therefore, be it

"*Resolved,* That in the departure from this life of one so good, noble and useful as the late President John Taylor, we have sustained a great loss, in which the community widely participates and while fully sensing this effect of his decease, we extend to his family, in the hour of their bereavement, our most heart-felt sympathy. Also,

"*Resolved,* That this expression of our appreciation of the character and ability of our deceased, venerated President, brother and friend be spread upon the minutes of this board meeting in full, and that a copy thereof be engrossed and presented to his family."

The *Deseret News*, a few days after his death, speaking again of him said:

"The departed servant of God, the tokens of whose decease still droop from the doors and depend from the places that once were dignified by his presence, needs no eulogy of the living to glorify his tomb. He has a pattern of integrity, intrepidity, firmness and calm reliance upon God and the truth. His record is clean and his course without a spot."

Such were a few of the expressions of mingled esteem and love which welled up from the hearts of the people, and found expression on their lips.

CHAPTER 48 - A FADED COAT

The story of President Taylor's life is before the reader. We may now consider his character as reflected in that story.

In person President Taylor was nearly six feet in height and of fine proportion, that combination which gives activity and strength. His head was large, the face oval and the features large, strong and finely chiseled. The forehead was high and massive, the eyes gray, deep-set, and of a mild, kindly expression, except when aroused, and then they were capable of reflecting all the feelings that moved his soul, whether of indignation, scorn or contempt. The nose was aquiline, the mouth well-formed and expressive of firmness, the chin powerful and well rounded. In early life he was of a fair complexion, but with age the face grew swarthy, and even in middle life his abundant hair turned to a silvery whiteness, which but added beauty to his brow and made his appearance venerable.

In his manner he was ever affable and polite, easy and gracious, yet princely in dignity. In his association with others he was familiar but never vulgar. He was not a man whom a friend, however intimate, would slap familiarly on the back or turn and twist about when shaking hands; such proceedings with him would have been as much out of place as with the proudest crowned monarch in the presence-chamber. Yet there was no affectation in his deportment, no stiffness; his dignity was that with which nature clothes her noblest sons. It did not spring from self-conceit, or self-sufficiency, or any spirit such as

"I am Sir Oracle, and when I speak

Let no man ope his lips!"

Nor was it studied, or copied, or put on for state occasions. He carried it with him wherever he went—into his own home, into the homes of his friends. It was with him in courts and palaces, among the refined and the titled nobility of this world; he never plucked it off on entering the humblest cottage of the poor. He was to his manners born, and they were suited to the man. In any assembly he would have been a striking figure.

There was a beautiful harmony in the character of his mind and the lineaments of his person. If the habitation was splendid, the inmate was worthy of it. His noble form and bearing were but the outward expression of the spirit within. A universal benevolence, powerful intellect, splendid courage, physical as well as moral, a noble independence of spirit, coupled with implicit faith and trust in God, a high sense of honor, unimpeachable integrity, indomitable determination, and a passionate love of liberty, justice and truth marked the outlines of his character—in short, the elements were, "So mixed in him, that Nature might stand up and say to all the world—'This is a man!"'

President Taylor believed absolutely in the universal Fatherhood of God and the brotherhood of man. From that grand cardinal doctrine sprang his liberal views as to the hand dealings of God with His children. He despised anything that savored of narrow-mindedness or bigotry. Who does not remember with what scorn he treated the spirit which led the man to pray:

"Lord, bless me and my wife,

My son John and his wife,

Us four, but no more. Amen."

"I think sometimes," he would remark, "that as a people we are a good deal sectarian in our feelings, and it is necessary for us occasionally to look at the pit from whence we were dug, and the rock from whence we were hewn. We are all too ready to cry out, as the sectarians do in their different orders:

"'The temple of the Lord, the temple of the Lord,

The temple of the Lord are we!'

"We say we are the children of God. That is true, we are. We are sparks struck from the blaze of His eternal fire. But what of the rest of the world—whose children are they? They are also the children of our Heavenly Father, and He is interested in their welfare as He is in ours; and as a kind, beneficent Father towards His children, He has been seeking from generation to generation to promote the welfare, the happiness and the exaltation of the human family.

"We sometimes talk about the hand of God being over us. Of course it is, and will be over us forever, if we will only serve Him, for He is always true. But His hand is over the nations of the earth also. He is interested in the welfare of this nation, and all other nations, and all other peoples, as well as in our welfare.

"I believe in God, in Jesus Christ, and in the exaltation of the human family, and consequently have acted and do act in accordance with that belief. If others choose to do otherwise, that is their business. 'But,' says one, 'don't you want to send them all to hell?' No, I don't; but I would be glad to get them out of it; and if I could do them any good, I would do it with pleasure. I do not believe in this wrath and dread, but if a man acts meanly I will tell him that he is a poor, mean cur. Then if I find him hungry, I would feed him; or if I found him naked, I would clothe him; for the gospel teaches me to do good and benefit mankind as far as lies in my power.

"I remember reading a few lines of some very zealous Protestant who wrote over some public building:

"'In this place may enter
Greek, Jew or Atheist,—
Anything but a Papist.'

"Now, I say, let the Papist come in, too, the Moslem, the Greek, the Jew, the pagan, the believers and the unbelievers, and the whole world. If God sends His rain on the good and the evil, and makes His sun to shine on the just and the unjust, I certainly shall not object. Let them worship as they please and have full freedom and equal rights and privileges with us and all men."

It will be seen from the foregoing that while he claimed absolute religious liberty for himself, he accorded the same right to others. "There are two things," he remarks, "that I have felt very decided upon ever since I could comprehend anything; one is that I would worship God as I pleased, without anybody's dictation; and that I would dictate to no man his faith, neither should any man dictate to me my faith; the other is that I would vote as I pleased."

Of the deep religious convictions of President Taylor it is scarcely necessary to speak. His whole life demonstrates how deep was the religious soil in his nature, into which the seeds of truth were sown to bring forth an hundred fold. His devotion to his religion was not only sincere, it was without reserve. He gave himself and his whole life to it. His faith, his trust and confidence in God were complete. "I do not believe in a religion that cannot have all my affections," he would sometimes remark, "but I believe in a religion that I can live for, or die for.

"I would rather trust in the living God than in any other power on earth. I learned [while on missions] that I could go to God and He always relieved me. He always supplied my wants. I always had plenty to eat, drink and wear, and could ride on steam-boats or railroads, or anywhere I thought proper: God always opened my way, and so He will that of every man who will put his trust in Him.

"I would rather have God for my friend than all other influences and powers outside."

Such were his sentiments, such his devotion to his religion, such his testimony to the goodness of God.

"He was a man," said one who knew him well-nigh half a century, "that could not get down to grovel with the low-lived, the vicious, the ribald, nor any who indulged in the follies and vanities of mortal life." Referring himself to those who did love the abomination of wickedness, with all its crookedness, deceitfulness and crime he ever exclaimed: "My soul, enter thou not into their secret; and mine honor, with them be thou not united!" In all these things he not only lived above reproach, but above suspicion.

The most prominent feature of his character, doubtless, was his ardent love of liberty. For this he was distinguished even among his brethren who as a group were remarkable for their love of and devotion to freedom. To other men the love of liberty was a principle; with him it was not only a principle but a passion: others may have been educated to love it; he loved it instinctively.

In a letter to one of his brethren, answering one that had laid rather hard conditions upon him, he expressed the following sentiments, in which it is difficult to determine which most appears, his love of liberty or his detestation, his utter abhorrence of slavery:

"I was not born a slave! I cannot, will not be a slave. I would not be slave to God! I'd be His servant, friend, His son. I'd go at His behest; but would not be His slave. I'd rather be extinct than be a slave. His friend I feel I am, and He is mine:—a slave! The manacles would pierce my very bones—the clanking chains would grate upon my soul—a poor, lost, servile, crawling wretch to lick the dust and fawn and smile upon the thing who gave the lash! Myself—perchance my wives, my children to dig the mud, to mold and tell the tale of brick and furnish our own straw! But stop! I'm God's free man: I will not, cannot be a slave! Living, I'll be free here, or free in life above—free with the Gods, for they are free: and if I'm in the way on earth, I'll ask my God to take me to my friends above!"

He never devoted himself to money getting. He never bowed at the gilded shrine of mammon. The yellow god of this world found in him no devotee. "Many men could see a sovereign or a half eagle a long way farther off than he could," remarked one who knew him. Yet the amount of property he accumulated at Nauvoo, and which he sacrificed in order to flee into the wilderness with the Church of Christ, is sufficient to prove that he was not without financial ability. But he had his eyes and heart fixed upon the better riches, those which moth and rust could not corrupt, neither mobs break through nor steal. These things filled his soul, engrossed his attention and left but a small margin of time to him in which to fall in love with the wealth of this world. His motto was—"Money is of little importance where truth is concerned."

"It is the crowns, the principalities, the powers, the thrones, the dominions, and the associations with the Gods that we are after, and we are here to prepare ourselves for these things—this is the main object of existence."

Still it must not be thought that he was indifferent to financial enterprises and the development of the resources of the country. His efforts at establishing sugar works after his return from France; building and running the first nail factory; the contracts he took and filled when the Union Pacific railroad was building; his interest in the mining industry of the Territory; his association with Z. C. M. I., all give evidence to the contrary. He merely gave financial affairs a subordinate place to the interests of the kingdom of God. He was cautious in his business methods, and scrupulously honest.

During a period that he was in straightened circumstances, a member of his family was out of fuel, and without the means to purchase any. She sent word of the situation to him; having no money, and not wishing to go in debt as long as he saw no prospect of repaying it, he sent to her his new overcoat as that was the only thing he had at hand which could be turned into money. It was accompanied with a kind note that directed one of his sons to dispose of it, and deplored the rather close circumstances in which they were placed. "I can get along very nicely with my old coat this winter," he wrote: "it is a little faded, but then *I prefer a faded coat to a faded reputation*; and I do not propose to ask for accommodations that I am not prepared to meet."

He was a skillful workman in his business of turner, and when not engaged in the ministry, like Paul, "his own hands administered to his necessities." We have already seen him in the saw-pit day after day manufacturing lumber with a whip saw before the erection of saw mills; building his own house, cultivating his own garden, fencing his own farm, constructing the first bridge over the river Jordan.

He had adopted in practice some most excellent maxims which would have insured him success in any business he might have chosen. What they were may be seen in this: If he plowed a field it must be done well. He was not content to skim over the ground merely. If the ground was hard or rocky in places, someone must ride on the beam and the plow made to do its work. Moreover, the furrows must be straight. If he planted trees the holes must be made large; in setting them in, the fibers of the roots must be spread out and the soil placed round them carefully, and then be well watered that they might have every chance to live.

He had some skill in drawing and was an adept at wood carving for which his patterns were of his own designing. Of this kind of work as of all other kinds he would often say: "If a thing is done well, no one will ask how long it took to do it, but who did it."

Of his skill and power as a writer, the reader who has followed us through this volume, has seen some evidence from the extracts from his writings. These, however, have been mainly from his discussions, editorials and newspaper articles in the defense of Zion and her interests; and from his theological works. Powerful as he was in his style of composition, he also had ability in other departments of literature. He wrote in part a drama founded on incidents recorded in the Book of Mormon. He never completed it, and the manuscript of it, unfortunately, is lost; but those who heard it read, speak of it as giving evidence of considerable dramatic skill in its construction, and applaud the speeches of the characters for vigor and elegance of diction.

President Taylor was also a poet; and from the deep religious nature of the man, it could but be expected that the grand themes suggested by the gospel would inspire his muse. The restoration of the gospel, the going forth of messengers of glory with it to the sons of men, furnished him with inspiration for several hymns published in the Latter-day Saints' Hymn Book. The one on page 295, beginning—

"The glorious plan which God has given,

To bring a ruined world to heaven,"

suggested by this passage of scripture—"For there are three that bear record in heaven, the Father, the Word and the Holy Ghost; and these three are one; and there are three that bear witness in earth, the Spirit, the water and the blood; and these three are one" —is not only a poem, but a discourse in which the harmony and beauty of the Triune witnesses in heaven and in earth are made to stand out in bold relief.

Friendship also inspired his muse, and his "Response" to Parley P. Pratt's "Fiftieth Year;" and "The Seer," written in memory of the Prophet Joseph Smith, are two of his noblest pieces in verse.

His friends speak of a number of his poems that were never published, written in different strains from those with which the public is familiar, especially of one written while crossing the Atlantic, highly humorous and exhibiting an extensive knowledge of mythology. This is not to be found among his papers.

The following in blank verse is worthy of preservation for the grandeur and sublimity of the theme. It was written September 5th, 1846:

LINES WRITTEN IN THE ALBUM OF MISS ABBY JANE HART, OF NEW YORK CITY

ABBY: knowest thou whence thou camest? Thine
Origin? Who thou art? What? And whither thou
Art bound? A chrysalis of yesterday:
Today a gaudy, fluttering butterfly—
A moth; tomorrow crushed, and then an end
Of thee. Is this so? And must thou perish
Thus, and die ingloriously without a hope?

Ah, no; thou art no such thing. Thou in the
Bosom of thy Father bask'd and liv'd, and
Mov'd thousands of years ago. Yes, e'er this
Mundane sphere from chaos sprung, or sun, or
Moon, or stars, or world was fram'd; Before the
Sons of God for joy did shout, or e'er the
Morning stars together sung—thou liv'd'st.
Thou liv'dst to live again. Ah, no! Thou liv'd
But to continue life eternal—to

Live and move, and act eternally. Yes;
Long as a spirit, God or world exists;
From everlasting, eternal, without end!
And whilst thou dwelt in thy paternal home,
And with thy brethren shar'd extatic bliss,
All that a spirit could, not clothed in flesh,
Thou through the vista of unnumbered years
Saw'st through the glimmering veil that thou would'st
Dwell in flesh—just as the Gods.

Tread in the
Footsteps of thine elder brother, Jesus—
The "Prince of Peace," for whom a body was prepared.

Thou heard; thou look'd; thou long'd; thou pray'd;
Thou hop'd for this, at length it came; and thou
Appeared on this terraqueous ball,
From the hands of Elohim—eternal
As himself—part of thy God. A small spark
Of Deity, struck from the fire of his eternal blaze.

Thou cam'st! Thou cam'st to live! Of life thou art
A living monument; to it thou still
Dost cling—eternal life! To thee all else
Are straw and chaff, and bubbles light as air;
And will be all, until thou gain'st once more
Thy Father's breast; raised, quickened, immortal;
Body, spirit, all; a God among the Gods forever bless'd.
Abby, and hast thou dared to launch thy
Fragile baroque on truth's tempestuous sea;
To meet the pelting storm and proudly brave

The dangers of the raging main; and through
The rocks and shoals, and yawning gulfs pursue
The nearest way to life, in hopes that thou
Woulds't speedily gain a seat among the Gods?

See'st thou the multitudes who sail in
Gilded baroques, and gently float along the
Silvery stream? Downward they go with sweet,
Luxurious ease, and scarce a zephyr moves
The tranquil bosom of the placid stream.
Unconscious of the greatness of the prize
They might obtain, they glide along in peace;
And as they never soar aloft, nor mount
On eagle's wings, nor draw aside the veil
Of other worlds, they know none else than this—
No other joys. They dream away their life,
And die forgot, just as the butterfly,
They gaily flutter on; today they live—
Tomorrow are no more.

And though, like thee
In them is the eternal spark, thousands
Of weary years must roll along er'e they
Regain the prize they might with thee have shar'd.
Regain it? Never! No! They may come where
Thou wert, but never can they with thee share
Ecstatic bliss.

For whils't in heaven's progressive
Science skilled, thou soard'st from world to world, clad
In the robes of bright seraphic light; and

With thy God, eternal—onward goest, a
Priestess and a queen—reigning and ruling in
The realms of light. Unlike the imbeciles
Who dared not brook the scorn of men, and knew not
How to prize eternal life.

Abby, the cup's within thy reach; drink thou
The vital balm and live!

How priceless the album containing such a gem!

It will be as a preacher of righteousness that President Taylor will be best remembered by the generation who heard him. His published sermons would make several large volumes if collected; but those published are insignificant in comparison with the number he delivered. The Saints who listened to him for half a century will remember as long as they live his commanding presence, his personal magnetism, the vigor and power of his discourses and the grand principles of which they treated. He spoke extemporaneously as indeed do all the Elders of Israel. The formal, set discourse, so common in the world, has never been favorably received in the Church of Jesus Christ. It may be said that in that Church a new school of oratory, quite distinct from the strictly scholastic oratory of the world, is being formed; a manner of speech which depends for its success rather upon the presence and operations of the Holy Spirit than upon the cunning or ability of the speaker. When the Lord sent the first Elders out to preach the gospel He gave them these instructions:

"Neither take ye thought beforehand what ye shall say, but treasure up in your minds continually the words of life, and it shall be given you in the very hour that portion that shall be meted unto every man."

"Verily I say unto you, lift up your voices unto this people, speak the thoughts that I shall put into your hearts, and you shall not be confounded before men; for it shall be given you in the very hour, yea, in the very moment, what ye shall say. But a commandment I give unto you, that ye shall declare whatsoever things ye declare in my name in solemnity of heart, in the spirit of meekness, in all things. And I give unto you this promise, that inasmuch as ye do this, the Holy Ghost shall be shed forth in bearing record unto all things whatsoever ye shall say.

"This is an example unto all those who are ordained unto this priesthood, whose mission is appointed to go forth [to preach the gospel]. They shall speak as they are moved upon by the Holy Ghost, and whatsoever they shall speak when moved upon by the Holy Ghost, shall be scripture, shall be the will of the Lord, shall be the word of the Lord, shall be the voice of the Lord, and the power of God unto salvation; behold this is the promise of the Lord unto you, O ye my servants."

This makes the kind of oratory which obtains in the Church of Christ today resemble closely that which existed in the Church among the first Christians. The reader will doubtless remember that the great apostle of the Gentiles said:

"And my speech and my preaching was not with enticing words of man's wisdom, but in demonstration of the spirit and of power."

In the primitive as in the modern Church the reason for instituting this manner of discourse, is the same: That the faith of believers should not stand in the wisdom of men, but in the power of God.

These instructions from the Almighty, President Taylor carried out as implicitly as any man engaged in the ministry; and while his discourses may lack the polish, the faultless rhetoric, the studied climax to be found in the set speeches of the learned orators of the world, they are full of great thoughts and the inspiration of God—an excellence which more than repays for the want of smoothness and the fine finish that a carping criticism demands.

It was not his manner to deal with nice distinctions of words, their derivations or the various shades of their meanings. His was not the skill to

"Distinguish and divide
A hair 'twixt South and South-west side."

He chose rather to deal with general principles, great truths and build on them such arguments, and draw thence such sound deductions as convinced the judgment, appealed to the feelings, increased the faith, reformed the wayward or more firmly established the convictions of those who believed. He was deliberate in speech, almost slow, but not more so than the great principles he was wont to treat of required. His voice was clear, strong, resonant, and of wonderful compass; and whether it sank, as it often did, to the tender tones which give expression to the deep pathos that sometimes moved his soul, or calmly reasoned upon some heavenly doctrine, or was raised to its grandest swell or thunder tones to denounce injustice or oppression, no one could grow weary of listening to it.

His eloquence was a majestic river full to the point of overflowing its banks, sweeping grandly through rich regions of thought. His discourse was mainly argumentative and abounding with occasional colloquialisms, not unfrequently of a humorous turn: for among his other qualities of mind he had a keen sense of the ridiculous. His gestures were few, but very significant. His manner was, in the main, calm and dispassionate, but when a train of thought more than ordinarily sublime stirred his emotions, he became more animated and impressive; the form dilated, the utterance was more rapid and the whole man was aglow with enthusiasm that it was impossible to resist.

If, as it often chanced, his theme was the wrongs of the Saints, or if he spoke in defense of the broad principles of liberty and the rights of man, he then had a theme which called forth all his powers. His denunciations of injustice and tyranny were terrible. At such times his brow, usually beaming with mingled intelligence and benevolence, grew dark as the coming storm approached. The form was drawn up to its full height, the gestures were majestic—the word suited the action, the action the word; eye and arm, voice and movement—the whole man, with the love of liberty burning like consuming fire in his bones, poured out impassioned utterances against tyranny in all its forms; and the demonstrations of the congregation as the climax was reached, is sufficient evidence that they were irresistibly borne along by that tempest of passion. Yet in these bursts of eloquence he never seemed to put forth all his strength. He always appeared to have still more force in reserve that he could have used had he so minded. Moreover, he had that rare faculty which in the very torrent, tempest and whirl-wind of passion exercised a temperance that gave it smoothness and never permitted it to become strained or incongruous.

These qualities in him sprang from nature, not from training. There was nothing of the schools, nor of the studied elocutionist in his manner. His style of speaking was peculiarly his own and was well suited to the man, and to him alone.

The great body of the Saints knew him principally as a public man; and so prominent was he as such that his private life and domestic virtues have attracted but little attention. Yet it is pleasant to know that his private life was in every sense as praiseworthy as his public career. The letters to his family published in this volume give all necessary evidence to the existence of deep solicitude for their welfare, comfort and happiness; as well as a true parental interest in the mental, moral and spiritual development of his children; an interest so intense that it was an anxiety, such as only generous, manly bosoms, big with hopes that reach beyond the grave, are capable of experiencing. While he was willing and did labor for the good of the human race, and possessed brilliant talents and a universal sympathy which eminently qualified him for that work, he looked upon his own family as being the nucleus of that kingdom over which he would reign as priest, as king, as God! He loved his family, but that love was sanctified and made devoid of all selfishness by the hopes and aspirations awakened in his breast by the glorious gospel of the Son of God. Love so sanctified could only result in making him a kind, noble father, a gentle and loving husband.

He possessed superb self-control, which, with his nice sense of justice and honor, enabled him to be remarkably successful in the patriarchal order of marriage. Each wife was treated as the equal of the others, and with her children shared equally in the blessings and material advantages he was able to bestow upon them.

The social circle offered him an opportunity for the exercise of all his generous impulses. He delighted in family gatherings, in neighborhood feasts, and the reunions of friends, especially of those tried and true. His genial manners, his delightful conversation, his powers as a vocalist, together with his great experience, and an inexhaustible fund of humor made him a central figure and often the very life of these social gatherings.

Such was the character of President John Taylor; such the qualities of his mind; such his public and domestic virtues: and if, as an old English writer hath it, the great man is he who chooses the right with invincible resolution; who resists the sorest temptations from within and without; who bears the heaviest burdens cheerfully; who is calmest in storms, and most fearless under menace and frowns; and whose reliance on truth, on virtue, and on God, is most unfaltering—the name of JOHN TAYLOR must be written high up on the column of fame where the names of the great are enshrined, for in all these things he was pre-eminent.

CHAPTER 49 - THE CHAMPION OF LIBERTY

The morning of Friday, July 29, 1887, dawned over Salt Lake Valley, rosy and beautiful; but it was a day of sadness in the chief city of the Saints, and throughout Israel. It was the day appointed for the funeral services of President Taylor. Shortly after day-light had broken over the eastern mountains, vehicles loaded with people could be seen coming into the city from all directions to do honor to the great departed. Later special trains loaded to their utmost capacity brought in those too far from the city to reach it with teams.

The remains of President Taylor were removed to the Gardo House on the night of the 26th, and at six o'clock in the morning of the 29th, the day of his funeral, his family assembled to take a mournful but fond *adieu* of the earthly remains of him who had been their head—their husband, father and their friend. At ten minutes before seven the body was removed to the large Tabernacle; and at seven the doors of the mammoth building were thrown open to the great throng which already surrounded it. The body was placed in the open space in front of the stand so that the people could pass in single file on each side. The coffin in which it was enclosed was made of Utah pine, stained and polished until it resembled mahogany. It was tastefully ornamented with silver trimmings, but there was an entire absence of any display. On a silver plate on the coffin was inscribed in neatly engraved lettering:

PRESIDENT JOHN TAYLOR.

DIED JULY 25, 1887

AGED 78 YEARS, 8 MONTHS AND 24 DAYS.

At the bottom of the plate was engraved:

HOLINESS TO THE LORD.

REST IN PEACE.

The Tabernacle was draped in mourning, the great organ and stands being covered with crape. In front of the organ was an excellent life sized portrait of the deceased. The stands were decorated with a profusion of beautiful flowers tastefully arranged. On the sacrament stand, in the center, was a fine piece of floral ornamentation, on which was inscribed the noble title won by President Taylor in his early manhood—

CHAMPION OF LIBERTY

Near it was a large sheaf of ripe wheat, bearing the inscription—

WELL DONE, GOOD AND FAITHFUL SERVANT

The countenance of the deceased President was peaceful, and much more natural than might have been expected. There was but little evidence of physical suffering, though he looked somewhat worn, by the anxiety and confinement through which he had passed in the last few years of his earthly career.

For four and a half hours there was a continuous stream of humanity passing in at the west gate of the Temple enclosure and into the Tabernacle by the north-west entrance. Fully twenty-five thousand people passed the coffin and gazed for a moment in sadness upon the countenance of the noble man they had learned to trust and love as one of God's most distinguished servants, a friend and leader. While the people were passing through the building, Professor J. J. Daynes played a number of appropriate selections on the grand organ. There were but few faces in that great throng that were not wet with tears, and many a bosom swelled with righteous indignation at the thought that President Taylor's life had been shortened by his enforced confinement, made necessary by the cruelty of relentless enemies.

At 12 o'clock, the hour appointed for commencing the services, the great Tabernacle was filled to its utmost capacity, even to the standing room, while thousands were unable to enter but waited without until the formation of the burial cortege. President Taylor's two Counselors, and many of the Apostles and other leading Elders in Israel could not be present at the funeral services without great danger of falling into the hands of their enemies. The stand of the First Presidency was therefore unoccupied. That stand so long graced by the majestic form and presence of President Taylor being vacant, and so many of the well-known leading Elders being absent from their accustomed places, made the feeling of loneliness doubly oppressive. But three of the quorum of Twelve Apostles were present—Lorenzo Snow, Franklin D. Richards, and Heber J. Grant. Daniel H. Wells, himself bowed with the weight of 73 years was there; as was also the Patriarch of the Church, John Smith. Angus M. Cannon, President of the Salt Lake Stake, and A. O. Smoot of Utah Stake, together with Patriarchs Lorenzo D. Young and Joseph B. Noble were seated in the second stand with the Apostles. In the third were Presidents Jacob Gates, Horace S. Eldredge, Seymour B. Young, Abraham H. Cannon of the first Council of Seventies, and others. The members of President Taylor's family occupied the seats immediately in front of the stands.

At fifteen minutes past 12, the services began by President Angus M. Cannon reading the following letter written by President Taylor some years before his death, in answer to one addressed by President Young to him and the other Apostles asking them to give a written account of how they wished to be buried:

"SALT LAKE CITY,

"November 17, 1873.

"President Brigham Young,

"DEAR BROTHER: Being asked to give a written account of the way I wish to be buried, I present the following:

"I have no desire for any particular formula, but I should wish my body to be washed clean, to be clothed in clean white linen garments and robes, with shoes, apron and cap, etc.; to be laid in a coffin sufficiently large to contain my body without pressure.

"Should I die here, let me be buried in my own lot in the grave yard. Let the coffin be neat and comely, but plain and strong, made of cedar or red wood, or of our own mountain pine; if of the latter, colored or stained, and placed in an outer strong box, with a light cotton or woolen mattress or bed and a convenient pillow for the head.

"The services such as prevail at the time among the Saints. A plain slab may be placed over the body, and a stone at the head and feet, on the stone to be given an account of my name, age and birth, as shall suit the feelings of my family.

"Should I die in Jackson County, Missouri, let the above directions be carried out as far as practicable.

"Respectfully your Brother,

"JOHN TAYLOR"

The choir and congregation united in singing the hymn by Wm. Clayton, beginning:

"When first the glorious light of truth
Burst forth in this last age,
How few there were with heart and soul
T'obey it did engage!
Yet of those few how many
Have passed from earth away,
And in their graves are sleeping
Till the resurrection day."

The fourth verse of the hymn refers to the martyrdom of the Prophets Joseph and Hyrum Smith, which, in view of the fact that these lines were being sung as a requiem over the remains of their fellow martyr, was doubly pathetic.

"Our Patriarch and Prophet, too,

Were massacred, they bled;

To seal their testimony

They were numbered with the dead.

Oh, tell me, are they sleeping?

Methinks I hear them say,

Death's icy chains are bursting—

'Tis the resurrection day!"

Bishop Millen Atwood offered the opening prayer; after which the choir sang,

"Thou dost not weep to weep alone,

The broad bereavement seems to fall

Unheeded and unfelt by none,

He was beloved—beloved by all."

Apostle Lorenzo Snow was the first speaker. He read his text from Paul's second letter to Timothy:

"For I am now ready to be offered, and the time of my departure is at hand. I have fought a good fight, I have finished my course, I have kept the faith."

The speaker then said:

"Paul, whose remarks I have just read in your hearing, was an apostle of the Lord, our Savior. The man whose remains now lie before us was also an apostle of our Lord and Savior Jesus Christ, the Son of the living God. And as Paul made this statement in regard to himself, so also could be made a statement similar by President Taylor, whose remains lie before us this afternoon.

"Paul, during his life, struggled and contended for the faith which was once delivered to the Saints—those principles which pertain to the exaltation and salvation of the human family; and he was willing to make any sacrifice and go through every scene of difficulty and trouble in order to accomplish this object, that his testimony in regard to the Son of God and those principles that he had espoused might be carried forth to the nations of the earth—to the whole human family. He suffered imprisonment; he suffered the lash of his persecutors; he suffered every indignity, and finally died a martyr to those principles he so laboriously and so effectually carried forth among the human family.

"So also we can say of President Taylor. Those principles made known to him by the revelations of the Son of God as being of a divine nature—principles that pertain to the interest and salvation and exaltation of the human family—he carried forth to the various nations of the earth: and he heeded not the difficulties that ensued, or that were in his path of progress. He has shown to the world, he has shown to the Latter-day Saints, he has shown to the angels and to the Lord our God, his willingness, his determination, his resolution to do all in his power to carry out and accomplish the work of the Most High God. This he has done, and there lie his remains. He has left this world of sorrow, of trials, of afflictions of every nature that the Saints have to endure. He has gone to a better world. And it may be said of him truthfully, as was announced to John the Revelator when upon the Isle of Patmos, who was commanded to write what he heard by a voice from the eternal worlds:

"'Blessed are they that die in the Lord from henceforth. Yea, saith the spirit, that they may rest from their labors; and their works do follow them.'

"In a few verses before those that contain this vision it says an angel was seen passing swiftly through the midst of eternity, coming down to the earth bearing the gospel of the Son of God, to be declared to every nation, and kindred, and tongue, and people. This message our dear, beloved brother has sought, during a part of his life covering a period of fifty years, to carry forth to the nations of the earth. And during this period it is well known to the Latter-day Saints, the sufferings, the trials, the afflictions, and the blood that he spent in announcing and carrying forward these principles of life and salvation to the world of mankind. He truly fought a good fight. He has finished his course; 'and henceforth,' his spirit could well proclaim, 'there is laid up, for me a crown of righteousness, which the Lord, the righteous judge, shall give me at that day; and not to me only, but unto all them also that love his appearing.'

"Of course we feel the affliction; we feel the sad stroke. The Latter-day Saints feel that they have lost a friend; that we have lost a mighty counselor; that we have lost one of the greatest men that have stood upon the earth since the days of the Son of God—a man whose virtue, whose integrity, whose resolution to pursue the path of righteousness is known, and well known.

"Now, we could apply this passage of scripture to many others who have gone before; they have fought the good fight and kept the faith to the end; and they have finished their course, and they now sleep in peace in the spirit world, and the influence of their grand doings and great accomplishments in the path of righteousness, extend over the land of Zion. The Latter day Saints feel those beautiful and glorious influences. Our hearts are made glad to contemplate their virtues, their fidelity, their faithfulness, their glorious integrity.

"This our beloved brother has not only been a father and friend to his wives and to his children—to his numerous family; he has been a faithful friend also to the world of mankind, which at some future period, though it may be for a thousand years to come, they will distinctly understand. He has stood firm to those principles that are a light to the world, that are a light to the human family. And did the world understand President Taylor and his motives during the last fifty years of his pilgrimage among the children of men, they would feel differently towards him than they do. Those who put themselves in the attitude of enemies to the Latter-day Saints and the servants of God, do so because they don't comprehend us; they don't understand our hearts, and don't understand our willingness to sacrifice in order to lay a plan or to carry out measures by which salvation may come to them also. We dedicate our lives which we hold as not dear to us, in order that the world may understand that there is a God in the eternal worlds; in order that they may understand that God has something to do at the present time with the affairs of the children of men. The world is passing into feelings and opinions of infidelity. Even among the Christian portion of the human family, thousands and tens of thousands, though they are not willing to confess it because of being unpopular, do not believe that

God has anything to do with the children of men. We have to stand forth and make sacrifices in order that that belief and knowledge may come to the children of men. That is the case with our beloved brother, President Taylor. He has shown himself willing to make sacrifices before he would deny or turn his back upon those principles that, when people understand them, lead them to the path of knowledge, of salvation and of immortality.

"Well, it is so ordered that one man's death, or the death of a dozen, though they stand in the highest positions in the Church, does not stop this work. The Latter-day Saints have advanced to that wisdom and that intelligence and that understanding, that this does not materially affect their interest. The kingdom of God moves forward. It is not dependent upon one man or a half dozen men. It was thought by some in the days of Joseph that this Church could not prosper except Joseph guided its destinies; and when the time came that he was to pass away from this world as a martyr, into the spirit world, the Saints throughout the kingdom of God were greatly agitated. It was something unexpected. They hardly knew how things would then move. The responsibility then devolved upon the quorum of the Twelve Apostles; and through the blessings of God upon them and the spirit of inspiration that dwelt in their bosoms, and under the guidance of the Almighty, the kingdom moved forward. And so in regard to the time when our beloved Brother Brigham Young was called from this state into the spirit life. He passed away almost unexpectedly. The Saints were hardly prepared for it. And yet the kingdom of God moved forward. The duties of guidance were still upon the Quorum of the Twelve Apostles.

"The Lord has seen proper now to call our beloved brother, President Taylor, away from these scenes of suffering, these scenes of martyrdom; and the Church still moves forward.

"Notwithstanding the duties and the obligations devolve again upon the quorum of the Twelve Apostles, for the third time, through the blessings of the Almighty and the spirit of inspiration that will be upon them as it always has been, the Church will move forward. We are gaining that experience that each man and each woman knows what his or her duty is; and they know the foundation upon which this kingdom and Church is founded; they know the foundation upon which each individual is established; and they know that God reigns over the children of men and over the affairs of the Latter-day Saints. They feel, now, perhaps, different to what they generally feel when circumstances of this kind occur. They feel more calm, more assurance in the providences of the Almighty.

"And so in regard to the beloved family of President Taylor. Of course they cannot but feel—and it is well that they do feel—that they have lost a parent, a father, a guide, to direct and counsel. But still there is nothing in the way of their progress, any more than there is in the way of the progress of the kingdom of God. They can move forward, and it is their duty to move forward in order that the word of the angel may be fulfilled which said: 'Blessed are the dead which die in the Lord henceforth; yea, saith the spirit, that they may rest from their labors and their works do follow them.

"And this family of President Taylor's, if they prepare themselves, can go onward notwithstanding they have lost their head. The road is still clear. They still have the counsels of the Holy Spirit, to which they are entitled, for guidance and direction, and they can move forward in the path of wisdom and knowledge, and in all those beautiful qualifications that make a Latter-day Saint; and they can prepare themselves, so that the words of the angel may be fulfilled. Elder Taylor's works follow him. His labors, so far as his family are concerned, follow him. Well, I have occupied sufficient time. There are a number here that we wish to speak. I ask God in His mercy to bless the family of President Taylor, that the Holy Spirit of life may be upon them, and that they may have consolation in their hearts. Their parent is now dwelling in glory, having a crown of righteousness upon his head; and he will be there to welcome them as they pass off one after another from this into the next world and to take them by the hand. God bless the family of President Taylor, God bless the Latter-day Saints; God bless the quorum of the Twelve Apostles, on whom rests the responsibility of moving forward the interests of the kingdom of God. God bless the authorities of the Latter-day Saints and bless the honest in all the world of mankind, is my prayer, in the name of Jesus. Amen."

Apostle Franklin D. Richards followed Apostle Snow:

"Beloved fellow-mourners: On occasions of this kind, when the great men whom God has raised up for our guidance, are released from their labors in this low estate and called to another of a higher and more glorious character, it appears to me suitable that we should spend a little time and dwell upon their virtues, their excellent examples, and those high, dignified traits of character which they have shown forth unto us as the exemplars of that which is right and proper before all good people, and which is most acceptable to God and the angels of heaven. We are called upon to part with one of God's noblemen—a brother, a father, a husband and a true friend to all that is praiseworthy among mankind. Many of the points of his character and of the transactions of this great and good man have already been noticed in the prints, and it is to be hoped that a correct, competent and creditable biography of his life may be given to the Saints and to the world, that his true character as a man of God may be known as a standing and abiding testimony to the whole human family. I, therefore, cannot—neither can any of us today—enter largely into a consideration even of the most important features of the busy and very profitable life which he has spent. But I wish to notice two or three of the prominent traits of his character, which as a fellow-laborer in the gospel, I have come personally to know.

"President Taylor was a man who could not get down to grovel with the low-lived, the vicious, the ribald, nor any who indulged in the follies and vanities of mortal life. When the gospel found him, he was aspiring from the measure of grace that existed among the most devout religious worshipers, and hungering and thirsting for something nobler and better; and the testimony of the glorious truths again revealed came to his ears by the Elders of the Church, and soon by the blessed testimony of the Prophet Joseph.

"Brother Parley P. Pratt had the distinguished honor to sound the gospel of Jesus Christ in his ears. He was the instrument to lead him into the Church of Christ. Brother Pratt found in him that right heart, and that open hand by which he was led to go right forward in the truth, and the new wine in the old vessel did no harm.

President Taylor was a man bold and daring for the truth. He knew no fear. I recollect well when he and I were on our missions in Europe together, he labored in France—on the coast of infidel France—if I mistaken not in Havre. He labored in that vicinity diligently; and at one time a number of religious divines combined together to put down this heresy, as they term it. President Taylor, with that boldness which ever characterized him, consented to meet a whole pack of them, all that were willing to conspire together to silence and turn away the testimonies from reaching the hearts of the people. I recollect well my feelings when in Liverpool at the time. Morally speaking it was like Paul when he writes about fighting wild beasts at Ephesus. He withstood them and he brought forth the truth, and souls were given him as the fruit of his labors; an interest was awakened, and some were gathered out. His labors were continued and incessant until he obtained a translation of the Book of Mormon in the French language.

"President Taylor was a man who in his bearing and nature was onward and upward. Who that is before me ever heard him indulge in ribaldry or light and trifling and vain conversation? He was always looking forward, from the moment he embraced the gospel, for a higher platform upon which he could climb, and raise until he could go back, a son of God, and associate as he did here upon the earth, with the prophets of the Most High. There were but very few men that attained the warm, personal relation that he attained to and maintained most successfully with the Prophet Joseph Smith till he died, and the story of that personal affection was consummated by the bullets he received in Carthage jail with the Prophet when he was slain. President Taylor was himself disabled. In the scene that he then passed through he experienced all that pertains to martyrdom. He never suffered greater pain, or more severe pain than he experienced in the jail with the Prophet Joseph. But it was not appropriate for him to give up the ghost then. He had to wait another forty years, that he might show forth his magnanimity, his Priesthood and his fervor, and be a blessing to God's people in these valleys of the mountains.

"At another time when President Taylor was laboring in New York, he went to work and with faith, and the co-operation of such brethren as he could find, established a paper, and published it in New York—one of the most successful enterprises of the kind that was ever undertaken in the last days. Some of the papers of New York undertook to run him out, thinking New York belonged to them. They dared President Taylor to an investigation. He proposed to meet as many of them as pleased to attend; but he was ready with so magnanimous a heart and so full a hand, that they declined the opportunity to meet him. I cite these instances of the high moral bravery that President Taylor possessed anywhere, everywhere and at all times in behalf of the truth while traveling and laboring in various countries. This has been his spirit and feeling. And while he has been of this magnanimous character, he has always entertained a most profound regard for legitimate authority. No man delighted more to receive and obey the counsel of those over him. This he did with the Prophet Joseph although some of the counsels given him, tested him and many of his brethren to the innermost soul and to the veritable life itself. President Taylor always delighted to serve the people. It was a notable trait in his character that he was not addicted to hankering after money. Many men could discover a sovereign or a half eagle a long way farther off than he could. He sought for the riches of eternal life. Blessed be God, he is rich in the possession of the knowledge he attained, and the skill and integrity which he exercised, and the authority with which he was entrusted until he has taken his departure and gone hence.

"President Taylor entertained the most profound regard for the superiority of the principles of the American government as embodied in the holy constitution, and the just laws of the land. I recollect well when the news arrived of the passage of those laws which have lately engaged the attention of the people, how with what consideration he sat down and conversed with myself and others upon that subject, and how he carefully and prayerfully adjusted the affairs of his household in a way that, in the honesty of his heart and the magnanimity of his soul, he felt that no man nor no government could take exceptions to. He felt to place himself in conformity with the law. He would rather do that than that any issue should arise. He therefore gladly bade family, kindred and friends *adieu* and went into retirement, went where, under certain circumstances he could still serve his brethren, still counsel them in the ways of life, still advise them as a man who was entrusted with the keys of eternal life to the human family, and this he did, blessed be God! Until the day of his death. And it will be pleasant to some who are present to know that President Taylor has not died of organic disease. He has died from the legitimate consequences of confinement, of limitation from exercise, just as everybody else would do if they were limited and could not get exercise. Their candle would go out from want of oil; the fires of their life would go out for want of fuel. He has attained to the age of four score, and the Lord has permitted him to finish his days in this, and to a great degree, happy manner, notwithstanding the unfavorable circumstances which surrounded him.

"When we recount the activity of his life, when we contemplate the dignity of his character and of his course, and how exceptional it has been, what an example it is for us! Should we not be trending upward too and continually so?

"But President Taylor, by the blessing of God was placed in a position in which he was not only a father and protector to his family, but God made him a great benefactor to many of the human race. There are numbers here today before me, who have been brought from distant lands—lands where poverty and want looked them in the face—and they have been brought to this land where there is room for enterprise and industry, whereby multitudes of the poor have come to have homes and the comforts of life around them. President Taylor has exercised this discretion and this authority with a liberality that was becoming a saint of God, and there are few in the Church more intimately acquainted with these facts than myself, and I wish to testify to them. A great man and a good man has fallen—fallen not from grace, not from any virtue, or any adornment of mortal life, but his mortal body is laid down that his spirit may go hence.

"And we are together in meeting, we are in his presence, though we may not discern it. God is bringing to light many wonderful developments of science, so much so that men are constructing eyes that they can look at the distant planets and tell their surface, and tell their distances, and comprehend those things that lie at very remote distances in space.

"And these things are made after the pattern of the human eye. Shall He who made the human eye not see? We are taught in the revelations that some men can see into the future. But God is able and He has power to see us continually. We are in His presence continually, and we ought never to forget it.

"He who has made the ear, shall He not hear? Behold! Men are already learning to talk to others at a distance of many hundreds of miles. If men can do this by the limited knowledge they possess, is it not true that greater things shall yet be revealed?

"Jesus said to marvel not at certain things; for the day shall come when all they that are in their graves shall hear His voice and live. We lay our bodies down, but it is as true to science as it is to revealed religion that these bodies shall be brought forth by the power of that resurrection which was attained to by Jesus, and though the wicked may scoff and the fool may say in his heart, 'There is no God,' Saints know their foolishness.

"Now, then, my dear friends, my brethren and sisters—friends and relatives of President Taylor—I feel thankful that I have been favored with an acquaintance of so great and noble a household. There are few households, indeed, in Israel or on the earth that are as honorable as that of President Taylor. My dear young brethren and sisters, endeavor and ask God to help you to strive to emulate those glorious qualities of your dear father, who has gone before you, as he has written in the song—for President Taylor, be it known, was a writer, he was an author and a poet and there are very few productions more exalted and ennobling and dignified than the one he composed, and which he used to sing with great *eclat*, beginning,

"'The seer the seer, Joseph the seer,
I love to dwell on his memory dear,
The chosen of God and the friend of men,' etc.

"He who had all these qualifications as a man here among us, is a great exemplar to all Israel, and a worthy instructor to my young brethren and sisters. I beg you to heed the counsels he has given, heed the testimonies he has left on record, and strive to follow the same, so that by-and-by, when you return to clay, he will be ready to welcome you to Zion's shore. He has gone to prepare a place for you. Be not discouraged. Be not afflicted. We mourn President Taylor's absence. We will lose his counsel. We cannot well spare such men. We need such men in the Church to establish righteousness and preach the gospel and build up Zion on the earth. You and I feel the loss—all Israel feel it. We are all mourners on this occasion. I feel to say, then, that while we bid President Taylor *adieu*, let us send with him congratulations. Oh what a joyful reception will be given him yonder, when he will shake hands with Joseph again, with Hyrum and Brigham, with Parley and Orson, and George A. and Willard, and all of the brethren of the Twelve! Why there is nearly a quorum of the Twelve Apostles to establish and carry on the work which we here but begin.

"My dear brethren and sisters, may the spirit of the gospel, the spirit of the Gods be with all those who seek to know and obey the gospel of the Lord Jesus Christ, to keep His commandments and to walk in His statutes and ordinances continually."

"May the Lord help us to cultivate and to follow the examples of so great and glorious men. May we acquire their virtues and like them seek more abundantly to become Saints of God; seek to stand without rebuke in this untoward generation; seek to overcome all evil, that we may ultimately gain the reward of the faithful. This is my desire, my purpose and my labor with you all, in the name of Jesus Christ. Amen."

Apostle Heber J. Grant said:

"I feel that it is much more appropriate that those men who have lived almost a life time with President Taylor should be the speakers on this occasion. However, inasmuch as I have been requested to make a few remarks, I will willingly do so. I can say of

President Taylor that he lived a faithful, honest and conscientious life; that he did all that was in his power for the advancement of the work of God upon the earth. He has been a faithful Latter-day Saint, and no more can be said of any man. He has lived unto a good old age. He has filled up the measure of his creation, and there is no man but can say that he has been true to his own conscience. No matter what has been the obstacle before him, he has never faltered. He has always been firm and steadfast in walking in the path of duty. May God bless his family. May God bless the Latter-day Saints everywhere, is my prayer in the name of Jesus. Amen."

Counselor Daniel H. Wells was the next speaker:

"I agree with the psalmist who said: 'I shall be satisfied when I arise in His likeness.' The Lord Jesus Christ has brought light and redemption into the world for the benefit of the human family, from the creation of the world to the redemption of every creature worthy of eternal life.

"President Taylor espoused this cause [referring to the work of the Lord in the last days] because he had the light of truth burning within him when it was first made known to him. He lived a fearless, noble and God-like life—let those who still live seek to emulate his noble example. President Taylor has been a friend to himself, a friend to his family, a friend to this people and a friend to God. He has been the champion of human rights, the champion of liberty, truth and freedom. He has lived a noble, useful life, full of honor and credit to himself and family, a satisfaction to the people and a glory to God. I take pleasure in bearing this testimony to the faithfulness and devotion of President Taylor, to his integrity to God and the love of his people. I knew him to be a man determined to do right, to see justice administered, truth upheld, and honor sustained among this people. He has lived to see this people pass through many changes. He sought to maintain the right in every instance, for which there are great and glorious crowns in the eternal worlds reserved for him."

He prayed for the divine providential care to rest upon the family of those who are called to mourn his absence, that they may follow in his footsteps, and ever cherish the love they now have for their father and husband, and that it may grow stronger and become brighter with the lapse of time, and that those remaining may live to meet him in his glorious and exalted estate.

Brother Wells bore his testimony that Mormonism is true, that Joseph Smith, Brigham Young and John Taylor were prophets, seers and revelators of the Church of Jesus Christ in the last dispensation. And as the people of God have twice before been called upon to part with their leader, and have survived, and the work been strengthened, so now God will raise up men who will continue it where President Taylor has left off, until shall become mighty and powerful over all the earth. The speaker extolled the example of the revered and honored President, and commanded all who would be great to follow in his path. He bore his testimony to the existence of God, the power of His work, having no fear of its final destiny; trusted all would fulfill the obligation incumbent upon them, and as President Taylor had kept his first estate, come here on earth, kept his second estate, and had now gone to the spirit world, so may those of his family, his brethren and all Israel do likewise—prove their integrity to God and finally meet the reward of an exaltation in His presence.

President A. O. Smoot:

"It is nearly forty-nine years since I first became acquainted with President John Taylor, whose remains now lie before us. I first knew him as a distinguished and successful missionary. I next knew him in the troubles of Missouri, in what are termed the wars of Missouri. I next knew him as an apostle of the Lord Jesus Christ. I knew him as a journalist in Nauvoo, as editor of the Nauvoo *Neighbor* and other periodicals. I knew him in crossing the plains from Winter Quarters to this city. I knew him as a distinguished Legislator in the councils of the Legislature of the Territory of Utah. I have known him in adversity, I have known him in prosperity, and in a great many capacities have I been familiar with Brother Taylor for forty-nine years. And in all the positions which I have known him to occupy, he has been eminently faithful and has filled them with ability and with unflinching integrity to the kingdom of God on the earth.

"We have come here to mourn with those who mourn, and we in reality have occasion to rejoice as well as to mourn. Brother Taylor has filled up the measure of his days in usefulness, and has never been known to waver, or to flinch, or to murmur, or to complain of his hardships. He stood up for the right. He supported the truth at home and abroad, for the salvation of the human family, and we have occasion to rejoice that he has thus filled up the measure of his days in usefulness.

"While we have reason to mourn his absence for the loss of his usefulness among the Latter-day Saints, as has appropriately been said others will be raised up in the midst of the people of God that will be qualified to magnify the callings and positions which he has filled, and the calling he filled at the time of his demise, and they will do honor to Israel as he has done. I do not feel to mourn for him as a man, and it is to be hoped that we may all be so happy as to pass the ordeal with the stars of honor with which he has done and with as little reflection of wrong, or of wrong-doings, either by friend or foe, as Brother Taylor has passed it. May it be our happy lot so to do. And I hold that we should not cleave to life longer than we are useful. God bless all those who are faithful in Israel. It is true this departure of our beloved President is a bereavement to his family and to all Israel. It is an occasion for mourning, and yet that mourning may be tempered with joy. I do not wish, my brethren and sisters, to detain you, or to enter into details in relation to his character. History gives this.

"Eulogy is not required in the case of President Taylor. History will tell his life, and his doings and his devotion to God and His kingdom upon the earth. May the comfort of the Holy Spirit rest upon the mourners.

"May the comforting influence rest abundantly upon them that they may feel to acknowledge the hand of God and to profit by Brother Taylor's example in life."

Lorenzo D. Young and Joseph B. Noble, Patriarchs in the Salt Lake and Davis Stakes respectively, made remarks, bearing testimony to the excellent character and nobility of soul of the deceased President.

Angus M. Cannon, President of the Salt Lake Stake, was the last speaker. He said:

"It is with feelings of solemnity that I arise before you on this occasion. In looking upon the remains of our late President, it brings to my memory many of his noble traits and actions. My acquaintance with him dates back a little over forty years ago, when I was a child, and when he brought the gospel to my parents. I have been familiar with his record from that day to this. When nigh unto death with leaden missiles, received through his integrity to the Prophet of Almighty God and his brethren and the servants of the Most High, he stood immovable, determined to maintain the testimony of the Lord Jesus Christ.

"If I ever abided in the truth—nourished and cherished by his testimony and God like qualities—within me, it has been under his divine instructions and by the aid of his holy example and by his self-denial and the integrity that he has exhibited for the testimony of the Lord Jesus Christ.

"I saw him last in enfeebled health, and when I asked him if he would have me bear a message to his loved ones—to his family, his wives and his children—he said, 'Yes, say unto them I remember them always. I love them individually, and never cease to plead with God for them. And although I am feeble now, I hope soon to be better.'

"He has been relieved from his pains. He sleeps in God; and I can imagine seeing the portal of heaven open through which he has entered. I see Joseph, I see Hyrum, I see the Patriarch, the father of Joseph, I see Don Carlos, Samuel and Heber, Brigham, Willard, David Patten, Jedediah and George A., and as he is free with them and in their society, I can imagine and rejoice in the joy and counsels and power of God that they who have gone exhibited, which they are now enjoying and which will animate and strengthen the hands and comfort the hearts of those brethren who remain.

"And I tell you this day that the work of God will roll on with greater rapidity than it has ever done, and God will be glorified. His servants' hands will be strengthened and Jesus' testimony will be maintained.

"Brother Taylor took the testimony that Joseph gave him, that Jesus delivered unto Joseph, that God bade Joseph to listen to from the lips of his beloved Son—and he bore those tidings to foreign lands, and made our hearts tingle with the words which he there enunciated. I say the joy and rejoicing with which President Taylor has met with his co-laborers beyond the veil, surrounded with apostles of Jesus Christ, is great.

"When I think of the glory that attends God's work, the increase of His servants, the growth of Israel born in the everlasting covenant, surrounded by these lofty crags and peaks, inspiring them with love of liberty, I trust that from the ashes of our beloved President—who obtained the title of Champion of Freedom and Liberty, the champion of the people's rights—I trust that from his ashes may spring innumerable champions who will stand in the image of their Maker, as has our departed president, and that they may maintain the right and the rule of truth of God as he has done. We cannot sacrifice principle. We can go to prison. We can endure death; we can separate ourselves from our families, with the hope that we will have them eternally with God. But we cannot forsake the work that He has assigned unto us. And I bear testimony today that Jesus is the Christ, the Son of the living God. Joseph was His prophet and sealed his testimony with his blood. Brigham Young his successor, and also John His servant, have gone from the earth, sealed their testimonies as Prophets, Seers and Revelators in this generation.

"May God our Heavenly Father nourish His loved ones who remain with us. May He inspire the hearts of His people that they may go on in good works, emulating the example of our beloved President and perform works that will exalt them to meet with him. May He cherish and nourish the little ones who are left; may He bless them in health, give them strength and enable them to follow in the footsteps of him whose body now lies before us. May God grant that his wives may set such examples and give such counsel to those of their children who remain that will make them worthy to be received of him and be cherished in his bosom eternally.

"And may God strengthen His Saints to maintain the rule of righteousness, extend the principles of truth and enable us to bring about greater good to humanity, that God may be glorified, His Church strengthened, and that we, as His people, may be qualified for every event in life, through Jesus Christ. Amen."

The choir sang the splendid anthem:

"Jerusalem, my glorious home."

The benediction was pronounced by Patriarch John Smith.

This closed the services in the Tabernacle. Although they had lasted for two hours and a half, and many in the congregation had been sitting in the building from early morning, there was no sign of weariness. The most profound silence was maintained. Nothing was heard in the vast building but the sweet strains of music, the voice of the speakers as they recounted the noble deeds and virtues of the illustrious dead. A spirit of profound sorrow brooded over that great congregation. Israel sincerely mourned the departure of their great leader.

As the congregation slowly and mournfully left the Tabernacle the funeral cortege was formed as follows:

Held's Cornet Band,

Pall Bearers—Twelve sons of the deceased,

Hearse,

Ogden Brass Band,

Family,

Garfield Beach Band,

First Presidency,

Apostles,

Patriarchs,

First Seven Presidents of the Seventies,

Olsen's Brass Band,

Presidents of Stakes,

High Councilors,

Choir,

Presidencies of High Priests' Quorums,

Sixth Ward Silver Band,

Presidencies of Elders' Quorums,

Presiding Bishopric,

Provo Silver Band,

Bishops and Counselors,

Salt Lake City Band,

Presidencies of Teachers' Quorums,

Presidencies of Deacons' Quorums,

Committee of Arrangements,

Citizens in Carriages and on Foot.

The cortege was of great length, and splendid in its appointments. It proceeded east on South Temple Street, to N Street, thence turned north, and entered the cemetery at the upper gates.

At the grave a select choir sang with exquisite sweetness that most beautiful and heaven inspired of hymns—

O, my Father, thou that dwellest
In that high and glorious place!

The dedicatory prayer was offered by Elder Richard Ballantyne, after which the earthly remains of the great Apostle and President of the Church of Jesus Christ were consigned to their temporary resting place, pending the construction of a stone vault, and the immense throng quietly and sadly dispersed.

Early in the morning of the 20th of August, the remains of President Taylor were removed, in the presence of his family, from the first grave to their permanent resting place. The sepulcher is of granite rock slabs twelve inches in thickness firmly clamped and doweled together with heavy bolts and rods of solid steel, thus forming a chamber seven feet by four, and five feet in depth. This is enclosed by a massive, solid cap-stone of the same material, eight feet six inches by six feet, one foot thick and weighing four and a half tons. It is secured in its position by a number of powerful steel rods, making a structure almost impregnable.

There sleeps in peace the body of the fearless CHAMPION OF LIBERTY, and the APOSTLE OF RIGHTEOUSNESS.

THE TESTIMONY OF JOHN TAYLOR

"Jesus came here according to the foreordained plan and purpose of God, pertaining to the human family as the Only Begotten of the Father full of grace and truth. He came to offer himself a sacrifice, the just for the unjust; to meet the requirements of a broken law, that the human family were incapable of meeting, to rescue them from the ruins of the fall, to deliver them from the power of death to which all peoples had been subjected by the transgression of a law."

(Deseret News Semi-weekly, July 9, 1881, 1.)

"I know that God rules and reigns in this nation and among the nations of the earth, and that He will direct all things, according to the counsels of His will. I know that the work that God has commenced in these last days will continue to go forth despite the powers of darkness and all the fiends of hell."

(Deseret News Weekly, Sep. 17, 1884, 547.)

"And this provision [the Atonement] applies not only to the living, but also to the dead, so that all men who have existed in all ages, who do exist now, or who will exist while the earth shall stand, may be placed upon the same footing, and that all men may have the privilege, living or dead, of accepting the conditions of the great plan of redemption provided by the Father, through the Son, before the world was; and that the justice and mercy of God may be applied to every being, living or dead, that ever has existed, that does now exist, or that ever will exist."

(The Mediation and Atonement [1882], 181.)

THE FAMILY OF JOHN TAYLOR

Wives and dates of marriage

Leonora Cannon Jan 28, 1833

Elizabeth Haigham Dec. 12, 1843

Jane Ballantyne Feb. 25, 1844

Mary Ann Oakley April, 1845

Sophia Whitaker April 23, 1846

Harriet Whitaker Dec. 4, 1847

Margaret Young Sept. 26, 1856

Children and dates of birth

George John Taylor Jan. 31, 1834

Mary Ann Taylor Jan. 23, 1836

Joseph James Taylor June 8, 1838

Leonora Agnes Taylor June 1, 1842

Josephine Taylor Mar 15, 1846

Thomas Edward Taylor Nov. 7, 1849

Arthur Bruce Taylor Oct. 9, 1853

Richard James Taylor Feb. 4, 1848

Annie Maria Taylor Oct. 21, 1849

David John Taylor Aug. 8, 1853

Henry Edgar Taylor Dec. 26, 1849

Mary Elizabeth Taylor Jan. 30, 1854

Brigham John Taylor Aug. 8, 1858

Ida O. Taylor Sept. 6, 1860

Ezra O. Taylor May 20, 1863

Harriet Ann Whitaker Dec. 7, 1847

James Whitaker Taylor Mar. 2, 1850

Hyrum Whitaker Taylor Jan. 10, 1854
John Whitaker Taylor May 15, 1858
Helena Whitaker Taylor Mar. 21, 1860
Moses Whitaker Taylor Mar. 9, 1862
Frederick Whitaker July 18, 1866
Sophia Elizabeth July 14, 1849
William Whitaker Sept. 11, 1853
John Taylor Mar. 19, 1855
Ebenezer Young Taylor Feb. 25, 1860
Frank Young Taylor Nov. 4, 1861
Leonora Young Taylor Mar. 25, 1864
Robert Young Taylor Mar. 2, 1866
Maggie Young Taylor Mar. 15, 1870
Nephi Young Taylor Oct. 25, 1872
Mary Young Taylor Dec. 6, 1875
Abraham Young Taylor Dec. 12, 1878
Samuel Young Taylor Nov. 20, 1881

As of the original publication of this book in 1892, the grandchildren and great-grandchildren of President Taylor numbered upwards of one hundred, so that in addition to a name and a fame for himself, he also is the founder of a family that is not likely to perish while the earth shall stand; nor is it likely that he will ever be without a man to stand before the Lord in the priests' office—a thing esteemed by the ancients as one of the greatest blessings.

Please look for more books written by B.H. Roberts, including:

THE MORMON BATTALION

B. H. ROBERTS

LATTER-DAY STRENGTHS

Made in the USA
Las Vegas, NV
27 January 2022